MIND *as* ACTION

MIND *as* ACTION

James V. Wertsch

New York   Oxford
OXFORD UNIVERSITY PRESS
1998

Oxford University Press

Oxford   New York
Athens   Auckland   Bangkok   Bogota   Bombay   Buenos Aires
Calcutta   Cape Town   Dar es Salaam   Delhi   Florence   Hong Kong
Istanbul   Karachi   Kuala Lumpur   Madras   Madrid
Melbourne   Mexico City   Nairobi   Paris   Singapore
Taipei   Tokyo   Toronto   Warsaw

and associated companies in
Berlin   Ibadan

Published by Oxford University Press, Inc.
198 Madison Avenue, New York, New York 10016

Oxford is a registered trademark of Oxford University Press

Library of Congress Cataloging-in-Publication Data
Wertsch, James V.
Mind as action / James V. Wertsch.
p. cm.
Includes bibliographical references and index.
ISBN 0-19-511753-0
1. Psychology.   2. Social psychology.   3. Culture—Psychological
aspects.   I. Title.
BF57.W46 1997
150—dc21   97-25636

1 3 5 7 9 8 6 4 2

Printed in the United States of America
on acid-free paper

To Nicholas Morgan Wertsch *and*
Tyler Peterson Wertsch

Acknowledgments

Bakhtin's claims about the inherent dialogicality of human life apply nowhere more obviously than in writing a book. In struggling with each paragraph, one is immersed in endless dialogic encounters with the voices of others, voices of one's earlier self, speech genres, previous and subsequent paragraphs of the book, and so forth. Everything one thinks and writes is shot through and through with dialogic overtones. As I reread the chapters of this book, I can't help but recount dialogic encounters I have had with others. In some cases, quotations, citations, and other forms of evidence have made the identity of my dialogic partners obvious. In others, the words of these partners no longer appear in the text, but it is nonetheless clear to me where they have shaped what I have said. And in still other—indeed most—instances, the voices to whom I have responded are sufficiently distant in time or embedded in intellectual tradition that I may not even recognize their impact.

Three figures whose influence *is* quite obvious in this book are Lev Semënovich Vygotsky, Mikhail Mikhailovich Bakhtin, and Kenneth Burke. I have never met any of these figures personally, and since none of them is alive today, I never shall. However, much of what I have to say is in the form of dialogic interchanges with them. In some cases, I have accepted and simply "rented" (Holquist, 1981) what they wrote; in others, I have tried to provide rejoinders or even rebuttals to their utterances; and in still others the influence may be less apparent and direct, even to me, but it nevertheless runs throughout my text.

Of course I have engaged these figures in dialogue through their writings, but this effort has not been mine alone. Instead, it has been heavily mediated by individuals whom I have been fortunate to know over the past two decades, individuals whom I now count as teachers as well as friends and colleagues. In the case of Vygotsky, the list includes Michael Cole, Aleksandr Romanovich Luria, and Vladimir Petrovich Zinchenko. In the case of Bakhtin, I am deeply indebted to Michael Holquist and Ragnar Rommetveit. And when it comes to Burke, I have in mind Bernard Kaplan. To the extent that my interpretation of Vygotsky, Bakhtin, and Burke is useful, it is in no small part due to the efforts of these teachers; to the extent it is unclear or unproductive, it is surely due to my unwillingness or inability to listen as I should have.

Given my concern in this volume with sociocultural context, I would be remiss not to recognize the contributions to my work made by several institutional, historical, and cultural settings. In this connection, I must mention Clark University, where I spent seven wonderful years on the faculty; the Universidad de Sevilla, where I was a visiting professor during my 1992–1993 sabbatical year; and Washington University in St. Louis, where I have been since 1995. Clark provided a rich context in which discussions with students—especially graduate students—and faculty pushed me to challenge old ideas and develop new ones. It was also at Clark that I was introduced to issues in history and the philosophy of history under the tutelage of Stefan Tanaka. In Sevilla and Madrid, colleagues such as Juan Daniél Ramirez and Alberto Rosa helped me come to a deeper understanding of Bakhtin and Burke, and at Washington University colleagues such as Andy Clark and Bill Bechtel have assisted me in seeing some of the connections that can be forged between contemporary cognitive science and the study of mediated action.

My efforts to produce this volume have also benefited from other forms of institutional suport over the past several years. In particular, the Spencer Foundation has supported my research as I sought to examine a set of empirical issues, many of which are discussed in what follows. And the International Research and Exchanges Board helped underwrite a 1994 conference in Moscow on Vygotsky's ideas in the human sciences, where the rich context of discussion gave rise to several of the ideas I have pursued here.

Finally, none of the work for this book could have been completed without the help, understanding, and support of those who sustain me in my day-to-day life at home. Hence my deepest thanks must be reserved for my family. My wife, Mary, has been a source of steady support and encouragement, and our boys, Nicholas and Tyler, have been an endless source of joy, pride, and amazement. Vygotsky, Bakhtin, and Burke shared a passion for understanding the world in which we live in the hopes of building a better one. Tyler and Nicholas have been a source of similar aspirations on my part. Like children everywhere, they make it possible for the rest of us to dream about a better future and find strength to continue trying to make these dreams become reality. For these reasons, I dedicate this volume to them.

Contents

MIND *as* ACTION

❋ 1 ❋

The Task of Sociocultural Analysis

The task of sociocultural analysis is to understand how mental functioning is related to cultural, institutional, and historical context. The relationship between mind and sociocultural setting has concerned scholars for decades, if not centuries, but in recent years it has received renewed attention as dissatisfaction has grown with analyses that limit their focus to one or another part of the picture. In addition, investigators are being asked to contribute to the understanding of pressing contemporary problems more than ever before, and one of the ground rules for participating in this effort is that we not begin with the assumption that such problems come in pre-sliced disciplinary pieces.

When it comes to dealing with such issues in a way that recognizes their complexity, the human sciences have all too often come up short. In many respects, the problems we have in dealing with complex, multifaceted reality are similar to those in the story of the three blind men trying to understand what an elephant is. Like these men with their different and incommensurable perspectives on an elephant, various traditions in the human sciences have had different and incommensurable ideas about the essence of human nature. Some traditions have viewed humans as political animals, others have argued that our essence lies in tool-using activities, still others define us as symbol-using animals, and so forth.

In the contemporary social sciences, these views have been updated, but often at the cost of further fragmentation. For example, in

3

economics humans are now often viewed as rational choice makers, some areas of anthropology start with the assumption that humans are essentially defined by their place in a kinship system, and in psychology one can find views ranging from images of humans as mindless machines to humans as complexly programmed computers to humans as governed by dark, unconscious forces.

As is the case with the three blind men with different images of the elephant, none of these ideas about human nature is simply or completely false. Instead, each provides a partial picture, but one that remains unconnected with others. Furthermore, and more problematic in the long run, each provides an image of human nature that seems to be incommensurable and hence not just unconnected but unconnectable with the others. The story of the three blind men ends with each insisting that his was *the* true account of the elephant. In the social sciences, there is a tendency for each of many traditions to argue that its idea of human nature is *the* true one. In all instances, this contributes to the predicament of having no way to connect the various partial images together into a more complete and adequate account.

There are of course limits to the analogy I have outlined between the case of the three blind men and that of the human sciences. One of these limits concerns the roots of the predicaments in the two cases. In contrast to the physical blindness of the three men, many of the forms of conceptual blindness in the human sciences have arisen due to forces that operate in large modern bureaucratic organizations. One needs only to encounter a professional organization or interdepartmental politics at a university to be reminded of the degree to which specialization and isolation are basic facts of modern institutional life.

In this connection, just consider the case *within* a single discipline of the social sciences. The largest professional organization in the discipline of psychology in North America today—the American Psychological Association[1]—currently has over 100,000 members, each of whom must have membership in at least one of *forty-nine* divisions. These divisions, which are devoted to issues such as "Consumer Psychology," "Psychology of Religion," and "Population and Environmental Psychology," have typically emerged when a group of scholars or practitioners wants to pursue a particular issue and has found it difficult to do so within the confines of other divisions. The result has been a proliferation of divisions and subdivisions that often have little or no contact with one another and a vast array of partial, unconnected (if not unconnectable) pictures of psychological functioning.

Problems of this sort loom even greater when we move from looking at relations within a discipline to looking at relations among disciplines. It is easy for psychologists to have very little professional contact throughout their careers with sociologists, anthropologists, historians, or representatives of other human sciences. While many important benefits derive from specialization, it also results in what Kenneth Burke (1966) called "terministic screens" that impair our vision of phenomena in all their complexity. Indeed, in some cases it can lead to what he termed "learned incapacities" associated with socialization into a professional discourse. The result is that various disciplines rest on ideas about human nature that representatives of other disciplines find naive, trivial, or ludicrous, but because scholars can spend their professional life insulated from others' perspectives, there is little need or professional reward for confronting the constructs and methods of others.

One of the major results of this kind of fragmentation and isolation is that the human sciences are often viewed as incapable of providing useful interpretations of problems in the "real world" of modern society. In contrast to the tendency of specialists to examine each segment of complex phenomena in isolation (and to have difficulty saying how these segments are related to others), a basic fact about contemporary social problems is that they typically involve many dimensions and complex interrelationships among these dimensions. For example, contemporary social issues inevitably involve psychological *and* cultural *and* institutional *and* other dimensions.

As an example of what I have in mind, consider what the human sciences have had to say about some of the most pressing cultural, social, and political problems in the global arena, problems that it seems no one (certainly not human scientists) saw coming. During the 1990s, many of the certainties about how the world would operate, at least for the foreseeable future, have proven to be wildly off the mark. The Soviet Union no longer exists and no one seems to know what will follow in its wake; ethnic strife in places like Eastern Europe and India has occurred in ways that few had anticipated; the globalization of finance, manufacturing, and communication is affecting virtually everyone's life in ways that we have yet to understand—the list could go on and on.

In each of these cases, the argument is often made that major psychological, cultural, and institutional changes are an essential part of the picture. Focusing for the moment on the psychological dimensions of such issues, it has been said that some of the most conservative forces impeding the transitions now so desperately needed in the former Soviet Union are psychological in nature: everything—the government, laws, currencies—have changed, but old ways of thinking make real change next to impossible. Or when speaking of national conflict in places like the former Yugoslavia, the point has often been made that we cannot hope to understand, let alone deal, with the issues until we understand the beliefs about history and their implications for identity held by the Serbs, Croatians, and Bosnian Muslims.

To make this point about the psychological dimensions of these problems is certainly not to argue that they can be reduced to a psychological level—one of the things I am arguing *against*. Instead, my concern is with why psychologists have had so little to say about these and other major social and political issues of our day. In particular, why have psychologists had such a difficult time entering into productive dialogue with members of other disciplines in addressing such issues?

I ask these questions believing full well that psychology *has* made major contributions in many areas (often by collaborating with other disciplines). For example, in collaboration with neuroscience, psychology has made major strides in understanding brain functioning, and thanks to efforts in psychology we now know a great deal more about issues such as infant development. However, when it comes to psychology's contributions to issues typically taken up in disciplines such as sociology or political science, there is a marked lack of a common language that would make discussion and synergy possible.

Some might assume that this silence simply reflects the interests of the members of the discipline, and to some extent this may be true. After all, psychology is typically defined as the science of the mental processes or behavior of the individual, and some might argue that practitioners of such a science need not concern themselves with politics, society, and culture. However, I think there are other, more powerful reasons for this silence. Indeed, when asked, most psychologists would say that their research, practice, or teaching does have implications for today's broader social and political issues. Difficulties, nonetheless, typically arise when one asks us to be specific or when one asks for how our work has been recognized by others as having the implications claimed on its behalf. Another reason for believing that the silence is not self-imposed is that many psychologists, at least in informal conversation, state that they very much would like to be involved in discussions of contemporary social problems. There clearly seems to be a will, but not a very productive way, to engage in this discourse.

What I have said so far suggests that much of the fragmentation within and between disciplines can be traced to the bureaucratic forces that shape our lives. But such fragmentation is reinforced by differing theoretical assumptions about the essence of human nature. My purpose in what follows will be to examine these assumptions— assumptions that often go unrecognized and hence remain beyond the scrutiny of critical reflection. When these assumptions *are* challenged, they are often defended on the basis of being reflections of reality—a problematic claim to be examined further in the pages that follow. Furthermore, these assumptions tend to be made with little thought given to how the particular image they generate might be connected or connectable with others.

Translation at the Crossroads

To address the problems of different and incommensurable perspectives in the human sciences, two issues need to be considered. First, we must find a way to link perspectives without simply reducing one to another. One guiding assumption for this volume is that attempts to account for complex human phenomena by invoking a perspective grounded in a single discipline are as unlikely to be productive as were the attempts of each of the three blind men to come up with *the* true account of an elephant. The goal, then, is to arrive at an account—a kind of "translation at the crossroads"—that would make it possible to *link, but not reduce,* one perspective to another.

When trying to understand various viewpoints and their limitations, I think it useful to recognize that the basic assumptions and units of analysis that guide any inquiry in the human sciences are tied to political, cultural, and institutional interests. These interests may not be consciously recognized and may not be overtly invoked in pursuing a research agenda, but the acceptance of a set of assumptions inevitably occurs, committing one to a perspective grounded in them. Such a claim will come as no surprise to some, and it will irritate others. Regardless of one's initial response to it in the abstract, however, I hope to demonstrate its importance when considering concrete research efforts in the human sciences.

There are many ways one can divide up the perspectives offered by the human sciences. One of the most general and widely used of these involves a distinction between individual and society. In this connection, analytic strategies often take one of two general paths, depending on what is given analytic primacy. One path is grounded in the assumption that it is appropriate to begin with an account of societal phenomena and, on the basis of these phenomena, generate analyses of individual mental functioning; the other assumes that the way to understand societal phenomena is to start with psychological or other processes carried out by the individual.

As an illustration of these two basic alternatives on analytic primacy, consider statements by Aleksandr Romanovich Luria, one of the founders of the "Vygotsky-Leont'ev-Luria" school of cultural-historical psychology in the former USSR, on the one hand, and by Paul Churchland, a philosopher of cognitive science, on the other. In Luria's view:

> *In order to explain the highly complex forms of human consciousness one must go beyond the human organism. One must seek the origins of conscious activity and "categorical" behavior not in the recesses of the human brain or in the depths of the spirit, but in the external conditions of life. Above all, this means that one must seek these origins in the external processes of social life, in the social and historical forms of human existence.* (1981, p. 25; emphasis in the original)

In contrast, Churchland (1988) argues for a reductionist account of human consciousness[2] based on principles of natural science and gives analytic primacy not even to psychological but to neurological "connectionist" processes. In response to "cultural embedding objections" to his reductionist program, Churchland notes that such objections are typically based on the observation that humans discriminate and respond to very complex aspects of the environment, including "all of the intricacies that make up a functioning culture" (p. 42). Churchland agrees that complexity must be addressed, but he argues that this is

> wholly consistent with a reductionist program for understanding the nature of human cognition. What the reductionist must do is explain how a physical system can come to address and manipulate such subtle and culturally configured features. While this is certainly a challenge, it no longer appears to be a problem in principle, for . . . with suitable teaching, the network generates an internal representation of [features] regardless [of complexity]. This does not mean that the features addressed are magical, or super-physical, or beyond the realm of natural science. It just means that the simplest possible definition or representation of them may well be the entire configuration of the successfully trained network! (p. 42)

These statements by Luria and Churchland are noteworthy for the explicitness of their underlying assumptions. Even in the absence of such overt formulation, however, I would argue that most scholars in the social sciences hold some position on this issue of analytic primacy. In some cases, this may simply be a matter of disciplinary orientation. Thus psychologists may assume that we can explain cultural, historical, or institutional phenomena by appealing to psychological processes, sociologists may assume that we can explain psychological phenomena by appealing to institutional processes, connectionists might try to account for both by reducing them to physical processes, and so forth. One's position on this issue may reflect other factors as well, but a major problem with virtually all such formulations is that there seem to be few bases other than personal preference or disciplinary affiliation for making a selection among the alternatives.

The fact that this debate seems to go on and on with no principled resolution in sight suggests that deeper issues may be at stake. Namely, it suggests that the academic dispute over whether to give psychological or societal processes analytic primacy may reflect an underlying debate—a debate that cannot be resolved through rational argument. Another way of putting this is to say that our discussions about these issues in academia are embedded in a broader sociocultural setting—something that should come as no surprise to anyone espousing a sociocultural position. My candidate for the relevant sociocultural setting is a long-standing debate about ethical and political issues in modern society. In particular, I have in mind a discussion grounded in an antinomy between individual and society.

Among the commentators on this antinomy, Elias (1991) has provided some important insight and wisdom relevant to my argument. According to Elias, this antinomy resembles a "curious party game that certain groups in western society are apt to indulge in over and over again" (p. 54). The two opposing groups he has in mind endlessly engage in encounters of the following sort:

> One says, "Everything depends on the individual," the other, "Everything depends on society". The first group says: "But it is always particular individuals who decide to do this and not that." The others reply: "But their decisions are socially conditioned." The first group says: "But what you call 'social conditioning' only comes about because others want to do something and do it." The others reply: "But what these others want to do and do is also socially conditioned." (p. 54)

Elias suggests that this "debate" is likely to go on endlessly and fruitlessly because there is no obvious way to resolve it rationally.

In his view, the reason for this is that at bottom the debate is not grounded in empirical fact or logic but in "valuations" of society and the individual. According to him:

> In their most popular form, the professions of one side present the "individual" as the means and the "social whole" as the supreme value and purpose, while the other regard "society" as the means and "individuals" as the supreme value and purpose. And in both cases these ideals and goals of political thought and action are often presented as facts. What one side says *should* be is thought and spoken of as if it *is*. For example . . . members of groups in which it is loyal to demand and wish that the claims of individuals *should* have priority over those of the group often believe they can observe that individuals are the true reality, that which actually exists, while societies are something that come afterwards, something less real and perhaps even a mere figment of thought, an abstraction. . . . In short, what one understands by "individual" and "society" still depends to a large extent on the form taken by what people wish for and fear. (pp. 83–85; emphasis in the original)

It is essential for sociocultural research to formulate its position vis-à-vis this antinomy between individual and society. If it does not, such research is likely to be misunderstood or falsely categorized. For example, investigators who presuppose analytic primacy for mental functioning in the individual might view sociocultural research as amounting to a form of social learning theory concerned with what Lawrence and Valsiner (1993) term "internalization as cultural transmission." Other investigators who give analytic primacy to mental functioning might be inclined to interpret sociocultural research as amounting to a call for rejecting the study of psychological phenomena altogether in favor of focusing on cultural, historical, and institutional issues.

Many such troubling interpretations are grounded squarely in the individual–society antinomy and the related opposition between mental functioning and sociocultural setting. The persistence of the interpretations reflects the power such antinomies have in shaping our thought and discussion. Once they are permitted to frame the debate, we are put in the position of having to choose between stark alternatives, a position from which it seems very difficult to extricate oneself.

As is the case with many antinomies, the key to dealing with one between individual and society may be to recognize that the very formulation of issues in either/or alternatives is counterproductive. This is precisely why the term "false" seems to appear so often as a modifier of "antinomy" in general and why I would argue that the individual–society antinomy in particular is problematic. A major part of the problem is how the terms placed in opposition are understood. They are typically understood as referring to essences or objects (Elias's "true reality") that have some kind of independent existence. As long as we give "mental functioning" and "sociocultural setting," or "individual" and "society," this kind of ontological interpretation, sociocultural research is likely to be confused about its agenda and methods.

An alternative that makes it possible to avoid this confusion is to keep in mind that these terms are hypothetical constructs or conceptual tools (tools that may be of only temporary use) in our process of inquiry. In this capacity, they are "inherently necessary for controlled inquiry," as John Dewey (1938, p. 263) noted in his account of general propositions, but they are not "linguistic expression[s] of something already known which needs symbols only for the purposes of convenient recall and communication." The implication of this is that it may be important to reflect on the conceptual tools we employ to formulate the issues we wish to investigate. In particular, it is important to consider whether these conceptual tools might encourage us to "take sides" or otherwise lead us to perceive one perspective on reality as the one and only truth, a truth that cannot be reconciled with others.

Multiple Perspectives on Human Action

An individual who has made major contributions to the discussion of these issues is Kenneth Burke (1966, 1969a, 1969b, 1972, 1984). Like several other figures whose ideas I will use, Burke is very hard to categorize in standard academic terms. His writings have obvious implications for literary studies, but they have also been recognized as being relevant to anthropology (Geertz, 1973), psychology (Bruner, 1986), social criticism (Lentricchia, 1985), and sociology (Gusfield, 1989). In general, it is very difficult to place Burke's writings within the confines of any single discipline. This is no accident; he wrote a great deal about the "learned incapacities" and "disciplinary pathologies" that restrict the horizons of modern academic discourse.

Burke's critical and philosophical focus gave rise to an approach whose primary implications have to do with method. In an extensive review of the implications of his writings for the social sciences, the sociologist Joseph Gusfield (1989, p. 4) observes that "Burke's importance . . . lies not so much in any particular content of any particular part of his writings, but in the development of a method, a perspective about perspectives." This claim applies equally well to Burke's potential role in what I am calling sociocultural analysis. Throughout this volume, I will rely on several of Burke's ideas as I try to develop an account of sociocultural research. His account of "dramatism" (Burke, 1968) will be of particular importance since it provides a framework for a set of more concrete methods and claims.

The starting point of Burke's dramatistic method is that it takes human *action* as the basic phenomenon to be analyzed. This assumption provides the groundwork for building links between Burke's ideas and those of figures such as Lev Semënovich Vygotsky (1978, 1981a, 1981b, 1981c, 1987; Wertsch, 1991; Zinchenko, 1985), Mikhail Mikhailovich Bakhtin (1981, 1984, 1986), and George Herbert Mead (1934; Joas, 1985). Although there are important differences among these figures, at a general level they all took human action to be their fundamental unit of analysis. In all cases, they were primarily concerned with describing, interpreting, or explaining action, as opposed to some other phenomenon such as behavior, mental or linguistic structure, or attitudes. Furthermore, they all viewed any attempt to break this unit down into more basic "elements" (Vygotsky, 1987) as misguided and as likely to distort the very phenomena to be investigated. For none of these figures did such assumptions imply that detailed analyses carried out by specialists could not contribute to an account of human action. Instead, their point was always that such specialized perspectives must take their place in a larger integrated effort.

In Burke's case, the notion of action was coupled with that of "motive"; he was fundamentally concerned with "what is involved, when we say what people are doing and why they are doing it" (1969a, p. xv). In his view, the forms of thought that go into understanding this "are equally present in systematically elaborated metaphysical structures, in legal judgments, in poetry and fiction, in political and scientific works, in news and in bits of gossip offered at random" (p. xv).

For Burke, the actions of persons contrast with the "sheer 'motions' of 'things'" (1966, p. 53):

> The splashing of the waves against the beach, or the endless cycle of births and deaths in biologic organisms would be examples of sheer motion. Yet we, the typically symbol-using animal, cannot relate to one another sheerly as things in motion. Even the behaviorist, who studies man in terms of his laboratory experiments,

must treat his colleagues as *persons*, rather than purely and simply as automata responding to stimuli.

Burke notes that he is "not pronouncing on the metaphysics of this controversy." Indeed, it is possible in his view that "the distinction between *things moving* and *persons acting* is but an illusion." The fact that Burke was concerned with the symbolic frameworks we use to interpret human motives and action means, however, that "illusion or not, the human race cannot possibly get along with itself on the basis of any other intuition." As will become obvious, this does not mean that Burke's approach succumbs to the critique of "folk psychology" that has been outlined in cognitive science (e.g., Stitch, 1983). Instead, his ideas turn out to be quite consistent with several contemporary developments in cognitive anthropology (D'Andrade, 1995; Hutchins, 1995a) and connectionism (A. Clark, 1993).

Burke's approach to human action is that it can be adequately understood only by invoking multiple perspectives and by examining the dialectical tensions that exist among them. This "perspective about perspectives" (Gusfield, 1989, p. 4) reflects Burke's strongly critical stance toward "the wisdom and infallibility of [any] deterministic and monist perspective." Burke's attempt to avoid the limitations, and even the arrogance, of such monist perspectives is concretized in his account of the "pentad" and its role in the dramatistic approach to human action and motives:

> We shall use five terms as generating principle of our investigation. They are: Act, Scene, Agent, Agency, Purpose. In a rounded statement about motives, you must have some word that names the *act* (names what took place, in thought or deed), and another that names the *scene* (the background of the act, the situation in which it occurred); also, you must indicate what person or kind of person (*agent*) performed the act, what means or instruments he used (*agency*), and the *purpose*. Men may violently disagree about the purposes behind a given act, or about the character of the person who did it, or how he did it, or in what kind of situation he acted; or they may even insist upon totally different words to name the act itself. But be that as it may, any complete statement about motives will offer *some kind of* answers to these five questions: what was done (act), when or where it was done (scene), who did it (agent), how he did it (agency), and why (purpose). (1969, p. xv)

There is a deceptive simplicity to Burke's pentad. The questions What? Where? Who? How? and Why? are what school children typically are taught to answer in essays, and they are questions newspaper stories are supposed to answer. However, when considered in their complexity, the methodological implications of Burke's ideas for sociocultural studies are wide ranging and profound.

The first point I would make in this regard echoes Gusfield's observation about Burke's importance for sociology: Burke's major potential contribution to sociocultural studies lies "in the development of a method" (1989, p. 4). Burke envisioned the pentad as a tool for conducting inquiry about human action and motives. He did *not* view it as a simple representation or reflection of reality. Relying once again on Dewey's formulation, the pentad does not constitute a "linguistic expression of something already known which needs symbols only for the purposes of convenient recall and communication" (1938, p. 263). To assume that pentadic terms were useful simply for convenient recall and communication would be to assume that terms such as "scene" and "agent" have some kind of counterpart in an independently existing reality. This was not Burke's intention.

The assumption that pentadic elements are tools for interpretation rather than reflections of reality is perhaps most obvious in Burke's analysis of scene. The basic notion of scene is that it is a kind of "container" within which agents act and acts occur:

> There is implicit in the quality of a scene the quality of the action that is to take place within it. This would be another way of saying that the act will be consistent with the scene. . . . Or, if you will, the stage-set contains the action *ambiguously* (as regards the norms of action)—and in the course of the play's development this ambiguity is converted into a corresponding *articulacy*. The proportion would be: scene is to act as implicit is to explicit. (1969, pp. 6–7)

When analyzing scenes, Burke made it clear that they do not have some kind of independent, static existence and simply wait to be accurately or inaccurately identified. Instead, like the other elements of his pentad, the scene is a tool for interpreting human action and motives. This surfaces quite clearly in his comments on the "circumference" of a scene:

> One has *a great variety of circumferences* to select as characterizations of a given agent's scene. For a man is not only in the situation peculiar to his era or to his particular place in that era (even if we could agree on the traits that characterize his era). He is also in a situation extending through centuries; he is in a "generically human" situation; and he is in a "universal" situation. Who is to say, once and for all, which of these circumferences is to be selected

as the motivation of his act, insofar as the act is to be defined in
scenic terms? . . . The contracting and expanding of scene is rooted
in the very nature of linguistic placement. And a selection of circumference from among this range is in itself an act, an "act of
faith," with the definition or interpretation of the act taking shape
accordingly. (1969a, p. 84)

This account of scene entails the assumption that what counts
as the scene when making one interpretation of an action may not
count as the scene when making another. When we argue over why
someone did something by arguing over whether it was just the immediate situation that person was in or whether it was, say, the whole
political situation in the United States today, we are arguing over
what the relevant circumference of a scene is. Such discussions make
it clear that there is often no simple, objective, a priori definition of
the scene and its boundaries, a point that does not deter us from relying heavily on the notion of scene when interpreting action.

Many of the points Burke makes throughout his writings stem
from his efforts to reflect on and criticize interpretations of action
in the human sciences. He clearly believed that some interpretations
are better, or at least more appropriate, than others, but he strongly
resisted the assumption that a deterministic and monistic perspective is capable of providing an adequate understanding of human
action. Given this, he viewed his role as being one of understanding
the limits of such understanding:

> We take it for granted that, insofar as men cannot themselves create
> the universe, there must remain something essentially enigmatic
> about the problem of motives, and that this underlying enigma will
> manifest itself in inevitable ambiguities and inconsistencies among
> the terms for motives. Accordingly, what we want is *not terms that
> avoid ambiguity*, but *terms that clearly reveal the strategic spots
> at which ambiguities necessarily arise.* (1969a, p. xviii)

Many of the points Burke made about human action and motives
surface in the writings of others in the human sciences, and in most
cases this is not due to any influence he may have had. For example,
it is fairly obvious that many investigators begin their analyses of
human phenomena from the perspective of one or another element
of the pentad, and in this sense they may be viewed as sharing Burke's
insights. However, the fact that investigators have typically used
one or another element of the pentad is precisely the problem in his
view; it is what Burke (1966, p. 52) saw as ensuing from employing
single terministic screens that result in "over-socialized," "over-

biologized," "over-psychologized," "over-physicized," or "over-poetized" pictures of human motives and action. Commentators such as Gusfield (1989) have argued that the reliance on single terministic screens may characterize—and plague—entire academic disciplines. Thus Gusfield argues that sociologists are more likely than psychologists to emphasize scene rather than agent, and psychologists are likely to do just the opposite. Implicit in Gusfield's comment is the assumption that no one perspective in isolation is likely to provide an adequate account of human action.

As an illustration of how an isolated focus on a single element of the pentad can lead a discipline astray, consider some comments the religious scholar Martin Marty (1994) has made about the role of psychology in contemporary studies of fundamentalism. He argues that there is a general tendency among many psychologists to focus exclusively on what Burke would call the agent when trying to understand major social and cultural problems, and this gives rise to vexing problems when it comes to understanding religious and national fundamentalisms. In Marty's experience, this tendency to focus on the agent in isolation has resulted in psychologists' often being told "to wait in the anteroom while experts from other disciplines first report" (p. 16). Psychologists are told to do so because they often "engage in psychological reductionism." Marty refers to such reductionism in discussions of fundamentalism as "nothing buttery" as in "'fundamentalists are *nothing but* crazy people who . . . ' or 'millennialists are *nothing but* frightened people who. . . . '"

Hence the first general point to be gleaned from Burke's writings is not that the human sciences should formulate issues in terms of one or another of the pentadic elements but that it is essential to *coordinate* the perspectives provided by these elements in some way. To be sure, this is no easy assignment, and Burke did not assume that it was. It often seems that we have reached the limits of human understanding when we try to coordinate two or more pentadic elements into a single account of action and motive. For example, some accounts of action that begin with an agent might attempt to incorporate information about the scene as well, but when it comes to extending this account even further by addressing, say, how the purpose or the instruments ("agency") used play a role, the picture gets impossibly complex.

The major problem that confronts us, then, is how to "live in the middle" (Holquist, 1994) of several different analytic perspectives. Each such analytic perspective involves a terminology, and as Burke

(1966, p. 45) notes, "even if any given terminology is a *reflection* of reality, by its very nature as a terminology it must be a *selection* of reality; and to this extent it must function also as a *deflection* of reality." Such warnings might tempt us to seek an approach that was not blinded by terminology and hence by terministic screens, but as Burke points out, such a hope is misguided. "We *must* use terministic screens, since we can't say anything without the use of terms; whatever we use, they necessarily constitute a corresponding kind of screen; and any such screen necessarily directs the attention to one field rather than another" (p. 50). Again, we are back to seeking a way to live in the middle.

Methodological Individualism in the Copyright Age

In this book, I outline a way to live in the middle. The specific approach I take involves *mediated action* as a unit of analysis. In Burkean terms, this involves a version of the dialectic between agent and instrumentality. I have chosen to focus on the "ratio" provided by these two elements in Burke's pentad for a specific reason. Namely, I believe that much of what we do in the human sciences is too narrowly focused on the agent in isolation and that an important way to go beyond this is to recognize the role played by "mediational means" or "cultural tools" (terms I use interchangeably) in human action. Burke's notion of agent represents one pole in the antinomy outlined by Elias, but in my view this pole has come to dominate contemporary discussions in the human sciences to such a degree that it deserves special critical attention.

The assumption that analytic primacy should be given to individuals as agents underlies discourse far beyond that found in contemporary social science. For example, the literary scholar Northrop Frye (1957, pp. 96–97) argued that there has been a "tendency, marked from Romantic times on, to think of the individual as ideally prior to his society." In this context, Frye believed that we have come to give authors and other creative artists more credit than they deserve for the aesthetic objects they produce. This is so because in our understanding of creative activity the role of convention has receded far into the background. Warning against such a view, Frye argued that "all art is equally conventionalized, but we do not ordinarily notice this fact unless we are unaccustomed to the convention. In our day the conventional element in literature is elaborately disguised by the law of copyright pretending that every work of art is an invention distinctive enough to be patented" (p. 96).

As Frye noted, this practice of viewing all art as a distinctive invention—that is, focusing on the individual's contribution rather than on the conventions (i.e., cultural tools) employed—is a relatively recent one, arising with the assimilation of literature into private enterprise in the "copyright age." In the copyright age, we have such a strong tendency to focus on the unique contribution of the individual that we overlook what Frye saw as the fundamental shaping force of conventions employed as a kind of tool in the creative act. Among other things:

> This state of things makes it difficult to appraise a literature which includes Chaucer, much of whose poetry is translated or paraphrased from others; Shakespeare, whose plays sometimes follow their sources almost verbatim; and Milton, who asked for nothing better than to steal as much as possible out of the Bible. It is not only the inexperienced reader who looks for a *residual* originality in such works. Most of us tend to think of a poet's real achievement as distinct from, or even contrasted with, the achievement present in what he stole, and we are thus apt to concentrate on peripheral rather than on central critical facts. For instance, the central greatness of *Paradise Regained*, as a poem, is not the greatness of the rhetorical decorations that Milton added to his source, but the greatness of the theme itself, which Milton *passes on* to the reader from his source. (1957, p. 96)

To the extent we are enmeshed in the assumptions of the copyright age, we are apt to resist such an analysis. To consider artistic creativity simply as a matter of passing on a theme from a source to a reader seems to demote it to something much less important and worthy of distinction than we normally assume. Frye's point, however, was that in the copyright age—an age of "literature which conceals or ignores its conventional links" (1957, p. 101)—we often lose perspective about the centrality of convention in the creative process, and we view the individual artist as the main, if not sole, source of a text or other aesthetic object.

Of course Frye was not saying that individuals make no contribution to the production of artistic objects. After all, poems and novels do not simply write themselves. He also was not saying that all poets, novelists, or other artists are of equal merit. However, he did believe that in the copyright age we are all too apt to "accept a critical view which confuses the original with the aboriginal" (1957, p. 97). And from this perspective we are all too likely to imagine "that a 'creative' poet sits down with a pencil and some blank paper and eventually produces a new poem in a special act of creation *ex nihilo.*" Frye contrasts this with a view that emphasizes that "the new baby is conditioned by a hereditary and environmental kinship to a society which already exists," a view that in his mind has "the initial advantage of being closer to the facts it deals with."

My goal in reviewing Frye's comments about authorship in the copyright age is not to produce an account of creativity or of the sociocultural underpinnings of cultural models of creativity. Instead, I see Frye's notions as having major implications for how we understand human action and mental functioning of all sorts. In my view, his claim about our tendency to focus on an individual's unique contribution and to ignore the role of "mediational means" applies to many of the analyses we carry out in the contemporary human sciences, especially those carried out in psychology. To paraphrase Frye, we could say that research in this discipline is all too often based on the pretense that every psychological act is an invention distinctive enough to be copyrighted by the individual producing it.

This criticism is hardly new. As I have argued elsewhere (Wertsch, 1991), critiques of the assumption that the individual acts ex nihilo can be found in the writings of Vygotsky (1978, 1981a, 1981b, 1987), Bakhtin (1986; Medvedev, 1978), Dewey (1938), Burke (1966), and Taylor (1985), figures whose writings have motivated writings in sociocultural studies such as those by Wertsch, del Río, and Alvarez (1995). Related critiques can be found in other areas of the human sciences as well. For example, it is interesting to consider points made by figures such as Lukes (1977, p. 180) in discussions of "methodological individualism." "Methodological individualism . . . is a prescription for explanation, asserting that no purported explanations of social (or individual) phenomena are to count as explanations, or . . . as rock-bottom explanations, unless they are couched wholly in terms of facts about individuals." Lukes traces the origins of methodological individualism to Hobbes, and he argues that it has come to occupy a dominant theoretical position in sociology, psychology, economics, political theory, and other areas of the human sciences.

Authors such as Vygotsky, Dewey, Burke, Bakhtin, and Lukes clearly differ over many issues. However, one on which they would all seem to agree is the need to go beyond the isolated individual when trying to understand human action, including communicative and mental action. While none of these authors used Frye's term, all of them would agree with the need to avoid the false assumptions of the copyright age.

Similar concerns have emerged in quite different disciplines. For example, in studies of artificial life (Resnick, 1994) major questions have arisen about the appropriateness of assuming that some sort of centralized control must be assumed to account for various phenomena. In artificial life research, these phenomena include processes other than human action—phenomena ranging from molecular interaction to robotics. As a result, the critique in artificial life writings of centralized control comprises a more general version of critiques we have already seen that call into question a too exclusive focus on the agent in the human sciences. Nonetheless, many of the problems that motivate the critique of centralized control models in artificial life research are parallel to those outlined by figures such as Frye and Lukes.

Resnick argues that the "centralized mindset" is pervasive in our thinking and leads to a host of problems:

> The centralized mindset can manifest itself in many different ways. When people observe patterns or structures in the world, they tend to assume that patterns are created either *by lead* or *by seed*. That is, they assume that a *leader* orchestrated the pattern (e.g., the bird at the front of the flock, the pacemaker slime-mold cell), or they assume that some *seed* (some preexisting, built-in inhomogeneity in the environment) gave rise to the pattern, much as a grain of sand gives rise to a pearl. (1994, p. 231)

Resnick believes that an important shift toward accepting decentralized models is now under way among scholars concerned with artificial life, and in this sense he is more optimistic about change than is someone like Frye, who sees such issues from the perspective of long-standing historical traditions. Even so, Resnick recognizes that the transition he envisions will not be easy to make:

> But seeing the world in terms of decentralized interactions is a difficult shift for many people. It requires a fundamental shift in perspective, a new way of looking at the world. At some deep level, people have strong attachments to centralized ways of thinking. When people see patterns in the world (like a flock of birds), they often assume that there is some kind of centralized control (a leader of the flock). And in constructing artificial systems, people often impose centralized control where none is needed (e.g., using top-down, hierarchical programming structures to control a robot's behavior). (1994, p. 230)

In many studies of cognitive science and artificial life, there has been a tendency to move away from the centralized mindset by invoking some notion of environment to account for how processes are organized. In summarizing a point made by Simon (1969), Resnick argues: "Don't underestimate the role of the environment in influencing and constraining behavior. People often seem to think of the environment as something to be *acted upon*, not something to be *interacted with*. People tend to focus on the behaviors of individual objects, ignoring the environment that surrounds (and interacts with) the objects" (1994, p. 239).

Hutchins (1995a, 1995b) has made parallel arguments about the role of the environment from the perspective of cognitive science. In contrast to the more general level of Resnick's analysis, where the environment was dealt with at a quite abstract level, Hutchins tends to focus on certain aspects of the sociocultural context—what he terms "sociotechnical systems." This is evident in his analysis of "how a cockpit remembers its speeds":

> Cognitive science normally takes the individual agent as its unit of analysis. In many human endeavors, however, the outcomes of interest are not determined entirely by the information processing properties of individuals. Nor can they be inferred from the properties of the individual agents, alone, no matter how detailed the knowledge of the properties of those individuals may be. In commercial aviation, for example, the successful completion of a flight is produced by a system that typically includes two or more pilots interacting with each other and with a suite of technological devices. (1995b, p. 265)

Many of the critiques raised by figures such as Resnick in artificial life and Hutchins in cognitive science echo lines of reasoning developed in quite different intellectual traditions such as literary analysis and social theory. In these cases, the point is that analytic efforts that focus too exclusively on one element in isolation are severely limited, if not misguided. For my purposes, the point is that analytic efforts that seek to account for human action by focusing on the *individual agent* are severely limited, if not misguided. One of the tasks of sociocultural analysis, then, is to find a way to avoid the pitfalls of such individualistic reductionism. Taking mediated action as a unit of analysis provides a means for doing just this.

Notes

1. A further point to note here is that in the 1980s a completely new organization, the American Psychological Society, was founded because

many psychologists believed that the APA had become dominated by particular factions and left inadequate room for their own interests to be pursued. The dispute in this case was largely between parties concerned with research and parties concerned with clinical and related areas of psychology, but the general implications for the present argument remain the same.

2. Although both Luria and Churchland use the term "consciousness," by no means should one assume that the two authors understand it in the same way. The terms fits into quite different theoretical frameworks in the two cases and hence has quite different interpretations.

❈ 2 ❈

Properties of Mediated Action

A fundamental claim of the sociocultural analysis outlined in this book is that its proper focus is human action. As understood here, action may be external as well as internal, and it may be carried out by groups, both small and large, or by individuals. In the view of many investigators, there are important parallels between action carried out on the social and individual planes and on the external and internal planes (e.g., Leont'ev, 1981; Vygotsky, 1978, 1981b, 1987; Wertsch, 1985). The fact that the notion of action is not tied solely to individual or to social processes means that analyses grounded in this construct are not inherently limited by the antinomic poles of "valuation" outlined by Elias. For my purposes, it is particularly important that analyses of action not be limited by the dictates of methodological individualism.

Of course this is not to say that action does not have an individual psychological dimension. It clearly does. The point is to think of this as a *moment* of action rather than as a separate process or entity that exists somehow in isolation. In what follows I often focus on the psychological moment of action, but my effort throughout will be to formulate psychological claims in such a way that their relationship to sociocultural context is always apparent.

Given that my focus has now expanded from mental functioning to a more general category of human action, I need to revisit my original formulation of sociocultural analysis. In the previous chapter, I stated that the task of sociocultural analysis is to understand how mental functioning is related to cultural, institutional, and historical context. This formulation could now be revised to read: The task of a sociocultural approach is to explicate the relationships between human *action*, on the one hand, and the cultural, institutional, and historical contexts in which this action occurs, on the other.

The specific notion of action I examine is *mediated action*. In the pentadic terms outlined by Burke, this involves focusing on agents and their cultural tools—the mediators of action. Such a focus gives less emphasis to other elements in the pentad such as scene and purpose, but I would argue that it makes sense to give the relationship between agent and instrument a privileged position, at least initially, in sociocultural research for several reasons. First, a focus on the agent–instrument dialectic is perhaps the most direct way to overcome the limitations of methodological individualism, the copyright age, the centralized mindset, and so forth. An appreciation of how mediational means or cultural tools are involved in action forces one to live in the middle. In particular, it forces us to go beyond the individual agent when trying to understand the forces that shape human action.

Second, analyses of mediated action, or "agent-acting-with-mediational-means" (Wertsch, Tulviste, & Hagstrom, 1993), provide important insights into other dimensions of the pentad—scene, purpose, and act. This is because these other pentadic elements are often shaped, or even "created" (Silverstein, 1985), by mediated action. To make this point is not to argue that one can reduce the analysis of these other elements to that of mediated action. Burke has demonstrated quite convincingly that such reductionism cannot work in the end. It is to say, however, that the perspective on human action provided by the agent–instrument relationship provides some important insights into the nature of other elements and relationships of pentadic analysis.

These first two points about mediated action point to a third—namely, that it is a natural candidate for a unit of analysis in sociocultural research. It provides a kind of natural link between action, including mental action, and the cultural, institutional, and historical contexts in which such action occurs. This is so because the mediational means, or cultural tools, are inherently situated culturally, institutionally, and historically. This is something I return to in more detail later in this chapter, but for now the point is that even when one focuses primarily on the individual agent's role in mediated action, the fact that cultural tools are involved means that the sociocultural embeddedness of the action is always built into one's analysis.

In the view outlined here, almost all human action is mediated action. Given this, one would expect that it is very difficult to provide an exhaustive list of action forms and mediational means, and this is indeed the case. My goal in this and the following sections is not to provide a rigid definition or system of categorization that would encompass every instance of mediated action or cultural tool. Any attempt to do so would be either so abstract or so expansive as to have little meaning. Instead, I outline a set of basic claims that characterize mediated action and cultural tools, and I illustrate each claim with some concrete examples. Specifically, I examine ten basic claims: (1) mediated action is characterized by an irreducible tension between agent and mediational means; (2) mediational means are material; (3) mediated action typically has multiple simultaneous goals; (4) mediated action is situated on one or more developmental paths; (5) mediational means constrain as well as enable action; (6) new mediational means transform mediated action; (7) the relationship of agents toward mediational means can be characterized in terms of mastery; (8) the relationship of agents toward mediational means can be characterized in terms of appropriation; (9) mediational means are often produced for reasons other than to facilitate mediated action; and (10) mediational means are associated with power and authority.

An Irreducible Tension: Agent and Mediational Means

Throughout this book, my analysis of mediated action focuses on two elements: agent and mediational means. This constitutes a selective emphasis on a subset of the elements one could take into account when examining human action, and indeed the other pentadic elements of scene, act, and purpose will make an appearance in what I have to say from time to time.

The essence of examining agent and cultural tools in mediated action is to examine them as they interact. Any attempt to reduce the account of mediated action to one or the other of these elements runs the risk of destroying the phenomenon under observation. But from time to time, it may be productive to abstract these moments, or aspects, as part of an analytic strategy, and this is what I often do. While we might isolate one element for an analysis, we need to keep in mind that these elements are phenomena that do not really exist independently of action.

The kind of analytic approach envisioned here has strong parallels with the basic methodological framework proposed by Vygotsky (1987). As van der Veer and Valsiner (1991, p. 399) have noted, Vygotsky took a "consistent *anti-reductionistic stance*" in outlining his account of human consciousness. Drawing heavily on Gestalt theorists of his time, he argued against Pavlovian and other elementaristic approaches when developing his claims about issues such as the development of thinking and speech. He insisted on the need to focus on *units*, which possess "*all the basic characteristics of the whole*" (1987, p. 46), rather than *elements* of analysis.

When warning against "the decomposition of the complex mental whole into its elements" (Vygotsky, 1987, p. 45), Vygotsky employed an analogy from chemistry about the relationship between water, on the one hand, and the elements of oxygen and hydrogen, on the other:

> The essential feature of this form of analysis is that its products are of a different nature than the whole from which they were derived. The elements lack the characteristics inherent in the whole and they possess properties that it did not possess. When one approaches the problem of thinking and speech by decomposing it into its elements, one adopts the strategy of the man who resorts to the decomposition of water into hydrogen and oxygen in his search for a scientific explanation of the characteristics of water, its capacity to extinguish fire or its conformity to Archimedes law for example. This man will discover, to his chagrin, that hydrogen burns and oxygen sustains combustion. He will never succeed in explaining the characteristics of the whole by analyzing the characteristics of its elements.

One of the results of focusing on the irreducible tension between agent and mediational means is that the boundaries between these two pentadic elements begin to erode. For example, the very notion of agent begins to be redefined. Instead of assuming that an agent, considered in isolation, is responsible for action, the appropriate designation of agent may be something like "individual-operating-with-mediational-means" (Wertsch, Tulviste, & Hagstrom, 1993). Such a description makes it possible to provide a more adequate response to the question, Who is carrying out the action? Or in the case of speech, Who is doing the talking? (Wertsch, 1991).

To illustrate the irreducible tension involved in mediated action I turn to a couple of examples. The first of these might at first glance seem out of place in an analysis devoted primarily to symbolic action and mental functioning. This is the track-and-field event of pole vaulting. I employ it, however, for a specific reason: unlike many cases of mediated action, especially those involving spoken language, where the mediational means appear to be ephemeral, the materiality of the mediational means in this case is obvious and easy to grasp. As is the case with most forms of mediated action, it is useful to approach the analysis of pole vaulting from a historical perspective.

Pole vaulting is thought to have originated in an early English practice of vaulting across streams with the aid of sticks made of hickory, spruce, or other strong woods. Vaulting for distance became a common sport, and this was succeeded by vaulting for height. The modern event of pole vaulting involves the vaulter running down a 125-foot runway with a pole in his[1] hands, planting the pole in a vaulting box at the end of the runway, and using the pole and his momentum to lift himself off the ground and over a bar that is held up by two uprights. Pole vaulting has been a part of the modern Olympic Games since their inception in 1896. Records in these games have increased over the years from a height of ten feet and ten inches in 1896 to over twenty feet today.

Pole vaulting considered as a form of mediated action provides a clear illustration of the irreducibility of this unit of analysis. For example, it is futile, if not ridiculous, to try to understand the action of pole vaulting in terms of the mediational means—the pole—or the agent in isolation. The pole by itself does not magically propel vaulters over a cross bar; it must be used skillfully by the agent. At the same time, an agent without a pole or with an inappropriate pole is incapable of participating in the event.

In this case, as in others, to recognize the irreducible tension between agent and mediational means is not to conceptualize mediated action as an undifferentiated whole. Instead, it is to conceptualize it as a system characterized by dynamic tension among various elements. It is important to keep sight of the elements within this system for at least two reasons. First, many of the analytic strategies for examining mediated action are made possible by the fact that one can isolate its elements. Among other things, such isolation allows various specialized perspectives to bring their insights to bear, and it also is often the key to understanding how change occurs in mediated action. Of course any analytic exercise involving the isolation of elements in mediated action must be carried out with an eye to how the pieces fit together in the end, but it cannot really get off the ground if mediated action is treated as an undifferentiated whole.

The second reason for considering various elements in mediated action is that it encourages the investigator to examine the various "mixes" of these elements. An analysis that focuses solely on the irreduciblity of mediated action as a bounded system all too naturally suggests a static system in which no dialectic tension is involved. While the elements of agent and mediational means are always involved in mediated action, one of these may take on special importance in particular cases. Furthermore, the transformations that mediated action undergoes often involve changes in this mix rather than the introduction of a new element. In all such cases an understanding of such dialectical complexities requires the separation and comparison of elements.

Returning to the case of pole vaulting provides an illustration of these points. As already noted, this form of mediated action is impossible without both the mediational means and the agent (as well as the other pentadic elements, but again, I am focusing on these two here). However, any attempt to understand this form of mediated action in more depth will often require specialized perspectives that focus on one or another of these elements in relative isolation, to examine how the contribution, or mix, of these two elements varies. For example, specialized analyses of the pole's material properties and how they do or do not make it heavy, flexible, and so forth could be quite relevant. And conversely, specialized studies of an agent's skills and how these skills can develop and be enhanced, say through an improved diet, are also quite relevant.

A second illustration comes from mathematics, an area that clearly qualifies as "semiotic mediation" (Wertsch, 1985, 1991). In this connection, consider the following multiplication problem:

$$\begin{array}{r} 343 \\ \times 822 \end{array}$$

If asked to solve this problem, you could probably come up with the answer of 281,946. If asked how you arrived at this solution, you might say, "I just multiplied 343 by 822!" and you might show me your calculations, which might look like this:

$$\begin{array}{r} 343 \\ \underline{822} \\ 686 \\ 686 \\ \underline{2744} \\ 281946 \end{array}$$

From the perspective of mediated action, the question to ask in such a case is, Was it really you (i.e., the isolated agent) who solved the problem? (After all, you said "*I* multiplied. . . . ") To see the force of this question, consider what we would do if asked to make one small change in the procedure. Namely, consider what you would do in response to the request to multiply 343 by 822, but without placing the numbers in the vertical array used above. Most of us would be stumped at this point, and even if we could solve this problem, others involving larger numbers would probably be impossible if we could not rely on the procedure of placing one number above the other as in the illustration. The first issue these questions raise, then, is whether it is really the agent alone who solved this problem. If this were the case, why do we have such difficulty in solving the "same" problem when asked to do so in the second condition? A seemingly slight change in how the problem is written out seems to make our ability to multiply disappear.

The answer to such questions clearly lies in the fact that a specific mediational means is involved, a mediational means that has certain "affordances" (Gibson, 1979; Still & Costall, 1989) that make solving the problem possible for us. Without the affordances provided by this cultural tool, it would be quite difficult to carry out complex multiplication problems. As Rumelhart, Smolensky, McClelland, and Hinton (1986, p. 46) have pointed out, the power of the mediational means in such cases comes from the fact that by using them "we reduce a very abstract conceptual problem to a series of operations that are very concrete and at which we can become very good." Most of us have become very good—or at least minimally proficient—at multiplying 2 times 3, 2 times 4, and so forth, as required in this case, but few of us are very good at multiplying 343 times 822 directly.

From the perspective of mediated action, this means that the spatial organization, or syntax, of the numbers in this case is an essential part of a cultural tool without which we cannot solve this problem. In an important sense, then, this syntax is doing some of the thinking involved. We might be unaware of how or why this syntax should work, and we might have no idea about how it emerged in the history of mathematical thought. In this sense, we are unreflective, if not ignorant, consumers of a cultural tool. The extent to which our performance relies on it, however, quickly becomes clear when it is not available. This leads me to suggest that when asked who carried out such a problem, the more appropriate answer might be, "I and the cultural tool I employed did."

There is much more to say about pole vaulting and multiplication as forms of mediated action, and I address some additional points as I use them to illustrate other claims in what follows. At this point, my point is simply that in both cases the form of action involved is defined by an irreducible tension between agent and cultural tool: either form of action is impossible, or at least very difficult, without a cultural tool and a skilled user of that cultural tool (i.e., agent). They are different in a variety of ways, the most important being that multiplication involves what Vygotsky (1987) termed mediation by a "psychological tool," or "sign," whereas pole vaulting falls under the heading of using a "technical tool."

At a general level, pole vaulting and multiplication are also alike in that the analytic strategy required to understand them as forms of mediated action involves the isolation and recombination of the elements of agent and mediational means. The usefulness of specialized inquiry will, however, depend on how it contributes to our understanding of a form of mediated action. Thus, studies of either the agent or the mediational means are useful and relevant insofar as they inform us about how these elements combine to produce the mediated action under consideration. Among other things, this means that cultural tools should not be viewed as determining action in some kind of static, mechanistic way. Indeed, in and of themselves, cultural tools such as poles in pole vaulting and the forms of syntax used in solving multiplication problems are powerless to do anything. They can have their impact only when an agent *uses* them.

The Materiality of Mediational Means

In outlining his account of mediation, Vygotsky focused primarily on language, but he recognized other semiotic phenomena as well. Among the signs and sign systems he mentioned are "language; various systems for counting; mnemonic techniques; algebraic symbol systems; works of art; writing; schemes, diagrams, maps, and mechanical drawings; [and] all sorts of conventional signs" (1981c, p. 137). Items such as maps and mechanical drawings have a clear-cut materiality in that they are physical objects that can be touched and manipulated. Furthermore, they can continue to exist across time and space, and they can continue to exist as physical objects even when not incorporated into the flow of action. These aspects of materiality are often associated with the term "artifacts" in the sense of historical artifacts that continue to exist after the humans who used them have disappeared. The kind of materiality of mediational means I have in mind has been discussed under the heading of "primary artifacts" by Wartofsky (1973), and this discussion has been extended by Cole (1996).

In some instances, mediational means do not have materiality in the way that prototypical primary artifacts do. The most relevant case of a seemingly immaterial cultural tool is spoken language. It is often easier to recognize the materiality of written language objects that continue to exist even when they are not being employed as mediational means (e.g., a manuscript that lies unused in a trunk for decades) than it is to recognize the materiality of spoken language. Unlike written language, the materiality of spoken language seems to evaporate after a moment's existence except for those rare instances when the speech is recorded. However, materiality is a property of *any* mediational means. The fact that the acoustic "sign vehicles" (Wertsch, 1985) in spoken language appear only momentarily may make the material dimension of this cultural tool more difficult to grasp, but it is no less real for that. In an attempt to keep cumbersome terms to a minimum, I do not employ terms such as "material mediational means," or "material cultural tools," but the modifier "material" may nonetheless be thought of as implicitly present in all cases.

In the view being outlined here, the use of material objects as cultural tools results in changes in the agent. I examine these changes in the following discussion where we look at mastery and appropriation of mediational means. At this point, however, I would simply point out that the external, material properties of cultural tools have important implications for understanding how internal processes come into existence and operate. Such internal processes can be thought of as skills in using particular mediational means. The development of such skills requires acting with, and reacting to, the material properties of cultural tools. Without such materiality, there would be nothing to act with or react to, and the emergence of socioculturally situated skills could not occur.

As Cole, Gay, Glick, and Sharp (1971) and others have argued, the notion of skill involved here is akin to that involved in riding a bicycle rather than the abstract and seeming immaterial mental processes often envisioned in psychology. One becomes skilled at bicycle riding by interacting with a material object over enough time to have mastered the challenges this particular object presents. The nature of this skill need not be understood in an overly narrow way. Once one becomes somewhat proficient at riding one bicycle, one is not limited to riding that bicycle alone. On the other hand, however, developing the skills required to ride a bicycle or bicycles in general does not seem to foster skill in carrying out other forms of action with other material objects.

The Multiple Goals of Action

This third property of mediated action—that it has multiple simultaneous goals— is related to Burke's pentadic elements of purpose. When writing of purpose Burke argued, "of the five terms, Purpose has become the one most susceptible of dissolution. . . . Implicit in the concepts of act and agent there is the concept of purpose. It is likewise implicit in agency, since tools and methods are for a purpose" (1969, p. 289). I argue that the notion of purpose is also often implicit in the pentadic element of scene, since scenes or contexts often strongly suggest, or delimit, the goal that will be pursued in them. Even though the temptation may exist to dissolve purpose into other pentadic elements, I concur with Burke that important benefits are to be derived from continuing to include it as a distinct element in an interpretive framework. For similar reasons, Leont'ev (1981) posited the notions of "goal" and "motive" as essential and distinct moments in his theory of activity.

My main reason for dealing with goal in an account of mediated action is to raise a point that often remains unexamined, even when some notion of purpose, goal, or motive is incorporated into an analytic framework. Specifically, I wish to address the point that mediated action typically serves *multiple* purposes. Furthermore, these multiple purposes, or goals, of mediated action are often in conflict. What this means is that in most cases mediated action cannot be adequately interpreted if we assume it is organized around a single, neatly identifiable goal. Instead, multiple goals, often in interaction and sometimes in conflict, are typically involved.

In the two examples I have employed so far, the issue of multiple goals emerges in different ways. In the case of pole vaulting, this issue is likely to arise in a less obvious way, but even here it is clearly present. At first glance, it would appear that the goal of pole vaulting is fairly obvious and singular—to get over the cross bar. However, just as the "circumference" of the pentadic element of scene may be enlarged or restricted depending on one's analytic perspective, the notion of goal can be similarly expanded and restricted. At one level, it would seem to be obvious that the goal of pole vaulting is to clear a cross bar, but this immediate goal can be envisioned as being part of a larger picture. For example, a pole vaulter may be motivated by the goal of impressing a particular audience, by the desire to overcome a general feeling of failure in life, by an irrational hatred of an opponent, and so forth. In fact, a pole vaulter may have as a goal the desire to let a competitor win for some reason and hence may actually forgo the goal of getting over the cross bar.

The picture of goals I have presented so far is somewhat restricted because it suggests that goals are attached to a specific, unique act rather than more general contexts and because it suggests that goals must have some sort of psychological reality for an individual. Assumptions about psychological reality suggest the kind of methodological individualism mentioned earlier, and focusing on specific, unique acts misses the point that in many instances goals are attached to the unexamined background framework, or "moral horizon" (Taylor, 1989) against which mediated action is carried out. For example, if we ask whether pole vaulting should be considered an Olympic sport or why competition and pride in individual accomplishment operate so powerfully in this context, we are dealing with goals whose circumferences extend beyond those concerned with individual efforts to get over a cross bar, and we are touching on issues that cannot be reduced to mental processes in the individual.

In the example of multiplication outlined earlier, the issue of multiple goals emerges even more clearly. If asked what the goal of multiplying 343 by 822 is, the first reply might be, "To get the right answer." As suggested earlier, however, such a response may not be sufficient since we really mean something like, "To get the right answer within the confines of a particular way of setting up the problem" (i.e., using Arabic numerals, using the syntax of multiplication outlined, not using a calculator, and so forth). The importance of these caveats touches on Burke's point about how purpose may dissolve into instrumentality. Rather than viewing this as dissolution, however, what I am suggesting is that the process may often be more adequately formulated in terms of multiple goals. Thus if asked to multiply the numbers, but to use Roman instead of Arabic numerals, the goal of the agent and the affordances of the mediational means come into conflict.

Since "tools and methods are for a purpose" (Burke, 1969, p. 289), and since the purposes of Roman numerals did not include that of carrying out multiplication, the goals of the agent and the goals "built into" the mediational means conflict, a situation that manifests the irreducible tension between agent and cultural tools in mediated

action. In subsequent chapters, I deal further with the issue of how
the goals of an agent may be shaped by, or come into conflict with,
the goals and purposes of particular cultural tools. For my present
purposes, the point is that mediated action is often organized around
multiple, and often conflicting, goals due to the fact that the goals
of the agent do not map neatly onto the goals with which the mediational means are typically associated.

Still, with regard to the task of multiplication, it is worth noting
that the goal of obtaining the right answer needs to be coordinated
with other aspects of the sociocultural setting as well. Is this mediated action being carried out in a context where one will be judged
on the performance (e.g., in a testing setting)? Is it being carried out
as part of formal instruction, in which case part of the goal may be
to practice for the sake of practice? Or is one carrying it out in a context not designed to encourage learning for learning's sake, a context
in which mistakes have practical consequences that go beyond low-
ering one's test score?

As will become obvious in subsequent chapters, multiple goals
and the complex relationships that exist among them are essential
issues to consider when trying to interpret mediated action. A major
shortcoming in many accounts of mediated action (including my own
in many cases) is that they interpret action as if it was motivated by
a single goal. This limitation often derives from utilizing a single
disciplinary viewpoint, a practice that is, I hope, less likely when one
approaches issues from the perspective of the complex dialectics
among the elements of mediated action.

Developmental Paths

The fourth claim—that mediated action is situated on one or more
developmental paths—is an elaboration of the general assertion that
mediated action is historically situated. Agents, cultural tools, and
the irreducible tension between them always have a particular past
and are always in the process of undergoing further change. This set
of issues is what led Vygotsky (1978, 1987) to employ a genetic, or
developmental method (Wertsch, 1985). Vygotsky's genetic method
was motivated by the assumption that we can understand many aspects of mental functioning only if we understand their origin and
the transformations they have undergone. Like theorists such as
Piaget and Werner, Vygotsky placed genetic analysis at the very foundation of the study of mind:

> To encompass in research the process of a given thing's develop-
> ment in all its phases and changes—from birth to death—funda-
> mentally means to discover its nature, its essence, for "it is only
> in movement that a body shows what it is." Thus, the historical
> [that is, in the broadest sense of "history"] study of behavior is not
> an auxiliary aspect of theoretical study, but rather forms its very
> base. (1978, pp. 64–65)

In Vygotsky's view, attempts to unpack the nature of mental processes by considering only the static products of development will
often be fruitless or misleading. Instead of correctly interpreting various aspects of these processes as emerging from the genetic transformation they have undergone, such attempts may be confused by
the appearance of "fossilized" forms of behavior.

To examine the implications of this sort of genetic method for
the analysis of mediated action, it is important to begin with an analysis of the notion of development. From the perspective employed here,
"development" is a term that applies to mediated action. This is simply one implication of the earlier claim that mediated action is the
relevant unit of analysis for sociocultural studies, and it contrasts
with claims or assumptions that what develops is the mind of the
individual or some other element of mediated action considered in
isolation.

To see the importance of this point, consider the following. In
the 1960s, the design of a new airplane might have involved dozens
of draftsmen working for months or years with slide rules, drafting
equipment, and other such cultural tools. Today, the same task might
be done in a much shorter time by a single computer operator using
the complex hardware and software that makes computer imag-
ing possible. The relevant issue to address in such cases is, "What
developed?"

It is fairly obvious that an explanation of the increased produc-
tivity cannot be grounded solely in an account of increased intelligence or skill on the part of the individuals involved. Indeed, some
might be tempted to argue that the single computer operator today
needs less intelligence or skill than what was required of the engi-
neers using slide rules, complex mathematical formulas, and other
instruments several decades ago. What the illustration does suggest
is that the intelligence involved is an attribute of the *system* created
by the irreducible tension between agent and mediational means.
Similar points have been made recently in cognitive science by authors such as Bechtel (1993), Clark (1997), and Hutchins (1995a).

A second point is that the development of mediated action involves a great deal of contingency and accident. This is something I explore in more detail later under the heading of another property of mediated action—namely, that cultural tools are often produced for reasons other than to facilitate mediated action, but more generally it is a point that parallels the ideas of Gould (1987) and others about the nature of evolution. Instead of viewing evolution as development toward some sort of preordained end point, I would argue, following Gould, that it is subject to all sorts of contingent events, many of which have major implications for how development occurs.

Yet another point about development has to do with the interpretive framework we use to understand it. While it may be the case that development in various "genetic domains" (Wertsch, 1985) has been shaped by all sorts of accidents and hence cannot be viewed as operating in accordance with a grand design, it is also the case that any analysis of development we conduct must be grounded in some assumptions about a "telos," or end point. Central to any account of development, and serving to distinguish it from chance or undirected change, is the notion of the intrinsic directionality of the developmental process. When, for example, we find comparative evaluations of development (levels, trajectories) meaningful in a given domain, the de facto implication is that we have posited a preferred direction that is pertinent to that domain. To make even the simplest observations about development, one must posit some a priori claims about where this development is headed. Such claims are often implicit rather than explicit, and they are often not particularly well formulated, but they always provide the background for an account of development. In short, one cannot coherently speak of development without positing an ideal end point.

As Kaplan (1983, p. 59) has pointed out, the recognition that development involves preferred directionality means that it "is a value, policy or normative notion." Hence to posit a telos—something that is part of any developmental theory—is to nominate a "virtue" or set of virtues in the sense outlined by figures such as MacIntyre (1984) and Taylor (1989); it is to identify the good. For this reason, a telos of development can be understood in terms of what Kaplan (1983, p. 59) calls a "mythos, dogma, theory, perspective, etc., that we use to evaluate, assess, and seek to regulate human actions and transactions, including those we call inquiry." Depending on the assumptions one makes in this connection, a developmental theory necessarily takes a stance with regard to what Kaplan terms "perfection-development." Such stances about a telos may be "dimly held or vaguely apprehended," but they nonetheless provide the grounds on which to "advocate different forms of education, different forms of therapeutic intervention, different forms of inquiry, different forms of governance, etc."

The issue of how to define an appropriate ideal end point for development is intellectually, ethically, and politically complex. For these reasons, developmental theorists often fail to spell out the form of perfection-development they have in mind or are ambivalent or confused about it. For example, Vygotsky had a difficult time resolving this issue and as a result ended up being ambivalent about the telos of human development (Wertsch, 1995d, 1996). At certain points in his writing, he was quite clear in positing a kind of Enlightenment rationality as the ideal outcome of human mental development, but at other points he seems to have envisioned the "harmony of imagination" as the ideal end point. Such complexity and ambivalence characterize most accounts of development. My point in noting this is to provide a reminder that, when we discuss development, we typically are positing some ideal end point or points. Hence when we speak of the development of mediated action, cultural tools, agents, and so forth, it is important to reflect on what end point we have in mind.

From the perspective of the agents involved in mediated action, one form of perfection-development that is obviously at issue is mastering the set of cultural tools provided to them by a sociocultural setting. While continuing to argue for the need to keep an analytic focus on mediated action, I also recognize that we engage in all sorts of efforts to assess and rank agents along some developmental path, and in so doing there is a strong temptation to treat individuals as if they possess some kind of abstract attribute such as intelligence, independent of any context provided by mediated action. By keeping mediated action at the center of our attention, however, we always carry out the assessment of agents' intelligence or skill against a set of background assumptions about what forms of cultural tools are to be used. In the previous illustration about designing a new airplane, the computer operator may have a kind of intelligence that is useful and highly valued in the context of computer simulation but would not be particularly useful in a context where people are expected to use slide rules or other tools—and vice versa. Just as information about genes is meaningful only in the context of knowledge about the physical environment in which an organism functions (Gould, 1981), information about intelligence is meaningful only in the context of knowledge about the cultural tools an agent will use.

Of course this in no way mitigates the point that there may be important differences between individuals, or even between groups of individuals, in the skills they have in using certain cultural tools. However, it suggests that, instead of concluding that such differences must reflect inherent attributes of individuals considered independently of any context of mediated action, the key might be these agents' particular experience with a specific set of cultural tools. I explore the nature of this experience later when I examine mastery and appropriation, but here I would note that each individual has a particular developmental history of experience with cultural tools, and the particular developmental history she has can provide fundamental insight into what sorts of skills and intelligence she has. This point is particularly apropos, given claims in evolutionary theory and connectionism that suggest that starting down a particular path of development has a profound impact on what is, and is not, likely to be possible at subsequent points.

Much of what I have just said about development focuses on how indivuduals encounter and master an existing set of cultural tools. As the illustration concerning airplane design suggests, however, a change in cultural tools may often be a more powerful force of development than the enhancement of individuals' skills. The irreducible tension between cultural tool and agent that defines mediated action means that, when considering how to enhance or change a course of development, the key may often be to change the cultural tool rather than the skills for using that tool. As we will see in what follows, there is often great resistance to changing a cultural tool even when it is recognized as being clearly outdated, so this is not always easy. Yet the perspective of mediated action suggests that it is an alternative that deserves more consideration than it is often given.

Constraint and Affordances

Most discussions of mediation view it in terms of how it empowers or enables action. For example, the Gibsonian notion of affordances (Gibson, 1979), when applied to mediation (Still and Costall, 1989), is concerned with the emergence of new and improved forms of thought, and Vygotsky (1978, 1987) viewed the development of language in ontogenesis primarily in terms of how it provides new capacities for human consciousness. There is little doubt that such a focus on how mediational means enable action is important when trying to understand action and the transformations it undergoes. However, a narrow focus on the kinds of empowerment provided by cultural tools gives us only a partial picture and one that is benign in an important sense. It does so because it overlooks a countervailing, though equally inherent, characteristic of mediational means —namely, that they constrain or limit the forms of action we undertake.

When trying to develop new cultural tools, the focus naturally tends to be on how they will overcome some perceived problem or restriction inherent in existing forms of mediated action. However, one of the points that follows inescapably from the view of mediated action I am proposing is that even if a new cultural tool frees us from some earlier limitation of perspective, it introduces new ones of its own. The aphorism coined by Mitchell (1990, p. 21) that there is "no representation without taxation" is quite apropos for any form of mediated action.

Authors who have examined issues related to mediated action can often be seen as falling into one of two basic camps, depending on whether one takes a "half-full" or a "half-empty" perspective. Those approaching mediation from the half-full perspective focus on what mediational means empower us to do; those approaching mediation from the half-empty perspective focus on the constraints mediation imposes. As I have already suggested, Vygotsky belonged to the half-full camp. In his writings, he tended to emphasize the enabling potential of mediational means, especially language. This is tied to that side of Vygotsky's worldview grounded in Enlightenment rationalism (Wertsch, 1995d, 1996). When operating from this perspective, he interpreted different forms of mediated action as levels in the development toward an ideal outcome of abstract thought. Hence he invoked a metric of "decontextualization" and argued that abstract concepts offered new, more powerful perspectives on reality than did more contextualized forms of thinking (Wertsch, 1985). In the course of making this argument, Vygotsky gave lip service to the idea that higher forms of decontextualization impose new constraints on our thinking as well, but his emphasis was clearly on the levels of empowerment it provided.

Burke is a representative of the half-empty perspective on mediation, and in this respect he provides an interesting contrast to Vygotsky. Like Vygotsky, Burke emphasized the power of language to shape human thinking and other forms of action throughout his writings. Furthermore, like Vygotsky, Burke recognized the power of language as a cultural tool to empower human action in essential ways. For example, in his definition of "the human actor" he argued that linguistic tools such as the negatives provide unique affordances

to human action. In his view, it is striking "that there are no negatives in nature, and that this ingenious addition to the universe is
solely a product of human symbol systems" (1966, p. 9).

However, a major theme that runs throughout Burke's writings
is that language imposes powerful constraints on us as we try to
understand and act in the world. For example, in writing about language as action, Burke (1966) had a great deal to say about "terministic
screens," which he understood as functioning in a way similar to
screens or filters used in photography. The essence of this notion is
that "culture and language not only open doors to experiences, they
also form a prison which constricts and narrows" (Gusfield, 1989,
p. 12). Such a perspective places strong emphasis on the notion that
any attempt to understand or act on reality is inherently limited by
the mediational means we necessarily employ. In a trenchant passage, Burke noted that "even if any given terminology is a *reflection*
of reality, by its very nature as terminology it must be a *selection* of
reality; and to this extent it must function also as a *deflection* of
reality" (1966, p. 45). In his view, this process affects not only how
we talk about reality but how we observe it in general:

> Not only does the nature of our terms affect the nature of our ob-
> servations, in the sense that the terms direct the *attention* to one
> field rather than to another. Also, *many of the "observations" are
> but implications of the particular terminology in terms of which
> the observations are made.* In brief, much that we take as observa-
> tions about "reality" may be but the spinning out of possibilities
> implicit in our particular choice of terms. (p. 46)

Burke's account of terministic screens is quite extended, and I make
no effort to explore all of its implications here. For the present, my
main point is that some theorists have tended to stress the constraints
that mediational means impose, whereas others have emphasized the
affordances they provide.

Regardless of whether a theorist belongs to the half-full or the half-
empty camp with regard to mediation, a further point that emerges is
that the constraints imposed by cultural tools are typically recognized
only in retrospect through a process of comparison from the perspective of the present. It is usually only with the appearance of new, further empowering (and constraining) forms of mediation that we recognize the limitations of earlier ones. As noted by Dewey:

> When we look back at earlier periods, it is evident that certain
> problems could not have arisen in the context of institutions, cus-
> toms, occupations and interests that then existed, and that even

if, *per impossible*, they had been capable of detection and formulation, there were no means available for solving them. If we do not see that this conditioning, both negative and positive, exists at present, the failure to see it is due to an illusion of perspective. (1938, pp. 487–488)

To return to one of my illustrations of mediated action—pole vaulting—the history of this event has been characterized by several such illusions of perspective. The main reason these illusions emerged and subsequently came to be recognized as such has to do with the various kinds of cultural tools employed. When pole vaulting was still an event whose goal was to leap horizontally across streams and during its first years as an event in the modern Olympics, vaulters used heavy and inflexible hickory, ash, or spruce poles. Bamboo poles, which were lighter, hence allowing competitors to reach greater speeds in approaching the vaulting box, were introduced in the 1900 Olympic Games. The greater affordances of bamboo poles—and by implication the constraints of earlier wooden poles—were quickly recognized, and bamboo poles quickly came to be universally adopted.

Records set with bamboo poles lasted until 1957. Cornelius Warmerdam, considered by many to be the greatest vaulter in the history of the sport, used bamboo poles to set six world records. He was the first vaulter to clear 15 feet, and he set a U.S. indoor record of 15 feet 8.5 inches, which lasted from 1943 to 1959. No one came close to Warmerdam's overall performance during the era of the bamboo pole, but after World War II vaulters' performances began to improve with the introduction of steel and aluminum alloy poles. The major change that made it possible to eclipse Warmerdam's and all others' records, however, was the introduction of the fiberglass pole in the 1960s. The much greater flexibility and strength of these poles led to a drastic change in vaulting styles. By bending the poles almost 90 degrees during their takeoff, competitors became capable of vaulting much higher than the records set using all previous poles. Fiberglass poles and their descendants have made it possible for recent vaulters such as Sergei Bubka to reach heights of over 20 feet.

Here again one can see the rise and fall of an illusion of perspective. No one seemed to recognize the constraints of aluminum poles until their fiberglass replacements came along. Pole vaulters viewed the cultural tool they had been using primarily, if not solely, in terms of the affordances it provided and did not seem to recognize any limitations or constraints it might have had. Indeed, after the appearance of fiberglass poles, users of aluminum poles argued that their instrument of choice was still the only legitimate one and that those using fiberglass poles were not really pole vaulting at all (more on this later).

An analogous point may be made with regard to the illustration involving the design of an airplane. In the age of the slide rule, reflections on the constraints of this cultural tool often focused on its material makeup (e.g., steel vs. bamboo vs. plastic). Such reflections were concerned with different rates of expansion and contraction of such materials and how these affected calculations based on adding logarithms. It was only with the appearance of powerful digital computers that this sort of reflection was considered to reflect an illusion of perspective and hence be beside the point. The general point here is that we are likely to live quite unreflectively with an illusion of perspective until some change comes along to challenge it—and bring a new illusion into existence.

The illustrations I have discussed so far might be termed instances of positive and negative affordances related to technological progress. By this, I mean that in these cases technological progress gave rise to cultural tools with affordances that were clearly superior to those offered by other cultural tools. The fact that no world-class pole vaulter today would use an aluminum pole and the fact that practically no one uses a slide rule reflect this point. In many cases, however, the reason for using a cultural tool is not so simply tied to superior levels of performance. Instead, the use of a particular mediational means is often based on other factors having to do with historical precedent and with cultural or institutional power and authority. I explore some cases of this sort in subsequent sections of this chapter and in subsequent chapters, but in general it should be clear by now that it is essential to recognize the role mediational means play in shaping human action. Only with such recognition are we likely to ask essential questions about why certain cultural tools and not others are employed and about who it is that has decided which cultural tools are to be used.

Transformations of Mediated Action

The sixth claim I make about mediated action is concerned with how the introduction of novel cultural tools transforms the action. This does not mean that the only way change is introduced is through new cultural tools. Changes often can be traced to different levels of skill or other facts about the agent. However, the dynamics of change caused by introducing new cultural tools into mediated action are often quite powerful and all too easily escape notice.

The importance of recognizing how new cultural tools transform mediated action was quite apparent to Vygotsky and provided a background assumption for much of what he wrote. He asserted that "by being included in the process of behavior, the psychological tool [sign] alters the entire flow and structure of mental functions. It does this by determining the structure of a new instrumental act, just as a technical tool alters the process of a natural adaptation by determining the form of labor operations" (Vygotsky, 1981c, p. 137).

One way of understanding the various ways in which the introduction of a new cultural tool "alters the entire flow and structure" of mediated action is to consider what happens in the different "genetic domains" (Wertsch, 1985) of phylogenesis, sociocultural history, ontogenesis, and microgenesis. For example, one could have in mind the transformations that occur in ontogenesis as children encounter new cultural tools such as written texts and numeral systems. Alternatively, one could focus on the emergence and influence of a new mediational means in sociocultural history where forces of industrialization and technological development come into play (Ong, 1982). An important instance of the latter sort is what has happened to social and psychological processes with the appearance of modern computers.

Regardless of the particular case or the genetic domain involved, the general point is that the introduction of a new mediational means creates a kind of imbalance in the systemic organization of mediated action, an imbalance that sets off changes in other elements such as the agent and changes in mediated action in general. Indeed, in some cases an entirely new form of mediated action appears.

I have already alluded to how this interpretation arose when a new mediational means in the form of the fiberglass pole was introduced into pole vaulting. The world record for this field event edged up only 2 inches between 1942 and 1960 during the era of bamboo and metal poles and seemed destined to stay forever at around 16 feet. With the introduction of the flexible fiberglass poles, however, this changed drastically, and the world record increased an astounding 2 feet in three years. Not surprisingly, the introduction of fiberglass poles was marked by great controversy. Pole vaulters argued heatedly over whether the introduction of this new cultural tool had transformed the event beyond recognition. For example, an article in the early 1960s reported that:

The astounding resiliency of fiber glass, . . . bending almost double
before slinging C. K. Yang of U.C.L.A. higher than pole vaulters
are supposed to soar, was the center last week of a crackling controversy. Yang and two other vaulters armed with fiber glass poles
had bettered the world's record three times in nine days, and the
onslaught was too much for purists objecting to vaulters becoming human projectiles.

The outcry was led by Don Bragg, Olympic champion [who
used an aluminum pole]: "It's ridiculous, and that's why I quit. Why
join the circus? There's a trick to the fiber glass style of hanging
on and letting the pole do the work." ("How far is a flip with a fiber
glass pole?" *Life*, February 22, 1963)

Such disputes reveal how powerful the transformatory effect of
a new mediational means can be. In this case, the effect was so great
that disputes arose as to whether or not the same action was indeed
being carried out. There is no simple way to adjudicate such arguments. Did the introduction of the fiberglass pole represent an extension of an existing type of mediated action, or did it create a qualitatively new one? The particular form this controversy took was over
whether the mix of elements involved in carrying out this type of
mediated action had swung so far in the direction of relying on a
cultural tool that the role of agent had been reduced below a reasonable level. If this indeed were the case, the question then arises as to
whether the agent should any longer be given credit for carrying out
the action.

These issues are apparent at several points in the way the controversy was described. In the passage above, the claims that the pole
is credited with "slinging" a vaulter, that vaulters have become "human
projectiles," and that the "trick" was one of "hanging on and letting
the pole do the work" are striking in this regard. The passage implicitly recognizes, however, the continuing contribution of the agents
involved since it is "they" (albeit "armed" with fiberglass poles) who
had broken the world record repeatedly.

Bragg specifically complained that "Fiberglass takes the human
element out of vaulting and makes the vaulter a catapulter" ("A pole
is a pole is a . . . ," *Newsweek*, February 19, 1962). But other vaulters
criticized him, arguing that "[Bragg] tried Fiberglass and couldn't
master it. He couldn't make 16 [feet] with either pole. He didn't com-
plain when he used an aluminum pole to break the record Warmerdam set with a bamboo pole." Here again, the two sides of this controversy reflect the two elements of agent—namely, the agent's skills
—and cultural tool in mediated action.

The major point to be made here is that mediated action can undergo a fundamental transformation with the introduction of new mediational means (in this case the fiberglass pole). The impact of introducing a new means into the action was so great in this case that it gave rise to a controversy over whether or not the event had been transformed into a qualitatively new form, one in which agents were only minimally present. Yet even in the midst of this controversy, no one thought agents were totally absent from this new form of action. So the issue remained one of whether the new *mix* of agent and mediational means was a legitimate one. Strong assumptions about the role of agent are manifested in the comments of those critical of Bragg. They formulated their argument in terms of how various agents, including Bragg, had not been able to develop the skills required to adapt to the new mediational means that had appeared, making the point that some athletes vaulted higher with aluminum poles than with fiberglass poles, and for others the opposite was true.

Such observations highlight once again an important implication of the study of mediated action—namely, that cultural tools provide the context and standard for assessing the skills of an agent. When answering the question of whether someone is a good pole vaulter, it becomes essential to specify whether one is asking the question in connection with the use of an aluminum or a fiberglass pole. That is, the skill of a pole vaulter must be assessed with regard to a particular cultural tool and is not something that can be defined, let alone assessed, in the abstract. In many cases, the standard cultural tool to be used when making such an assessment becomes fixed, but the illusion of perspective associated with this standard should not blind us to the fact that it reflects the cultural tools of a contingent sociocultural setting rather than some kind of timeless, natural state of affairs.

So when asking about someone's ability level, we are usually asking about someone's skill in functioning with a particular cultural tool. It is crucial to address this question since agents may demonstrate outstanding skills when functioning with one cultural tool but only average skills when functioning with others. This point is easy to overlook because the cultural tool to be employed in any particular assessment is usually a fixed and unquestioned part of the particular sociocultural context. For this reason, it would not occur to us today to claim that someone who can vault higher than anyone else using a bamboo or hickory pole is the best pole vaulter in the world. Such facts again raise general questions about who decides which cultural tools are to be used as means for assessing our skills and abilities.

Analogous points emerge when considering the illustration of multiplication I outlined above. It would be unusual today for someone to argue that it is unfair to assess our abilities in multiplication when we use Arabic numerals. Given the almost universal usage of this numeral system, no one expects us to demonstrate our multiplication skills using Roman numerals. However, major controversy *has* emerged in connection with another cultural tool that has become ubiquitous in our everyday lives—the calculator—and the controversy has some important parallels with those that emerged over the use of fiberglass poles in pole vaulting: namely, whether the use of a calculator to carry out multiplication problems counts as a legitimate case of multiplication at all.

This controversy has emerged in discussions of what mathematical skills need to be taught to schoolchildren. In the age of calculators, should they be required to demonstrate their skills at using an old cultural tool, or should we encourage them to become proficient at using a new cultural tool? Again, there are two sides to this debate and there is no completely obvious way to resolve it. The positions taken in this argument are sufficiently familiar that I need not review them in any detail. In certain important respects, an action may be the same, but the systemic organization of agent and cultural tool often ends up being quite different, indeed so different in some cases that controversy emerges as to whether or not the same action is being executed.

Internalization as Mastery

In discussing the materiality of mediational means, I touched on the issue of an agent's skills needed to use these tools. My point was that such skills emerge through the use of mediational means. From this perspective, the emphasis is on how the use of particular cultural tools leads to the development of particular skills rather than on generalized abilities or aptitudes. This is not to say that there are no such things as generalized abilities and aptitudes that distinguish one individual from another, but it is to warn against the temptation to mistake facility for using a particular set of cultural tools for some kind of general aptitude or intelligence.

In addition to conflating differences in facility for using particular cultural tools with differences in general intelligence when comparing one individual with another, a great deal of research about group differences is open to question on these grounds. Investigators such as Cole (1996) and Scribner (1977; see also Scribner & Cole, 1981) have argued that many studies in cross-cultural psychology are particularly open to this criticism. Their critique has been aimed at the tendency among many Western investigators to ask nonliterate subjects to perform tasks that basically reflect one's facility with literacy and then to interpret the lower performance of the nonliterate subjects as an indication of lower general intelligence. In such cases, there is no doubt that nonliterate subjects perform differently and usually less well than literate subjects *on such tasks*, but when using other cultural tools, ones with which nonliterate subjects were well acquainted, the opposite results often emerged. Hence the tendency to interpret differences in performance on particular tasks (i.e., tasks requiring the use of cultural tools with which the subjects were not particularly familiar) as differences in general reasoning abilities, intelligence, and so forth may be quite misguided. In principle, the possibility still remains that groups differ in something that might be conceptualized as general intelligence, but the writings of figures such as Cole and Scribner suggest that this may not have been what was being assessed. Instead, studies aimed at this issue may actually have been examining differences in the facility of groups to use particular cultural tools.

This question may be asked about Homo sapiens as a whole. Evidence from physical anthropology suggests that it is quite likely that certain aspects of the human brain, hand, and other aspects of our physical makeup may have evolved to provide a predisposition for using certain mediational means. Such a predisposition is still the result of using cultural tools, but unlike individual differences, which emerge in ontogenesis, or group differences, which emerge in sociocultural history, the predisposition in this case arose over thousands or millions of years in phylogenesis. It amounts to a kind of "protoskill" for using language, hand tools, and so forth. Such protoskills facilitate the use of certain general kinds of mediational means and make others difficult or next to impossible to use. For example, based on evidence from physical anthropology, Geertz (1973) and others have argued that morphological characteristics of humans such as the speech area of the cortex evolved during the long period of hominidization in response to early forms of speech. This morphological characteristic, which reflects an adaptation to a form of mediated action, may thus be viewed as predisposing humans to learn language.

Such claims about the predisposition for speech and other forms of tool use tell us something about what it is to be human, about the neurological underpinnings of human action, and about what forms of tool and symbol systems might be easy, difficult, or nearly impossible for us to master. These claims, however, operate at a quite abstract level. Namely, they tell us what our species will find relatively easy and difficult. To say that I have the potential for learning Japanese, Yoruba, and other human languages tells us nothing about whether I actually have mastered any of them. To understand which forms of mediated action an individual is actually likely to carry out, we must switch genetic domains (i.e., from phylogenesis to sociocultural history, ontogenesis, and microgenesis) and examine the history of actual encounters with material mediational means.

Analyses of how cultural tools are mastered by individuals in ontogenesis are often formulated in terms of "internalization." As I have argued elsewhere (Wertsch, 1993, 1995a), this term can be quite misleading. For starters, it encourages us to engage in the search for internal concepts, rules, and other such mental entities that are quite suspect in the eyes of philosophers such as Wittgenstein (1972; see also Williams, 1985) and cognitive scientists such as Clark (1993, 1997). The construct of internalization also entails a kind of opposition, between external and internal processes, that all too easily leads to the kind of mind–body dualism that has plagued philosophy and psychology for centuries.

However, the term "internalization" is so widely used—both in everyday and professional discourse—that I will not try to avoid it or substitute another term in its place. I have attempted to pursue such lines of argument elsewhere (e.g., Wertsch, 1993, 1995a), but this has sometimes been interpreted as simply trying to replace one term with another with no attendant change in the conceptual landscape. Hence my goal here is to clarify what I see as two of the viable meanings of the term "internalization" when applied to mediated action.

Debates over internalization are often quite problematic, if not fruitless, because different parties have quite different phenomena in mind when they use the term. Rather than thinking of internalization as a construct that can be abstractly defined and then applied to concrete examples, I would argue that it is more appropriate to view it as a term whose definition is closely bound up with particular phenomena and examples, and thus a term that takes on a variety of interpretations.

My claims on this issue are similar to what Burke (1969) said about "representative anecdotes" and what Kuhn (1970) had to say about the "shared examples" or "exemplars" that characterize scientific paradigms. In the postscript of the second edition of *The Struc-*

ture of Scientific Revolutions, Kuhn (1970, p. 187) stated that "the paradigm as shared example is the central element of what I now take to be the most novel and least understood aspect" of the argument he had been attempting to formulate. Instead of viewing the practice of solving particular empirical problems as the application of abstract theories and constructs, he viewed such theories and constructs as being grounded in the problems:

> Philosophers of science have not ordinarily discussed the problems encountered by a student in laboratories or in science texts, for these are thought to supply only practice in the application of what the student already knows. He cannot, it is said, solve problems at all unless he has first learned the theory and some rules for applying it. Scientific knowledge is embedded in theory and rules; problems are supplied to gain facility in their application. I have tried to argue, however, that this localization of the cognitive content of science is wrong ... at the start and for some time after, doing problems is learning consequential things about nature. In the absence of such exemplars, the laws and theories [the student] has previously learned would have little empirical content. (pp. 187–188)

Although Kuhn and others have questioned whether the notion of paradigm applies to the social or human sciences, his claims about the role of exemplars in inquiry would seem to be quite relevant to discourse in these areas. Specifically with regard to internalization, it seems that many different interpretations clutter the conceptual landscape and that these are tied to different exemplars. The problem is that we often attempt to carry on discussions about internalization in the abstract, but the interpretations given to it by the parties involved are grounded in specific and quite different exemplars. For example, when a Piagetian uses the term, he may have sensorimotor action in mind, whereas when a Freudian uses the term, she may have in mind phenomena that concern the ego and superego. In general, different exemplars are taken by different parties to be representative anecdotes for understanding internalization, and the result is that there may be as many meanings of this term as there are parties to the discussion. Because we do not share examples, we do not share constructs in such cases.

In this connection, it is important to remember that the present discussion of internalization is embedded in an analysis of mediated action. Hence my comments focus on internalization as it applies to the use of cultural tools. This is not to say that the internalization of mediated action must serve as a representative anecdote for everyone.

The choice of an exemplar depends on what one is trying to argue and how it fits into a larger theoretical framework. One thing that *is* clear, however, is that unless one specifies the exemplar one has in mind when discussing internalization, such discussions will often be frustrating and fruitless.

Limiting my discussion to the internalization of mediated action means that I am distinguishing my interpretation of this term from other accounts, but it still leaves a great deal unresolved. This is true in part because there is an extensive array of exemplars that might be considered under the heading of mediated action. In the rest of this section, I focus on one widely employed notion of internalization, and do so using only a few exemplars. But I would argue that this notion of internalization applies to virtually all cases of mediated action. The notion of internalization I have in mind can be termed "mastery." When speaking of mastery, I have in mind "knowing how" (Ryle, 1949) to use a mediational means with facility.

The terms "mastery" and "knowing how" have some advantages over the more general notion of internalization in several respects. The first of these is that it makes it possible to avoid some unneeded conceptual baggage that comes with the term "internalization." Many forms of mediated action are, and indeed must be, carried out externally. It may not be a necessary entailment of the term, but "internalization" suggests an image in which processes that were once carried out on an external plane come to be executed out of sight on some kind of internal plane. This is the kind of image encouraged by discussions such as those by Vygotsky (1978) about how counting originally occurs on an external plane with the help of material cultural tools such as sticks or one's fingers and then disappears as it is internalized.

What is striking in this regard is that many, and perhaps most, forms of mediated action never "progress" toward being carried out on an internal plane. This is not to say that there are not important internal dimensions or changes in internal dimensions in those carrying out these external processes, but it is to say that the metaphor of internalization is too strong in that it implies something that often does not happen. In this connection, consider again the example of pole vaulting. It is unclear what it could mean to talk about carrying out this form of mediated action on an internal plane. Indeed, a great deal of contemporary research in cognitive science deals with processes that are never intended to be internalized, a point made by many of those who analyze "socially shared cognition" (Resnick, Levine, & Teasley, 1991) and "socially distributed cognition" (Hutchins, 1991). For example, Hutchins (1995a) has examined what is involved in navigating a large naval vessel into a harbor. In his analyses, the cognitive system extends to a group of individuals as well as a set of complex tools. Instances such as this suggest that an answer to the question of how internalization occurs in cases of mediated action will often be: it doesn't, at least in a standard sense. Such observations lead me to prefer the terms "knowing how" and "mastery" over "internalization."

While the absence or incompleteness of internalization may be apparent in cases such as those outlined by Hutchins, where several people using external means of cognition and communication are involved, or in seemingly noncognitive cases such as pole vaulting or bicycle riding, it also characterizes many, if not most, cases of individuals working alone on a cognitive task. In this connection, consider the example of multiplication once again. My point when examining this example was that, while an agent must be involved, the mediational means does a great deal of work as well. As Rumelhart, Smolensky, McClelland, and Hinton (1986) point out, the external means does its work by allowing us to simplify the problem into a series of pattern recognition tasks that we can easily manage. The overall process of using the mediational means to solve the problem of multiplying 343 by 822 is one that for most people is never fully internalized. Instead of speaking of internalization in such cases, it would again seem to be more appropriate to speak of mastering the use of a cultural tool.

Developments in cognitive science under the heading of "connectionism" offer some striking parallels to what I am arguing. In outlining his particular version of connectionism, A. Clark (1993, p. 3) argues that it is "genuinely developmental," "process based," and "independent of folk psychology." All these claims are open to interpretation and dispute, but the way they are elaborated by A. Clark and others makes them quite interesting from the perspective of the study of mediated action: connectionism provides a level of description and analysis concerned with mental and even neural processes that is quite consistent with the claims about cultural tools, including their materiality and externality, that I am developing here.

I will not delve into the complexities of various strands of connectionism; I will point out only that connectionist models provide a way to formulate how processes in an agent might be said to "wrap around" cultural tools in such a way that mediated action does not "disappear" into the agent. For example, investigators such as Rumelhart and McClelland (1986a) and Plunkett and Marchman

(1989) have developed connectionist simulations of how past-tense forms in English are learned. In these accounts, the use of such forms is not based on a set of explicit rules (e.g., "add -ed to the ends of words ending in a consonant") that exist inside the agent (in this case a computer system). Instead, correct use of the past-tense form emerges over a series of trials during which a computer system forms a complex set of associations in response to encountering past-tense forms. The emergence of this complex set of associations makes it possible for the computer system to produce correct past-tense forms, including past-tense forms for nonsense words. To an observer unaware of the connectionist network involved, it may appear that the computer system is operating in accordance with an explicit rule that has been programmed into it—a form of "knowing that" (Ryle, 1949). However, the focus in connectionism is on developing systems of "knowing how" to use cultural tools in such a way that explicit rules need not be invoked, placed inside the head of the agent, and so forth.

In short, connectionist accounts provide ways of describing the skills involved in using such tools and how these skills emerge in the practice of using them, and they do this without invoking constructs from folk psychology that all too often are associated with the tenets of methodological individualism. The key to this potential is to be found in the nature of connectionist architectures. In describing such architectures, Bechtel and Abrahamsen (1991, p. 21) write: "Connectionist networks are intricate systems of simple units which dynamically adapt to their environments. Some have thousands of units, but even those with only a few units can behave with surprising complexity and subtlety. This is because processing is occurring in parallel and interactively, in marked contrast with the serial processing to which we are accustomed."

What I have said here hardly amounts to a complete account of how connectionist models might inform an analysis of mediated action, and indeed it seems to me that there are several points where such models will necessarily fall short in this enterprise. However, connectionist accounts are very suggestive when it comes to trying to understand some of the skills involved in using mediational means and how these skills might develop. In this sense, internalization involves a version of what Leont'ev (1981) emphasized—namely, the *formation* of an internal plane, but the internal plane at issue is quite material, being in the form of neural networks. The internal plane at issue here is quite different from the kind of psychological plane envisioned by many authors concerned with internalization. Indeed, this is the kind of folk psychological plane that those concerned with connectionism seek to avoid. I have argued elsewhere (Wertsch, 1993, 1995a) that there is actually no need to invoke the terms "internal" and "internalization" in such cases. Instead, less loaded and less misleading terms such as "mastery" and "knowing how" would seem to be preferable, and this is precisely why I have discussed processes such as riding a bicycle or speaking a language in these terms rather than in terms of internalization.

The compatibility I have outlined between connectionism and analyses of mediated action has been alluded to by others (e.g., Bechtel & Abrahamsen, 1991; Rumelhart & McClelland, 1986b) writing from the perspective of connectionism, but it has been little developed. In general, this would seem to have major possibilities for the development of both fields of inquiry.

Internalization as Appropriation

In addition to being characterized by level of mastery, the relationship of agents to mediational means may be characterized in terms of "appropriation." In most cases, the processes of mastering and appropriating cultural tools are thoroughly intertwined, but as I illustrate here and in subsequent chapters, this need not be the case. The two are analytically and, in some cases, empirically distinct.

"Appropriation" as used here derives largely from the writings of Bakhtin (1981). Since Bakhtin wrote in Russian, it is worth taking a moment to examine the actual term he employed: *prisvoenie*. The root of *prisvoenie* and the related verb *prisvoit'* is related to the possessive adjective *svoi*, which means "one's own." *Prisvoit'* means something like to bring something into oneself or to make something one's own, and the noun *prisvoenie* means something like the process of making something one's own. Following the practice of scholars such as Holquist and Emerson (1981), I use "appropriate" and "appropriation" to translate these Russian terms, with the understanding that the process is one of taking something that belongs to others and making it one's own.

As Holquist and Emerson (1981, p. 423) have noted, Bakhtin understood the notion of "one's own" word as being inherently related to that of others, to the "alien" word:

> *Chuzhoi* [alien, another's] is the opposite of *svoi* [one's own] and implies otherness—of place, point of view, possession or person. It does not (as does "alien" in English) imply any necessary estrangement or exoticism; it is simply that which someone has made his own, seen (or heard) from the point of view of an outsider. In

Bakhtin's system, we are all *chuzhoi* to one another by definition:
each of us has his or her own [*svoi*] language, point of view, conceptual system that to all others is *chuzhoi*. Being *chuzhoi* makes
dialogue possible.

For Bakhtin, language and words were understood in terms of this
necessary, ever-present tension between *chuzhoi* and *svoi;* indeed,
"language, for the individual consciousness, lies on the borderline
between oneself and the other" (1981, p. 293).

From this perspective, producing utterances inherently involves
a process of appropriating the words of others and making them, at
least in part, one's own. To quote Bakhtin again:

> The word in language is half someone else's. It becomes "one's
> own" only when the speaker populates it with his own intention,
> his own accent, when he appropriates the word, adapting it to his
> own semantic and expressive intention. Prior to this moment of
> appropriation, the word does not exist in a neutral and impersonal
> language (it is not, after all, out of a dictionary that the speaker gets
> his words!), but rather it exists in other people's mouths, in other
> people's contexts, serving other people's intentions: it is from there
> that one must take the word, and make it one's own. And not
> all words for just anyone submit equally easily to this appropria-
> tion, to this seizure and transformation into private property:
> many words stubbornly resist, others remain alien, sound foreign
> in the mouth of the one who appropriated them and who now
> speaks them; they cannot be assimilated into his context and fall
> out of it; it is as if they put themselves in quotation marks against
> the will of the speaker. Language is not a neutral medium that
> passes freely and easily into the private property of the speaker's
> intentions; it is populated—overpopulated—with the intentions of
> others. Expropriating it, forcing it to submit to one's own inten-
> tions and accents, is a difficult and complicated process. (1981,
> pp. 293–294)

Bakhtin's comments about how words may "resist" speakers'
attempts to appropriate them point to an important aspect of appropriation—namely, it always involves resistance of some sort. In the
more general terminology I am employing, Bakhtin's point was that
cultural tools are often not easily and smoothly appropriated by
agents. Instead, there is often resistance, and there is minimally something that might be called "friction" between mediational means and
unique use in mediated action. Since Bakhtin's position is fundamentally opposed to any kind of methodological individualism, he tended
to emphasize the resistance put up by cultural tools, arguing that

"many words stubbornly resist" or "put themselves in quotation marks against the will of the speaker."

Some form of such resistance or friction is the rule rather than the exception. Words are not formed de novo to reflect or convey what we intend to say on a particular occasion. Instead, whenever we speak, we must "buy into" an existing set of linguistic terms and categories. In the case of language, this means that one buys into a set of terministic screens when speaking. As noted by Burke, this does not constitute some kind of avoidable mistake or shortcoming. Instead, it is impossible to speak without employing terministic screens; it is simply part of the human condition when it comes to speaking and thinking.

As an example of the terministic screens we employ whenever we speak, consider how languages represent time in systems of tense and aspect. As authors such as Whorf (1956; also see Lucy, 1992) have noted, any particular representation of time is one of several possible alternatives, but in speaking a language we are buying into only one of them. Speakers often view their particular language's treatment of time as the only possible one and may indeed believe that the terministic screens are not screens at all but are "transparent" conveyors of meaning that allow them to convey their intended meaning perfectly. However, as Lucy and Whorf have argued, such impressions may reflect the "habitual thought" engendered by that language. Comparative analyses remind us that, like any other cultural tool, a language, through its system of tenses and aspects, offers a unique set of affordances and contraints.

The appropriation and resistance involved when employing a language's system for representing time typically are associated with an absence of awareness on the part of the agent. For example, until we learn, or at least learn about, a second language we are quite unlikely to be aware that our native language has fundamental constraints built into it for representing time. The point is that by using the cultural tools provided to us by the sociocultural context in which we function we usually do not operate by choice. Instead, we inherently appropriate the terministic screens, affordances, constraints, and so forth associated with the cultural tools we employ. Unlike Lewis Carroll's Humpty Dumpty, then, speakers are not in a position to assert that "When I use a word, it means whatever I want it to mean" (Carroll, 1872, p. 189).

Carried to its extreme, this view on appropriation would seem to suggest that agents are mindless, helpless consumers of the mediational means provided by their sociocultural settings. Such a perspective reduces the role of agent to such a degree, however, that it loses sight of the irreducible tension between agents and cultural tools that characterizes mediated action. In actuality, just as fiberglass poles do not sling "human projectiles" over cross bars, languages do not make agents speak. Bakhtin clearly recognized this and left room for the agent in several respects. When borrowing, or "renting" (Holquist, 1981), the words of others, Bakhtin viewed those words as being only "half someone else's" (1981, p. 293) and hence half the speaker's. He went on to state that the speaker populates the words of others "with his own intention, his own accent." Such terms clearly refer to the contribution of the agent involved in the mediated action of producing utterances. In making his point, Bakhtin also wrote of the process of "forcing [the word] to submit to one's own intentions and accents" (p. 294), a statement that endows the agent with clear powers of volition.

In some cases, such willful grappling with words may involve conscious reflection. For example, Morrison (1992) has reflected on the "chains" in existing literary conventions that prevented her from writing in the way that she wished. In other cases, the process may be one in which unnoticed differences in perspective result in "tactics of consumption" (de Certeau, 1984) of cultural tools, tactics that may be quite beyond conscious awareness. In all such cases, however, there is recognition of the active agent in the process of appropriation. On the one hand, then, agents must appropriate the words of others whenever they wish to speak; there is no alternative to using terministic screens, even if they "remain alien, sound foreign in the mouth of the one who appropriated them" (Bakhtin, 1981, p. 294). On the other hand, agents have in their power a range of possibilities for how these words will be appropriated, a range extending from actively embracing to strongly resisting them.

Returning to the issue of how mastery and appropriation are related, it is worth noting that in many instances higher levels of mastery are positively correlated with appropriation. However, this need not be the case. Indeed, some very interesting forms of mediated action are characterized by the mastery, but not by the appropriation of, a cultural tool. In such instances of mediated action, the agent may use a cultural tool but does so with a feeling of conflict or resistance. When such conflict or resistance grows sufficiently strong, an agent may refuse to use the cultural tool altogether. In such instances, we might say that agents do not view that cultural tool as belonging to them. If agents are still required to use this mediational means, their performance is often characterized by clear forms of resistance such as dissimulation.

An illustration of the kind of phenomenon I have in mind can be found in Gamoran's (1990) account of how non-Christian children in the United States participate in the celebration of Christmas in public schools:

> In American public life, Christmas is defined as a civil religious holiday, with the same stature as Thanksgiving and Memorial Day. Schoolchildren learn the signs and songs of Christmas, and come to see it as a holiday. They learn that Americans celebrate Thanksgiving, Christmas, and Memorial Day each year. This produces a paradox for non-Christian children who, seeing themselves as Americans and adopting the full range of norms, values, and beliefs corresponding to their emerging citizenship, do not take part in a holiday that is defined as one in the sequence of civil holidays. . . . Jewish children have a variety of ways of coping with the observance of Christmas in public school. From my own experiences, I recall that during Christmas songs one common strategy was to stop singing when a song referred to Jesus. This response, and others that set the child apart from his or her Christian peers, confirms one's identity as a Jew, but disallows one from complete participation in American civil religion. (pp. 249–250)

In his comments on this issue, Gamoran invokes terms such as "norms" and "values," but it is at least as legitimate, and perhaps closer to the evidence, to formulate an analysis in terms of mediational means and agents' uses of them. For my purposes, the interesting point about the example Gamoran cites is that the problem in performing the action (i.e., of singing the religious song) is not that the agent has not mastered the text. Indeed, it seems that the agent in this case knew the text quite well. Instead, the issue is whether the text that has been mastered is something with which the agent identifies and is willing to rent. In Gamoran's example, the answer is clearly no, and this is precisely what caused the problems for him as he sang (or did not sing) the song.

In subsequent chapters, I outline additional examples of appropriation and resistance. In all cases, the point is that the appropriation of mediational means need not be related to their mastery in any simple way. In some cases, mastery and appropriation are correlated at high or low levels, but in others the use of cultural tools is characterized by a high level of mastery and a low level of appropriation. Thus these two forms of "internalization" need to be differentiated and may operate somewhat independently of one another in mediated action.

Spin-off

In analyzing the first eight properites of mediated action, I have focused primarily on how cultural tools are taken up, used, or "consumed" (see chapter 5) by agents. In my comments about the materiality of mediational means, the irreducible tension defining mediated action, the empowerment and contraints imposed by mediational means, and other properties, I have said very little about how cultural tools are *produced*. For example, I said nothing about how and why fiberglass and the fiberglass pole came into existence. In the absence of an understanding of the processes whereby mediational means come into being, analyses of mediated action will often be quite incomplete. In particular, we are likely to be hindered by the illusion of perspective Dewey outlined, and we are likely to be quite unreflective and uncritical of the forces shaping mediated action.

Many analyses in the human sciences focus on the consumption or production of culture in isolation, and my contention is that we will continue to need to conduct such specialized analyses, at least to some degree, since the analytic questions and tools involved when examining these two processes are often quite complex as well as distinct. In the end, however, I hope to show that the best studies imaginable of either production or consumption in isolation will be essentially incomplete. Even an ideal account of the production of mediational means cannot guarantee an understanding of their consumption, and vice versa. The point, then, is that production and consumption of mediational means need to be examined in tandem in a broad vision of sociocultural studies.

One of the biggest problems that arises from examining mediated action solely from the perspective of consumption is that cultural tools tend to be viewed as emerging in response to the needs of the agents consuming them. This involves a kind of reductionist perspective that assumes that the mediational means we employ are designed to facilitate the forms of action we wish to undertake. Pole vaulting lends itself to such an interpretation. After all, pole vaulters switched to bamboo, aluminum, and fiberglass poles because they provided increased strength-to-weight ratios and increased flexibility. In these cases, there was obviously a great deal of reflection and conscious decision making involved, and those analyzing the needs of the agents recognized how existing constraints could be overcome and new forms of empowerment could be introduced.

If one expands the "circumference of the scene" (Burke, 1969a), however, it becomes apparent that even in this case the process whereby new cultural tools emerged cannot be traced solely to reflection and conscious decisions about what would serve best as mediational means. Specifically, if one turns to the issue of how the materials of aluminum and fiberglass made their appearance, it is clear that they were not devised in order to make better poles for pole vaulters. Instead, these materials were developed in the context of scientific, industrial, and military institutions and only later were taken over and employed in making poles. The process involved in such cases may be labeled "spin-off," to employ a term often used by military spokespersons when making the case for why it would be wise to support research and design efforts in the armed forces.

In the pole-vaulting illustration, the point is that aluminum and fiberglass poles would never have made their appearance had these two materials not been developed in response to forces of production that had nothing to do with pole vaulting. For example, fiberglass was developed as part of research and development efforts in the military and industry to devise lighter, stronger materials for aviation. The fact that it turned out to be useful to pole vaulters (as well as manufacturers of automobiles, fishing rods, and many other objects) was a quite unanticipated spin-off of these efforts. From the perspective of the mediated action of pole vaulting, the appearance of fiberglass was an accident that had the unanticipated potential to transform this action.

Such accidents and unanticipated spin-offs may be the norm rather than the exception when it comes to cultural tools used in mediated action. Such a claim has some quite striking implications. Among other things, it means that most of the cultural tools we employ were not designed for the purposes to which they are being put. Instead, they often emerge in response to forces that have nothing to do with the ideal design of a mediational means. In a sense, one could say that we are in a position of always "misusing" poles, words, patterns of speaking and thinking, and so forth in carrying out our actions. Indeed, in many cases we may be trying to speak, think, or otherwise act by employing a cultural tool that, unbeknownst to us, actually *impedes* our performance.

An example of how a cultural tool may actually have been designed to impede our performance in ways that have escaped our conscious reflection can be found in the very instrument I am now employing to produce this text, a word-processing keyboard. (For a detailed case study, see Norman, 1988.) The organization of this keyboard stems from the work of its designer, Christopher Latham Sholes. In 1868, Sholes arrived at a layout that represented a compromise dictated by several demands. One of these demands had to do with the mechanics of typewriter keys. Early versions of his machines were "slower" than typists' fingers, and as a result the type bars often jammed. Sholes's solution was to redesign the keyboard in an effort to slow down the typist. For example, as Hoffer (1985) has reported, the most common letters—E, T, O, A, N, I—became widely distributed, frequent combinations such as E–D were arranged such that they had to be struck by the same finger, and the typist was required to use the weaker left hand 57 percent of the time. In general, then, the familar "QWERTY," or universal keyboard that resulted was specifically designed to ensure a kind of inefficiency. It is also interesting that marketing considerations may have played a role in arriving at a final design. In this connection, David (1986, p. 36) writes that "it has been suggested that the main advantage of putting the R into QWERTY was that it thereby gathered into one row all the letters which a salesman would need, to impress customers by rapidly pecking out the brand name: TYPE WRITER."

In the twentieth century, several alternative keyboard layouts have been devised to overcome the inefficiencies of the QWERTY system. For example, "the Maltron keyboard, devised by a British team, offers to save typists time and motion by dividing keys into more efficient groups: 91 per cent of the letters used more frequently in English are on the Maltron 'home row,' compared with 51 per cent on the QWERTY keyboard" (David, 1986, pp. 32–33).

The best known of the post-QWERTY keyboards was patented in 1932 by August Dvorak, a distant relative of the Czech composer Anton Dvorak, and W. L. Dealey. Using the well-known principles of time and motion studies—namely, simple motion, short movement, and rhythmic sequence—they created the "Dvorak simplified keyboard" (DSK) grounded in the very principles of efficiency that Sholes had sought to circumvent. For example, "all five vowels and the five most common consonants are on the center, or 'home' row—right under the fingertips. With those letters—A,O,E,U,I,D,H,T,N,S—the typist can produce nearly 4,000 common English words (compared with about 100 on QWERTY's home row). Seventy percent of typing is done on the home row" (Hoffer, 1985, p. 38). For those who have familiarized themselves with the Dvorak keyboard the benefits are obvious. Hoffer notes that in several studies it has been found to be faster and easier to use, and since its introduction it has been used every time an international typing speed record has been set (see, however, Liebowitz & Margolis, 1990).

Thus mediational means are shaped by historical context and in turn shape our mediated action. At the time of Scholes's original design of the QWERTY keyboard, it may have been the most efficient and appropriate one imaginable. It was precisely by slowing down typists that he was able to overcome the problem of having keys jam, a problem that caused serious inconvenience and loss of speed. To some degree, it was an accident that the QWERTY keyboard was designed at a particular point in the developmental path of this technology, but that accident has had major implications well beyond the time when the design was adaptive. What is striking is not only that you are unlikely to use the Dvorak or another newer keyboard but that you are unlikely to know of their existence—despite the fact that since the mid-1990s computer software has made it easy to switch to the Dvorak layout. Furthermore, unless you have read or heard about the Dvorak or other keyboards, you are likely to have a misguided theory about why the QWERTY keyboard is the one made available to you, a theory that assumes that someone designed the QWERTY keyboard to make typing easy and fast.

This brief comparison of QWERTY and Dvorak keyboards reveals something about the power that historical context may have in shaping mediational means. This power is manifested in the fact that the QWERTY keyboard, which from today's perspective is purposefully inefficient, has retained its dominance even though the original reason for using it has long since disappeared. For several decades now, the technology of typewriters, let alone the capabilities of electronic keyboards, has obviated the necessity of using the QWERTY keyboard. Furthermore, Hoffer (1985) notes that studies have demonstrated that in about twenty hours those trained on the QWERTY system can master the much more efficient Dvorak system, and users report that it is not difficult to switch back and forth between the two. This example illustrates the power that historical and economic forces of standardization may have long after the reasons for the original design of a mediational means have disappeared.

In most cases, there is no such direct conflict between the demands for efficiency and inefficiency in mediational means as in the case of the QWERTY keyboard. Furthermore, mediational means typically are not the product of conscious design as they were in this example. Nonetheless, the case of the QWERTY keyboard provides a clear starting point when considering the claim that the cultural tools that shape mediated action may have been produced in response to forces other than the conscious requirements of agents currently carrying out such action. In other cases, the forces of production of cultural tools may be much less consciously directed, but the impact of these cultural tools on mediated action nonetheless remains quite powerful.

One of these other cases can be found in the development of writing and its effects on the mind. David Olson (1994, p. 100) has argued that "writing systems provide the concepts and categories for thinking about the structure of spoken language." In contrast to standard views that writing maps onto preexisting models of language, Olson argues that such models typically come into existence as a result of the imposition of writing systems, a process whose sequence is often subsequently misinterpreted. "Awareness of linguistic structure is a product of a writing system, not a precondition for its development. If true, this will not explain the evolution of writing as the attempt to represent linguistic structures such as sentences, words, or phonemes for the simple reason that prewriters had no such concepts."

The implications of Olson's claims for what I am calling spin-off take two basic forms. The first concerns the processes that give rise to writing systems in general. In this connection, Olson argues that writing systems usually do not evolve in response to the need to reflect on language. Instead, their emergence is largely in response to the demands of mnemonic and communicative processes, and any role they play in reflection is largely an unanticipated consequence. Hence this is a case in which a cultural tool is harnessed for a purpose other than the one that shaped its evolution. This suggests that at least in some instances the tool we use to reflect on and model language and thought may not be ideally designed for that purpose.

The implications of Olson's line of reasoning come across even more clearly when we turn to a second, related claim having to do with instances in which one language community borrows another's writing system. Olson notes that it is a common historical occurrence for a graphic system that has evolved and is used in connection with one language (a language for which it may therefore be reasonably well suited) to be employed in another language for which it is not at all well suited. In reviewing the history of how the Greek alphabet came into existence by borrowing from a Semitic language script, he writes:

> it is now recognized that the development of the alphabet, like that of the syllabary, was a rather straightforward consequence of

applying a script which was suitable for one language to a second language for which it was not designed, namely, of applying a script for a Semitic language in which vocalic differences were relatively insignificant, to the Greek language in which they were highly significant. (1994, p. 112)

Interestingly, even in this case where the process of spin-off resulted in using a script that would seem to be clearly inappropriate for reflecting on a language, the writing system ended up having a powerful mediating impact. One of the results of employing it as a mediational means in these circumstances was the emergence of a highly modified cultural tool: "equipped with such signs representing vowel sounds, the Greeks were in a position to 'hear,' perhaps for the first time, that those sounds also occurred within the syllables represented by the Semitic consonant signs. In this way syllables were dissolved into consonant-vowel pairings and the alphabet was born" (Olson, 1994, p. 112).

In sum, Olson's line of reasoning about how "awareness of linguistic structure is a product of a writing system" (1994, p. 100) touches on two points that are relevant to this discussion of spin-off in mediated action: (1) the cultural tools that mediate human action may not have evolved for the purposes they have come to have and (2) in many cases the concrete cultural tools used have been borrowed from quite distinct sociocultural contexts. In a sense, then, we often "misuse" tools, and this may have the consequence that our action is shaped in ways that are not helpful or are even antithetical to the expressed intentions and assumptions of agents about the design of the tools they employ.

The phenomenon of spin-off I have outlined involves the historical dynamics of sociocultural settings. Del Río and Alvarez (1995) have outlined several more general points in this connection. In their view, many forms of everyday action can be understood only by taking into consideration how they are shaped by complex cultural tools. The complexity they envision results from the fact that cultural tools are historically situated, and this history typically leaves its traces on mediational means and hence on mediated action.

Of particular interest in this respect is an argument del Río and Alvarez outline with regard to "vestigial systems of representation." In their view, the cultural tools (e.g., language) that we employ today with the assumption that they serve certain modern purposes often shape our action in ways that reflect the quite different demands of the settings in which they emerged. In other terms, the "primitive . . . has never ceased to play a role" (1995, p. 234), it has never ceased to be a fundamental force shaping human action. Thus like Cassirer (1944), del Río and Alvarez have been concerned with what happens when old forms of semiotic mediation are put to new uses.

Such historical analyses often lead investigators to see fundamental connections rather than discontinuities between earlier forms of mediated action and those of today. For example, in their analysis of the "encultured nature" of a traditional rural Castilian setting, del Río and Alvarez (1995) cite the continuing influence of traditional forms of rituals and forms of speech on individuals' overall "psychological architecture," an architecture that involves both rational and "nonrational" (Shweder, 1984) aspects of human action and consciousness.

Power and Authority

In my discussion of mediated action so far, I have focused primarily on the cognitive and communicative functions of cultural tools and have had very little to say about how issues such as power and authority might be involved. This amounts to treating mediational means as if they were neutral cognitive and communicative instruments, an approach that could be taken to reflect a narrow concern with "cognitive-instrumental rationality" (Habermas, 1984). Given that the larger goal of my analysis is to explore how human action is socioculturally situated, and given that sociocultural settings inherently involve power and authority, any analysis that focuses on cognitive-instrumental rationality alone would have to be viewed as having essential shortcomings. In outlining this tenth property of mediated action, and in subsequent chapters, I wish to turn to the issue of how power and authority are involved in mediated action in some detail.

Accounts of power and authority tend to focus on one of the pentadic elements in Burke's analysis—namely, the agent. In many instances, this involves locating authority in an individual. For example, when we say that someone is worth listening to because she is intelligent, or when we say that someone's powerful personality is the reason he occupies a position of authority, we are accounting for power and authority in terms of attributes of the individual agent. Other sorts of agents are also possible. For example, we often speak of institutions as agents when we say that we pay taxes in the United States because the Internal Revenue Service or the U.S. government has the power to make us do so.

When trying to account for power and authority, perspectives that focus on the agent obviously have great appeal. However, by not taking the role of mediational means into account, they come up short in at least two respects. First, such accounts overlook ways in which the emergence of new cultural tools transforms power and authority. It is not as if cultural tools, in and of themselves, operate as independent, causal factors, but they can have a potent effect on the dynamics of human action, including the power and authority relationships involved in it. For example, scholars such as Ong (1982) and Eisenstein (1978) have argued that the rise of print media and literacy have had a fundamental transformatory effect on how power is organized and exercised in society. Second, by focusing on the agent, analyses of power and authority often reproduce the kind of individual–society antinomies outlined by Elias (1991). Instead of engaging in endless arguments over whether it is *either* the agent *or* society that really exists and is the foundation of power and authority, a focus on mediated action and the cultural tools employed in it makes it possible to "live in the middle" and to address the sociocultural situatedness of action, power, and authority.

One of the places where Bakhtin dealt with issues of power and authority is in his account of "authoritative," as opposed to "internally persuasive," discourse (1981, pp. 342–348). In his account, "the authoritative word (religious, political, moral; the word of a father, of adults, of teachers, etc.) . . . demands that we acknowledge it, that we make it our own; it binds us, quite independent of any power it might have to persuade us internally; we encounter it with its authority already fused in it" (p. 342). In such cases, the kinds of appropriation available are bipolar: "one must either totally affirm [the authoritative word], or totally reject it" (p. 343). One is not invited to engage in the give and take of dialogue, to "divide it up—agree with one part, accept but not completely another part, reject utterly a third part."

In contrast, internally persuasive discourse does not rest on such hierarchical differentiation of authority between interlocutors. Instead of being put in a position of either totally accepting or totally rejecting the words of another, we are encouraged to engage in a kind of dialogue with what others say because "the internally persuasive word is half-ours and half-someone else's" (Bakhtin, 1981, p. 345). In contrast to authoritative discourse, which is characterized by the dogmatism attached to words, one is invited to take the internally persuasive word as a "thinking device" (Lotman, 1988), as a starting point for a response that may incorporate and change the form and meaning of what was originally said.

Bakhtin wrote about this in terms of how the authoritative word presupposes and enforces a kind of distance whereas the internally persuasive word encourages contact and dialogue. One of the ways such enforcement may occur involves overt, coercive action aimed at silencing others' voices. For example, it is possible to shout down, imprison, or kill speakers, and it is possible to burn books—practices with which Bakhtin was all too familiar. The cases that are of primary interest for my purposes, however, do not involve such overt coercion. Instead, they rely on a kind of acceptance of a position on the part of listeners themselves. Specifically, it is tied to the notion of appropriation I outlined earlier.

It is important to note in this regard that the acceptance of a particular utterance by an individual agent is not simply a matter of dispassionate, reflective choice. Instead, it is often shaped by the power and authority associated with items in the "cultural tool kit" (Wertsch, 1991) provided by a sociocultural setting. In this sense, mediational means are differentially imbued with power and authority and can be ranked in terms of "privileging" (Wertsch, 1991) or "cognitive values" (Goodnow, 1990). Under the heading of cognitive values, Goodnow includes issues such as why it is that certain knowledge is publicly available and openly taught while other forms of knowledge are not and why certain solutions to a problem are viewed as being inherently more appropriate or powerful when other solutions would work equally well, at least from a purely cognitive perspective. As she notes, the socialization of knowledge does not occur in an environment unstructured by values. Instead, a major part of what children learn is "what problems are considered worth solving and what counts as an elegant rather than simply an acceptable solution" (p. 259).

Since the end of the Middle Ages, a cognitive value that has attained extraordinary authority is that abstract rationality provides the best solution to problems in most, if not all, areas of human life. The power of this form of discourse has been noted by authors such as Habermas (1984) in his treatment of "cognitive-instrumental rationality" and Taylor (1985) in his account of modernity. In his volume *Cosmopolis: The Hidden Agenda of Modernity*, Stephen Toulmin (1992) has outlined some of the philosophical commitments to abstract rationality in modernity. Specifically, he has argued that we generally overestimate the accomplishments of modernity in the sphere of abstract rationality. Toulmin's principle goal is to challenge the "*standard account* or *received view* of Modernity" (p. 13). As outlined by Toulmin, the received view generally takes two statements about the origins of modernity as given—namely, "that the modern age began in the 17th century, and that the transition from medieval to modern modes of thought and practice rested on the adoption of rational methods in all serious fields of intellectual inquiry—by Galileo Galilei in physics, by René Descartes in epistemology—with their soon being followed in political theory by Thomas Hobbes."

One of the specific ways Toulmin sees these claims as being instantiated is in the tendency for modern philosophy to insist on a move "from the local to the general" (1992, p. 32). In this connection, he writes:

> Descartes saw the curiosity that inspires historians and ethnographers as a pardonable human trait; but he taught that philosophical understanding never comes from accumulating experience of particular individuals and specific cases. The demands of rationality impose on philosophy a need to seek out abstract, general ideas and principles, by which particulars can be connected together. (p. 33)

Toulmin summarizes this attitude among the founders of modern philosophy as "*abstract axioms were in, concrete diversity was out.*"

In the following pages, I would like to examine how the received view is routinely appropriated by people in our sociocultural setting and how such appropriation results in viewing certain utterances and arguments as convincing despite the many critiques of this tendency (cf. Lloyd, 1984; Rosenau, 1992). To pursue this line of analysis, I turn to an illustration concerning the power of a form of speaking and reasoning. This illustration comes from a transcript of a full day of the verbal and nonverbal behaviors of a nine-year-old girl, "Tanya" (Rupert, 1991; also see Wertsch & Rupert, 1993). The specific segment of Tanya's day I examine takes place at a restaurant while Tanya and her parents are eating dinner. It follows directly after Tanya's father has finished reading a story she wrote in school about pyramids.

1 FATHER: How many sides to a pyramid Tanya?//
2: TANYA: Sides/ three// No no/ four/ four/ four//
3: FATHER: Four//
4: TANYA: The bottom//
5: FATHER: No//

6: TANYA: No/ one/ two/ three/ and the bottom// If you/ if you/ meant/ lines that would be

7: FATHER: No// There's four sides to a pyramid//

8: MOTHER: How's that?//

9: FATHER: Pyramids have four sides// not counting the bottom//

10: MOTHER: Oh//

11: FATHER: It's one/ two/ three/ four//

12: MOTHER: Um hum//

13: TANYA: There's five sides//

14: FATHER: If you want to count the bottom but you don't count the bottom as one of the sides//

15: TANYA: Well/I count the bottom because I'm used to Euler's formula//

16: FATHER: Cause you what?//

17: TANYA: I'm used to Euler's formula//

18: FATHER: I'm sorry I don't quite understand//

19: TANYA: I'm used to Euler's formula//

20: FATHER: Euler's formula// And what is Euler's formula?// Since I don't know//

21: TANYA: E

22: MOTHER: I didn't know either//

23: TANYA: $V + F - E$//

24: MOTHER: Now, see?//

25: FATHER: $V +$

26: TANYA: $V + F - E$//

27: FATHER: I see/ can you tell me what they stand for?//

28: TANYA: Verticity minus faces plus/ Mom/ what was that E thing?//

29: MOTHER: Edges//

30: TANYA: Edges//

31: MOTHER: You count the number of vertices

32: FATHER: Vertices/ yes// Oh/ vertices/ I see/ yeah//

33: TANYA: And and and then you count the of the number of faces//

34: FATHER: Yeah//

35: TANYA: And then you count the number of edges// And so you put/ and so the number of it would be// vertices plus faces minus edges it will always equal 2//

For my purposes, this interaction can be divided into two basic segments. The first extends from utterance 1 through utterance 14.

In this segment, Tanya's father assumes an authoritative position in the discourse by asking Tanya an "instructional question" (Mehan, 1979) in utterance 1. This is a question to which he knows the answer, and its purpose is to evaluate Tanya's knowledge. Operating on the assumptions inherent in the use of an instructional question, Tanya's father evaluates her answer. Specifically, he evaluates it as incorrect (utterance 5) when he realizes that Tanya has come up with what he considers the right answer but has done so incorrectly (i.e., by counting the bottom of the pyramid). The authority structure characteristic of this segment of interaction is further reflected in the fact that Tanya's attempt to explain herself (e.g., utterance 6) is cut off by her father who states (utterances 7, 9, and 11) that there are four sides to a pyramid not counting the bottom.

The interaction in this segment is very similar to that documented by Mehan (1979) in his analysis of teacher–student discourse in formal instructional settings. Such discourse generally is organized around "I-R-E" sequences (i.e., sequences composed of *initiation* by a teacher, followed by a *reply* by a student, followed by an *evaluation* by the teacher). The organization of discourse grounded in the I-R-E sequence is such that the person making the initiations and evaluations (in this case Tanya's father) occupies a position of authority. Given this set of assumptions (at least on the part of Tanya's father), it is not particularly surprising that Tanya's repeated attempts to get her opinion heard do not succeed.

Utterance 15 marks a major turning point in the interaction between Tanya and her father. Tanya introduces "Euler's formula" at this point in her argument about why the bottom should be counted as one of the sides of a pyramid. Her father makes a major shift in the way he interacts with Tanya here by switching to a noninstructional question (utterance 16) about the topic Tanya has introduced. In this case, his question is a genuine request for information rather than an attempt to get Tanya to make her private knowledge public so it can be evaluated.

Two aspects of his question index the change in the structure of authority at this point. First, the question serves to indicate that Tanya's father is now willing to switch to a topic Tanya has introduced. Instead of ignoring or denying the relevance of Euler's formula, he responds by following Tanya's line of reasoning. Second, his question is explicitly motivated by the fact that "I don't know [what Euler's formula is]." As a result, it is now Tanya who has the authority to control the topic and access to information about it.

Utterances 15 through 35 reveal that Tanya does not have a very strong grasp of Euler's formula. She turns to her mother at one point (utterance 28) to ask what one of the letters in the formula stands for. Furthermore, in the end she does not produce the correct combination of variables and operators. Instead of the "$V + F - E = 2$" that she produces, the correct formula is $V - E + F = 2$. Therefore, even if Tanya had thoroughly understood what all the letters stood for, she would not have been able to use Euler's formula to support her point effectively. Working with her formula $V + F - E = 2$, Tanya and her parents attempt to see whether it holds for a pyramid. For a variety of reasons, perhaps the most important of which is that they are using the wrong formula, their answer never equals 2. Before they are able to come to a definitive resolution to the problem, however, their dinner arrives and Tanya asks if she can begin eating. The topic is therefore dropped and never picked up again during the dinner conversation.

There are many points of interest in this transcript. However, for my present purposes, the issues to address are (1) why did Tanya introduce Euler's formula into the conversation? and (2) why did her use of Euler's formula change the authority structure of the interaction? If one views this from the perspective of the agent involved, the answer would probably have to do with the application of strategies and concepts in the course of a problem-solving effort. While I do not deny that Euler's formula can be used effectively in such a problem-solving situation, its use in this case does not seem to be based primarily on instrumental rationality. A simple piece of evidence in support of this is that the transcript suggests that Tanya had a somewhat confused understanding of the formula but still insisted on using it.

The assumption that factors other than cognitive-instrumental rationality were at issue here is further supported by information from an interview with Tanya. In this interview, conducted by the adult observer who had made the day's recording, Tanya was asked why she talked about Euler's formula. She replied, "Well, I said it because . . . well, *I* don't know. I just felt exasperated, and well, what *could* I say? I felt like saying that I was used to something in school that you [i.e., her father] didn't learn" (Rupert, 1991).

Tanya's response suggests something quite specific about why she invoked Euler's formula. In her view, this was not simply a neutral suggestion whose sole function was to push the cognitive process forward. Instead, her invocation of Euler's formula seems to have had much more to do with her attempt to be recognized as an authoritative contributor to the conversation. Without going into the myriad factors that might have motivated Tanya's use of this mediational means in this interchange, we can state that it seems to be highly unlikely that her utterance was intended simply to contribute to a problem-solving process, at least as problem-solving processes are typically understood in traditional studies of cognition. Instead, the utterance seems to have had another function that is in many respects more important than its cognitive function. This is the function of gaining the floor in a capacity other than as a student responding to instructional questions.

For my purposes, the essential point is that it was *by employing certain mediational means* that Tanya succeeded in being recognized, or gaining the floor, in the way she wanted. During the early part of the interaction, Tanya made several statements and became increasingly adamant about them. They did not serve to alter the basic authority structure of the discourse, however. Her father continued to organize the discourse on the basis of assumptions similar to those employed by a teacher in a formal instructional setting. His role was to pose instructional questions (i.e., questions to which he knew the answer) and to judge the correctness of answers, and Tanya's role was to respond to these instructional questions as a way of displaying her mastery of a subject. It was this process that seems to have led to Tanya's becoming "exasperated."

Tanya's response to this situation was to invoke a mediational means that was relevant to the problem *and at the same time* was capable of gaining the floor in the way she wanted. This latter function is by no means reducible to the former. Instead, Tanya's strategy was to gain the floor by invoking a cultural tool that she knew her parents would respect and listen to. In this connection, it is worth noting that both of Tanya's parents are academics. As a result, they tend to "privilege" (Wertsch, 1991) or "value" (Goodnow, 1990) certain forms of speaking and reasoning over others. In particular, they value forms of speaking and reasoning that reflect the "speech genre" (Bakhtin, 1986; Wertsch, 1991) associated with the institutional setting of formal instruction. These claims were clearly borne out in an interview with Tanya's mother. In this interview, she remarked that "since we are both academics, we use this kind of talk often. Tanya also uses this style."

An essential point about Tanya's attempts to be heard as an authoritative participant is that it was not simply Tanya considered in isolation who managed to gain the floor. Several of her attempts to be heard during the early phase of the interaction were ignored by her father. Her increasing insistence on the correctness of her answer did little to change this. It was only when she invoked Euler's formula that the authority structure of the discussion changed.

This pattern of interaction raises the question, What is the source of authority in such cases? In an important sense, the source of authority is not to be found in Tanya alone. There is obviously something about the mediational means she invokes (i.e., Euler's formula) that provides the authority in this setting. It is not Euler's formula somehow operating in isolation that has the impact of course. It cannot speak for itself. However, Tanya operating by herself does not manage to change the authority structure of the discourse. Instead, one must turn to an account of mediated agency (in this case, Tanya-operating-with-Euler's formula) to account for the shifts in the discourse. In sum, there are many idiosyncrasies to this particular episode involving Tanya and her father, but the dynamics involved will be familiar to anyone; the general point is that by invoking the appropriate cultural tools it is possible for one's actions to take on a kind of power and authority.

In this chapter I have examined the interchange between Tanya and her father and several other phenomena from the perspective of mediated action. My intent throughout has been to outline some basic properties of mediated action, broadly understood. The following chapters narrow this broad understanding in one way or another by focusing on particular properties or on particular empirical examples. In chapter 3, I begin this focusing process by considering a cultural tool that has not been considered up to this point—narrative.

Note

1. To date, only men participate in this athletic event.

❊ 3 ❊

Narrative as a Cultural Tool for Representing the Past

In chapter 2, we looked at how human action is fundamentally shaped by cultural tools. Pole vaulting, multiplication, and using keyboards—all these actions illustrate the notion of mediated action. In this chapter, I narrow my focus somewhat and examine how a particular set of cultural tools—those involving language—shapes mediated action in particular ways.

In the terminology I am employing, *language is a cultural tool* and *speech is a form of mediated action*, and for this reason the general claims I have made about mediated action apply to speech. Particular instances, or performances, of speech occur in the form of *utterances*. The notion of utterance I employ derives from Bakhtin (1986, p. 71), who viewed the utterance as "the *real unit* of speech communication." In Bakhtin's view, "speech can exist in reality only in the form of concrete utterances of individual speaking people, speech subjects. Speech is always cast in the form of an utterance belonging to a particular speaking subject, and outside this form it cannot exist."

At first glance, Bakhtin's focus on "individual speaking people" might tempt one to think that utterances can be understood as the products of an agent in isolation, that utterances are simply the product of a "speech subject" (i.e., an agent), unconstrained by other factors. As I have emphasized elsewhere (Wertsch, 1991), however, this was not the case for Bakhtin, and it is not my argument here. Instead,

Bakhtin viewed various forms of language as providing different organizing foci of replicable elements that are taken up and used by speakers in unique ways when producing utterances:

> Behind each text stands a language system. Everything in the text that is repeated and reproduced, everything repeatable and reproducible, everything that can be given outside a given text (the given) conforms to this language system. But at the same time each text (as an utterance) is individual, unique, and unrepeatable, and herein lies its entire significance (its plan, the purposes for which it was created). This is the aspect of it that pertains to honesty, truth, goodness, beauty, history. With respect to this aspect, everything repeatable and reproducible proves to be material, a means to an end. This notion extends somewhat beyond the bounds of linguistics or philology. The second aspect (pole) inheres in the text itself, but is revealed only in a particular situation and in a chain of texts (in the speech communication of a given area). This pole is linked not with elements (repeatable) in the system of the language (signs), but with other texts (unrepeatable) by special dialogic . . . relations. (1986, p. 105)

Bakhtin's analysis of the utterance as simultaneously involving repeatable and unrepeatable aspects can be taken as a special case of the irreducible tension between the basic moments of mediated action—namely, cultural tools—and agents' particular uses of these tools. As I argued in the previous chapter, any account of mediated action that focuses exclusively on one or another of these moments in isolation is bound to be incomplete, if not seriously misleading—a point that can be found in Bakhtin's analysis of the utterance as well.

Bakhtin's notion of languages involved in utterances was not confined to "national languages" such as English, Thai, or Russian. Indeed, his primary concern was with "speech genres" and "social languages," two patternings of utterances defined by criteria quite distinct from those employed to identify a national language. In both cases, he was concerned with types, or categories, of utterances, a concern that distinguished his approach from that typically followed in linguistics, where generalization is based on types of linguistic form or meaning abstracted from the speech situation. In the case of speech genres, the categorization of utterances is tied to classes of speech situations, and in the case of social languages this categorization is tied to classes of speakers.

In outlining his notion of speech genre, Bakhtin stated:

A speech genre is not a form of language, but a typical form of utterance; as such the genre also includes a certain typical kind of expression that inheres in it. In the genre the word acquires a particular typical expression. Genres correspond to typical situations of speech communication, typical themes, and consequently, also to particular contacts between the *meanings* of words and actual concrete reality under certain typical circumstances. (1986, p. 87)

Bakhtin's characterization of speech genres makes it clear that they qualify as mediational means. In this connection, they play a role in both the production and comprehension of speech:

Speech genres organize our speech in almost the same way as grammatical (syntactical) forms do. We learn to cast our speech in generic forms and, when hearing others' speech, we guess its genre from the very first words; we predict a certain length (that is, the approximate length of the speech whole) and a certain compositional structure; we foresee the end; that is, from the very beginning we have a sense of the speech whole, which is only later differentiated during the speech process. (1986, pp. 78–79)

The theoretical observations provided by Bakhtin can be illustrated by a host of observations from everyday life. Whether we are conscious of it or not, we constantly employ speech genres to produce utterances and to understand the utterances of others. The power they have in shaping communication and thought is reflected, among other things, in the fact that we may become uncomfortable when utterances do not seem to be organized in accordance with a recognizable generic form. In this connection for example, consider the following excerpt from *The Adventures of Tom Sawyer* about Tom's experiences during a church service:

And now the minister prayed. A good, generous prayer it was, and went into details: it pleaded for the church and the little children of the church; for the other churches of the village; for the village itself; for the county; for the state; for the state officers; for the United States; for the churches of the United States; for Congress; for the President; for the officers of the government; for the poor sailors, tossed by stormy seas; for the oppressed millions groaning under the heel of European monarchies and Oriental despotisms; for such as have the light and good tidings, and yet have not eyes to see nor ears to hear withal; for the heathen in the far islands of the sea; and closed with a supplication that the words he was about to speak might find grace and favor, and be as seed sown in fertile ground, yielding in time for a grateful harvest of good. Amen. . . .

The boy whose history this book relates did not enjoy the prayer, he only endured it—if he even did that much. He was restive all through it; he kept tally of the details of the prayer, unconsciously— for he was not listening, but he knew the ground of old, and the clergyman's regular route over it—and when a little trifle of new matter was interlarded, his ear detected it and his whole nature resented it; he considered additions unfair and scoundrelly. (Twain, 1989, pp. 38–39)

The humor in this passage derives from Twain's play off a speech genre overwhelmingly recognizable to the readers of his day—the Sunday church service prayer. Indeed, much of the humor flows from the fact that Twain's rendition of this speech genre is so standardized as to be parodic. Because of its standardized form, Tom Sawyer, as well as Twain's readers, could easily "predict a certain length (that is, the approximate length of the speech whole) and a certain compositional structure" (Bakhtin, 1986, p. 79), and it was precisely the alterations in length and compositional structure (especially the length) that disturbed Tom Sawyer.

Bakhtin included a wide range of utterance patternings under the heading of speech genre. On the one hand, he included instances in which utterances are relatively tightly constrained with regard to form and content, items such as prayers and "various everyday genres of greetings, farewells, congratulations, all kinds of wishes, information about health, business, and so on" (1986, p. 79). On the other hand, he included the "freer and more creative genres of oral speech communication" (p. 80) that do not involve such tight constraints on the form and content of utterances. In this second category, he had in mind items such as "genres of salon conversations about everyday, social aesthetic, and other subjects, genres of table conversations, intimate conversations among friends, intimate conversations with the family, and so on." In all cases, a defining characteristic of speech genres is that they are associated with "typical situations of speech communication, typical themes" (p. 79).

In contrast to speech genres, which are tied to types of speech situations, Bakhtin associated social languages with particular *groups of speakers*. In this connection, he wrote of professional, social, generational, and gender "stratifications" of language. For example, with regard to professional stratification he stated:

there is interwoven with this generic stratification of language a *professional* stratification of language, in the broad sense of the term "professional": the language of the lawyer, the doctor, the businessman, the politician, the public education teacher and so forth, and these sometimes coincide with, and sometimes depart from, the stratification into genres. It goes without saying that these languages differ from each other not only in their vocabularies; they involve specific forms for manifesting intentions, forms for making conceptualization and evaluation concrete. (1986, p. 289)

Although it may appear straightforward to characterize speech genres as being tied to types of situations and social languages as being tied to types of speakers, these two ways of categorizing utterances are in reality often connected in complex ways. Bakhtin noted this in his comment that generic stratification is "interwoven" with professional stratification. In what follows, my main focus will be on social languages, but Bakhtin's point about how they are interwoven with speech genres means that I will often touch on these speech genres as well.

In Bakhtin's account of social languages and speech genres, the notion of a form of speaking *belonging* to someone or to some situation is central. Indeed, it runs throughout his whole analysis of meaning. In contrast to most linguistic and even discourse analyses, words, sentences, social languages, and so forth were viewed by Bakhtin as inherently and essentially belonging to settings, groups, or individuals. In his view:

> there are no "neutral" words and forms—words and forms that can belong to "no one"; language has been completely taken over, shot through with intentions and accents. For any individual consciousness living in it, language is not an abstract system of normative forms but rather a concrete heteroglot conception of the world. All words have the "taste" of a profession, a genre, a tendency, a party, a particular work, a particular person, a generation, an age group, the day and hour. Each word tastes of the context and contexts in which it has lived its socially charged life; all words and forms are populated by intentions. (1981, p. 293)

Bakhtin's analysis of the utterance, then, involves both "speaking people, speech subjects" making unique, unrepeatable utterances, on the one hand, and language systems belonging to someone that organize these utterances, on the other. In this view, "the word in language is half someone else's. It becomes 'one's own' only when the speaker populates it with his own intention, his accent, when he appropriates the word, adapting it to his own semantic and expressive intention" (1981, p. 294). In other words, the picture Bakhtin outlines is one of an irreducible tension between agent and mediational means.

According to Bakhtin, the process of appropriating the words of others is characterized by "heteroglossia." Drawing on a range of Bakhtin's texts, Holquist and Emerson (1981, p. 428) note that heteroglossia is "the base condition governing the operation of meaning in any utterance." They go on to write that heteroglossia

> is that which insures the primacy of context over text. At any given time, in any given place, there will be a set of conditions—social, historical, meteorological, physiological—that will insure that a word uttered in that place and at that time will have a meaning different than it would have under any other conditions; all utterances are heteroglot in that they are functions of a matrix of forces practically impossible to recoup, and therefore impossible to resolve. Heteroglossia is as close a conceptualization as is possible of that locus where centripetal and centrifugal forces collide; as such, it is that which a systematic linguistics must always suppress.

There is little doubt that it is a "difficult and complicated process" to appropriate the words of others and populate them with one's own intention as Bakhtin said. Not only is this process difficult to carry out, it is difficult to analyze. As in the case of mediated action more generally, it is possible to specify some of the factors and moments that need to be taken into consideration when trying to understand heteroglossia, but it is very difficult to determine how the process will occur in various contexts. Instead of continuing to discuss the nature of utterances, social languages, heteroglossia, or mediated action at a general level, then, I turn to analyzing some concrete cases to see how these notions play out. This is not simply a matter of applying these notions; it is also a matter of providing further specification of what the very terms employed in such an approach mean.

Representing the Past with Cultural Tools

In what follows, I look at cultural tools and forms of mediated action used to represent the past. In particular, I am interested in how nations and nation-states represent their past—that is, in national history. As is the case with any form of mediated action, the starting point is that this process involves an irreducible tension between cultural tools and the unique use of these tools.

At a general level, the basic cultural tool for generating the historical representations I examine is language, but my focus is on particular forms of language used in history, especially *narrative*. As authors such as Scholes and Kellogg (1966) have noted, the use of narrative forms to represent the past is not as natural as it might appear today, having evolved in complex ways over the history of historical writing. Indeed, there are several alternative ways to represent the past, alternatives that can be taken to reflect the use of different cultural tools. White (1987, p. 4) presents an overview of these when he writes "the *doxa* of the modern historiographical establishment has it that there are three basic kinds of historical representation—the annals, the chronicle, and the history proper—the imperfect 'historicality' of two of which is evidenced in their failure to attain to full narrativity of the events of which they treat."

As outlined by White, the annals form of history consists simply of listing events in their chronological sequence. There is little tendency toward narrativity, a point he makes using the *Annals of Saint Gall* as an illustration. This text consists of a series of entries for years, some of which have nothing reported beside them and others of which have one or more events listed. In those years when events are reported, they are usually presented as if they existed in isolation from others preceding or following them. There is little or no tendency toward formulating them in terms of a plot with a beginning, middle, and end. In White's view, these annals clearly do not have the essential properties required to make something a narrative:

> Although this text is "referential" and contains a representation of temporality . . . it possesses none of the characteristics that we normally attribute to a story: no central subject, no well-marked beginning, middle, and end, no peripeteia, and no identifiable narrative voice. In what are, for us, the theoretically most interesting segments of the text, there is no suggestion of any necessary connection between one event and another. (1987, p. 6)

The chronicle stands in contrast to the annals form. According to White (1987, p. 5), the chronicle "often seems to wish to tell a story" and "aspires to narrativity." However, unlike a narrative, it fails to achieve this in the way a genuine story would. In particular, it "is marked by a failure to achieve narrative closure"; it "does not so much conclude as simply terminate." White goes on: "It starts out to tell a story but breaks off *in media res*, in the chronicler's own present; it leaves things unresolved, or rather, it leaves then unresolved in a storylike way. While annals represent historical reality as if real events did not display the form of story, the chronicler represents it as if real events appeared to human consciousness in the form of unfinished stories."

From his description of the annals and chronicle form, one can infer White's notion of narrative: it is organized around temporality; it has a central subject, a plot with a well-marked beginning, middle, and end, and an identifiable narrative voice; it makes connections between events; and it achieves closure, a conclusion, a resolution. Furthermore, when describing plot, White goes on to describe it as "a structure of relationships by which the events contained in the account are endowed with a meaning, by being identified as part of an integrated whole" (1987, p. 9).

The importance of narrativity for human consciousness has long been obvious to scholars from a variety of perspectives in the human sciences. In addition to being a major topic of discussion in historiography, it has recently reemerged in disciplines such as psychology, where Bruner (1986, 1990) has emphasized the need to examine narrative as well as a "paradigmatic" mode of thought, and in moral philosophy, where, for example, MacIntyre (1984, p. 216) has argued that "man is in his actions and practice, as well as in his fictions, essentially a story-telling animal." My purpose in what follows is not to provide a review of the vast literature on this topic. Instead, I take up the issue of what happens when we consider narrative as a cultural tool in forms of mediated action whose purpose is to represent the past. Furthermore, instead of being concerned with the practices and tools of professional historians and other producers of history, I will focus on citizens as consumers of history.

Historical Texts as Cultural Tools

Among the narrative texts that children everywhere encounter in one form or another are historical accounts of their nation's past. The ways in which these texts are produced and the nature of agents' relationship to them are quite varied and complex. My immediate concern is with a related but more limited set of issues. Namely, I am concerned with how the structure of historical texts as cultural tools both empower and constrain those who use them. Several properties of historical narratives (outlined in the previous section) have been identified by authors such as White. These include being temporally organized, having a central subject, plot, and narrative voice, and achieving closure around a conclusion. These various properties are moments or aspects of narrativity that contribute to its basic tendency to present the "integrated whole" mentioned by White. Mink (1978, p. 144) made a similar point in arguing that "the cognitive function of narrative form . . . is not just to relate a succession of events but to body forth an ensemble of interrelationships of many different kinds as a single whole."

The historical accounts I examine are concerned with the origins of the United States The events covered include the arrival of European settlers, the French and Indian War, the Revolutionary War, the Declaration of Independence, the U.S. Constitution, and so forth. Throughout this analysis, I look at accounts that come from "official history," which contrast with "unofficial history" (Tulviste & Wertsch, 1994) in various ways to be explored in chapter 5. For the present, it is sufficient to say that official history is what tends to be presented by school textbooks and by teachers as they engage in formal history instruction.

Mastering Historical Texts: Knowing Too Little

Throughout the twentieth century, there have been numerous discussions in the press and among politicians about how much (or little) American students know about their history. Such discussions have often included some strong claims about how little is being taught and learned in schools and have variously identified textbooks, teachers, students, television, and other factors as the source of the perceived shortcomings (e.g., Cornbleth, 1995; Loewen, 1995). At the same time this discussion has been going on, several researchers have employed a host of techniques from cognitive psychology and other disciplines to examine the processes of teaching and learning history. I can make no attempt to review all this research. Instead, I focus on a set of studies carried out by one investigator, Isabel Beck, and her colleagues.

In recent years, Beck and her colleagues (Beck, McKeown, & Gromoll, 1989; Beck, McKeown, Sinatra, & Loxterman, 1991; Beck & McKeown, 1994) have conducted a number of studies on how information about the American Revolutionary period is presented and mastered by elementary school students. In a 1989 study Beck et al. analyzed how widely used fifth-grade history textbooks depict the events of this period and concluded that they were inappropriate for two reasons. First, these texts were based on "unrealistic assumptions about what students already know that is related to the topic" (p. 239), and as a result the students had a very difficult time understanding them. Second, Beck and her co-authors concluded that there were "problematic features of the text presentation, chiefly a lack of coherence and explanation."

In a longitudinal study, Beck and McKeown (1994) examined some of the implications these problems in textual organization had for students' understanding of the American Revolutionary period. They examined thirty-five students' understanding of this period before and after fifth grade, and they then interviewed twenty-six of these same students both before and after eighth grade. These two grade levels were selected because they were the first two major instructional encounters students had with historical material about this period. Beck and McKeown report that

> the impression left from students' responses across the 3 years was that students entered their first encounter with American history with very little prior knowledge and took from their initial instruction some facts and some very general ideas about the period of the American Revolution. The information students took was often incomplete, sometimes confused. This pattern of confusion was quite evident before their next encounter with instruction in eighth grade, suggesting that what students had learned [in fifth grade] had not remained with them. After eighth-grade instruction, much of the confusion ceased, but the same basic results seen after fifth grade—of factual details combined but not integrated with a general impression—still characterized many students' knowledge. The picture of how their country began was not complete or coherent for these students. The versions of history they had developed seemed like events pasted together, lacking connections and motivations. (p. 253)

On the basis of interviews with students about the American Revolutionary period, Beck and McKeown identified several ways in which students' knowledge about history changed between fifth and eighth grades. Some students began with sketchy but basically correct information and then improved over the fifth grade and maintained this knowledge until eighth grade; some students began with incomplete but accurate information and then improved over fifth grade, only to regress by the beginning of the eighth grade; and others began with little or no accurate information and never made progress.

Although there are some grounds for optimism when reviewing the students who made steady progress, Beck and McKeown report that "the single most striking pattern across all the data was the amount of confusion that was manifested in students' responses after fifth-grade instruction and before eighth-grade instruction" (1994, p. 250). For example, they give the example of Eric, who provided the following account after fifth-grade instruction (interviewer's comments are in brackets): "I thought it was the north and the south, or is that the Civil War? [That's the Civil War. Repeats question: A long time ago there were 13 colonies . . .] The British came in and put their forts up on our land. The French were trying to get the forts out. . . . [End?] We won and we wrecked [the British] forts." In this case, the hint provided by the interviewer only served to set Eric off in another direction that seemed almost as confused as the one he initially followed.

In the response he provided before eighth grade, Eric seems to have even less access to accurate information and introduced some information he apparently had obtained from accounts of then-current events:

> [Sides?] A country and us. [Can you remember what country it was?] Russia. [What were we fighting about?] Russia wanted to make our country colonist (sic, Communist). We wanted to be free and they didn't want us to be free. . . . [What do you mean by free in that case?] Well, like freedom of speech and stuff like that . . . [and Russia] wanted it run their way. [And what was their way?] It was Communist. (Beck & McKeown, 1994, pp. 250–251)

Such patterns of responses to the interviews conducted by Beck and McKeown were by no means rare and led them to conclude that "it seems that for many of these students, under the kind of instruction they receive, confusion begins immediately" (1994, p. 251). Instead of being a problem of forgetting the characters and events or the plot structures that organize them into a coherent whole, it seems that such organization was never apparent to the students in the first place.

The nature of this undifferentiated information is reflected in the findings Beck and McKeown (1994) reported in another analysis of children after they had completed their fifth-grade studies of American history. They reported that in response to the query, "Tell me anything you know about the American Revolution," 60 percent of the students gave no information about why the Revolution occurred, 57 percent did not mention Great Britain as the opponent, and 40 percent offered no information about which side won. In general, the students in this study responded to specific questions with simple answers that were not consistent with other answers they provided, and they showed little indication of any overall narrative organization to their knowledge. Figure 3.1 is a schematic representation of the "associative knowledge structure" that McKeown and Beck (1990) provided of the events of the Revolutionary period; this structure represents what would be acceptable for a student finishing fifth-grade instruction. In this figure, which may be taken as a kind of visual presentation of narrative organization, all the events, protagonists, and causal relations are placed in a kind of integrated whole.

In striking contrast to this picture of an acceptable representation, McKeown and Beck mapped out the associative structure of the text provided by Tony, one of the students who had completed fifth-grade history, and the result appears in Figure 3.2. Unlike the picture presented in Figure 3.1, Tony's response was fragmented into four "islands." For example, his answers showed no apparent connection between information about the thirteen colonies, the Revolutionary War, and the "no taxation" motto.

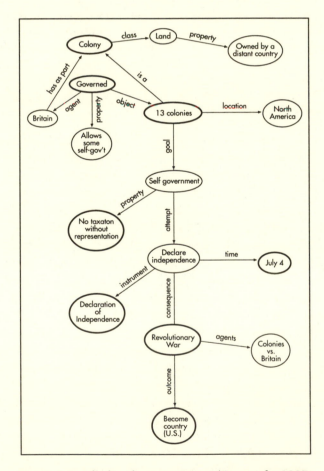

Figure 3.1 Idealized semantic net (Copyright 1997 by the American Educational Research Association. Reprinted by permission of the publisher.)

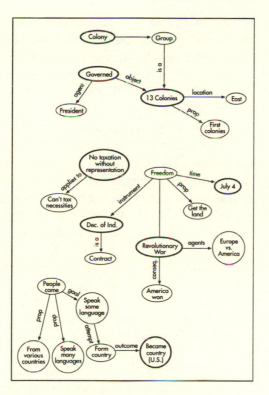

Figure 3.2 Semantic net for Tony
(Copyright 1997 by the American
Educational Research Association.
Reprinted by permission of the publisher).

Based on the findings from this and other studies, Beck and
McKeown (1994, p. 254) go on to argue that much of the responsibility for this disappointing instructional outcome rests with history
textbooks, which "are simply not adequate to the task of presenting
students with coherent, comprehensible accounts of history." They
stress the need for increased coherence in textbooks' presentations
of historical material, noting that several studies (e.g., Beck,
McKeown, Sinatra, & Loxterman, 1991; McKeown, Beck, Sinatra, &
Loxterman, 1992) have demonstrated that texts with more coherence
"bring about enhanced understanding of the causal sequence of events
and ideas" (p. 254). In addition, Beck and McKeown argue that teachers and textbooks try to cover too much material and as a result do
so very superficially. In their view, "it would be better to select a few
topics and explore them with the kind of reflective attention that can
bring about understanding and learning" (p. 255).

The notions that Beck and her colleagues invoke when talking about coherence in history texts and the coherence, or incoherence, of students' knowledge about the American Revolution are in many respects quite similar to those outlined by historiographers such as White (1973, 1987) and Mink (1978) in their comments about narrative. In particular, Mink's description of the cognitive function of narrative form as one of "body[ing] forth an ensemble of interrelationships of many different kinds as a single whole" (1978, p. 144) is relevant. Viewing narratives as cultural tools involves recognizing coherence as a basic organizing device, and this in turn provides clues about the affordances and constraints one can anticipate when examining the mediational means employed in representing the past. In the case of the fifth- and eighth-grade students studied by Beck and her colleagues, it would seem that there is often little in the way *either* of affordances or constraints because the cultural tool is poorly organized and mastered. The implication is certainly not that fifth graders or eighth graders cannot master narratives in general. However, it is quite clear that they have not mastered those used in school to present the story of the origins of the United States. Indeed, Beck's studies suggest that even after schoolchildren have two encounters with U.S. history in fifth and eighth grades, the textbooks and instruction do not result in their mastery of this basic narrative.

Mastering Historical Texts: Knowing Too Much

The general claim that textual information cannot be well understood, let alone remembered, in the absence of narrative organization has been made in psychology at least since Bartlett (1932) and has been the focus of numerous studies over the past several decades in developmental psychology. The general upshot of this research is that, unless it is integrated into a coherent schema (i.e., narrative in the cases I am considering here), information is very hard to comprehend and retain. In the studies reported by Beck and her colleagues, the absence of narrative organization was precisely the problem, and as a result the students had a difficult time understanding and remembering information that had been the object of many hours of classroom instruction.

In terms of mediated action, the point is that students had not mastered the cultural tool—namely, a historical narrative—and for this reason they could not take advantage of the affordances this cultural tool offered as they sought to carry out the form of mediated action involved in reproducing accounts of the American Revolution. These students knew too little in the sense that they had not mastered the narrative form that consists of an ensemble of interrelationships organized into a single whole. It is such findings that occasionally lead commentators to conclude that American schools are not doing their job.

I would like to turn to another set of findings that presents a seeming paradox in light of this conclusion—namely, that in at least some respects it seems that American schools have done their job almost too well when it comes to history instruction. Like the studies of Beck and her colleagues, the results I examine concern accounts of the early period of American history, but unlike her studies I report results from studies involving college students—subjects who have had least one more year of instruction in American history and who are of course older and more experienced with narrative organization and other aspects of instructional materials. But here I go beyond a focus on the degree of basic mastery and examine issues of appropriation as well.

To make this argument about the complex and dynamic relationships between agent and cultural tool, I examine results from other empirical studies carried out by O'Connor (1991, 1992), Wertsch and O'Connor (1994), and Wertsch (1994b). I begin by going into detail about some of the basic properties of the cultural tool employed by the subjects in these studies. I outline these basic properties under three general headings: (1) events, (2) theme, and (3) the construction of main characters. These three aspects of narrative contribute to the process of bodying forth an ensemble of interrelationships of many different kinds as a single whole. As will become evident, an analysis of the texts produced by the subjects in terms of these three aspects can tell us a great deal about how a narrative form can enable and constrain what individuals say about the early period of American history.

Subjects and Procedure

The texts I examine come from a study conducted by O'Connor (1991, 1992). In this study, 24 college students from a small university in New England were asked to spend 30 minutes to an hour writing an essay that would "provide an account of the origin of your country." They were told that the procedure was not a test of memory or of what they had learned in history classes but was instead intended to elicit how they would normally present information about the origin of their country. Students in this group, who were all U.S. citizens, included 18 women and 7 men, and they ranged in age from 18 to 21 years.

The texts generated by this procedure ranged from 203 to 856 words, with a mean length of 533. There were other variations in these texts as well, but the overriding impression one obtains upon reading them is of their striking similarity, which might be expected, given that all the subjects had studied a fairly standard curriculum of American history at least three times by the time they had graduated from high school.

EVENTS

Much of the uniformity of these texts derives from the similarity in the events included in them. In particular, five events were mentioned quite regularly. Columbus's arrival was mentioned by 13 students, the arrival of the Pilgrims by 18 students, the Declaration of Independence and the Revolutionary War by 19 students, the U.S. Constitution by ten students, and the Civil War and Emancipation Proclamation by 9 students. The strong tendency to include the arrival of the Pilgrims and the Declaration of Independence and Revolutionary War in these accounts is noteworthy, and in what follows I focus on these events in particular.

THEME

The strong similarity among participants about what events to include in their accounts is echoed by a second pattern having to do with textual themes. The notion of theme at issue here has to do with the goals attributed to the actors and the motives underlying these goals. Although multiple goals often appeared in a given narrative, one occurred particularly frequently (in 23 of the 24 cases) and served as an organizing point for the greater part of most of the narratives. On this basis, it was taken to be a central theme to consider. O'Connor (1992) labeled this the "quest for freedom" theme.

A subject's text was categorized as including the quest-for-freedom theme when it included a description of actions by groups of people indicating either an intention to escape a social system or ruler deemed by the groups as persecuting them or depriving them of their individual freedom, or an intention to establish a social system based on ideas of individual freedom. The criteria for categorizing a participant's narrative as including the quest-for-freedom theme were quite conservative: there had to be some explicit mention of the theme such as in the following example (segments concerning the theme are italicized):

> Hundreds of years ago our founding fathers were greatly *dissatisfied with their inability to exercise certain rights which they felt necessary to their happiness*. These people were finding out that England was not permissive of certain religions and beliefs. These people banded together to sail across the Atlantic Ocean to the little-known continent of North America, referred to as the New World. *Hundreds of people risked their lives for a chance of freedom and a new start that might bring about a nation that better served its people.* (from O'Connor, 1991, p. 10)

The fact that 23 of the 24 participants in this study used the quest-for-freedom theme as a major organizing device is of course closely related to the tendency to include the Pilgrims' arrival and the Declaration of Independence and Revolutionary War as key events. Indeed, it is hard to imagine what theme *other* than the quest-for-freedom could emerge, at least for individuals who learned history in American high schools, if these events are included.

THE CONSTRUCTION OF MAIN CHARACTERS

On the basis of what I have said so far, it would seem probable that the main characters in these texts would be the European settlers of America. After all, it is likely that their motivations and actions would be viewed as being essential for understanding events such as the Revolutionary War and the writing of the U.S. Constitution. Not that other individuals and groups would not be mentioned, but the frequency with which these other individuals and groups appeared, and the ways in which they are represented, might differ from patterns associated with the European settlers. To examine this supposition and hence further explore the organization of the narratives produced by the subjects in this study, three analyses concerned with the "construction of main characters" were conducted.

The term *construction* of main characters emphasizes that I am dealing with an aspect of narrative organization rather than with a set of statements that provide a complete account of "what really happened" in a direct, unmediated way. This is not to say that the propositions included in these essays were untrue—that is, inaccurate if taken in isolation. Instead, the focus is on which of several narratives, and hence which of several sets of main characters, the subjects employed to "grasp together" (Mink, 1972) the elements in their essays.

The relation between the accuracy of individual statements included in a narrative and what Mink (1978) called the "narrative truth" of the whole is a complex one. In outlining his account of narrative truth, Mink rejected the assumption that narrative form can be treated as a logical conjunction of assertions. From this perspective, the "truth-value of the text is . . . simply a logical function of the truth or falsity of the individual assertions taken separately: the conjunction is true if and only if each of the individual propositions is true" (pp. 143–144). Mink saw this misguided assumption as underlying the thinking of "philosophers intent on comparing the form of narrative with the form of theories, as if [narrative] were nothing but a logical conjunction of past-referring statements" (p. 144).

Such an approach overlooks Mink's concept of "narrative truth." Indeed, "it is not a model of narrative form at all. It is rather a model of *chronicle*" (Mink, 1978, p. 144). In the terminology outlined earlier that White employs, Mink's criticisms and claims apply more accurately to the form of annals than to chronicle, since in White's view the latter tends more toward narrative. Regardless of how one differentiates among such terms, the general point is clear: there is an important distinction to be made between the truth of the past-referring statements that might be included in a narrative and the "narrative truth" of the whole.

The issue of the truth of past-referring statements came up at several points in the results reported by Beck and McKeown (1994). For example, a student who had completed fifth-grade instruction made the false assertion that in the Revolutionary War "there was us and China [as enemies]." Indeed many past-referring statements in the students' interviews were inaccurate, primarily because of confusion over who the characters were. Indeed, as Beck and McKeown note, "confusion about agents was prevalent throughout the texts" (p. 243).

Mink pointed out that it is possible for all the past-referring statements in a narrative to be true and still not agree on the narrative truth of the text. This is because the conditions contributing to narrative truth are quite distinct from those determining the truth of individual statements:

> historical narrative claims truth not merely for each of its individual statements taken distributively, but for the complex form of the narrative itself. Only by virtue of such form can there be a story of failure or of success, of plans miscarried or policies overtaken by events, of survivals and transformations which interweave

with each other in the circumstances of the individual lives and the development of institutions. (1978, p. 144)

The notion of narrative truth, in short, has to do with whether one has employed the "correct" story when grasping together a set of events and characters into a narrative. For example, it has to do with whether the Boston Tea Party is best interpreted as an event in the quest-for-freedom narrative or as part of a story about the desires of the mercantile class in the colonies. Such arguments are the center of debates among schools of historical interpretation. For example, in the early twentieth century the historian Charles Beard (1921) and his Progressive followers argued that economic interest and class conflict, rather than the quest for freedom, were the forces behind American history, and in the view of some commentators the result was that "for the first time, the nation's professional historians parted company with the guardians of American exceptionalism" (Appleby, Hunt, & Jacob, 1994, p. 139).

Once we have differentiated narrative truth from the truth of past-referring statements, we are confronted with the relationhip between these two constructs. This is so, first of all, because "the same event, under the same description or different descriptions, may belong to different stories, and its particular significance will vary with its place in these different—often very different—narratives" (Mink, 1978, pp. 144–145). Furthermore, different narrative lines typically dictate different sets of characters and events. To paraphrase Burke (1969), this follows from the fact that even if any given narrative is a *reflection* of reality, by its very nature as a narrative it must be a *selection* of reality; and to this extent it must function also as a *deflection* of reality. In short, events, characters, and narrative truth are tightly bound together into what Mink called a "single whole" (1978, p. 144).

All of this suggests that the construction of main characters in a historical narrative is closely related to its narrative truth. The construction of main characters is a process concerned with questions such as Who is at the center of the narrative? and Who is responsible for the events that make up the story's main theme? Indeed, the use of "theme" in this last question reveals the close connection between the analysis of theme and main characters.

Returning to the college students' accounts of the origins of the United States, I use three measures to examine the construction of main characters: (1) frequency of mention; (2) patterns of agency; and (3) patterns of presupposed presence.

Frequency of Mention

Using the appearance of nouns and pronouns in surface form as a criterion, it is possible to examine how often various groups, or members of those groups, appeared as actors in these texts. Differences in the mention of groups were quite striking. In the 24 texts produced by the subjects, European settlers were mentioned 505 times, Native Americans were mentioned 94 times, the British were mentioned 48 times, and African Americans were mentioned 40 times. Other groups such as Spanish and French colonizers were also mentioned, but at much lower frequencies. Every one of the 24 subjects in this study mentioned European settlers more frequently than any other group, and in many cases they mentioned no other group at all. This measure of frequency of appearance is quite simple, but on its basis alone it seems that the European settlers occupied the role of main characters in the texts produced by these subjects.

This simple frequency measure reveals nothing about *how* the characters mentioned in noun phrases were represented. For example, a group that is mentioned most frequently, in connection with what Burke called the scene or in the role of what he termed a "counteragent," may not be the main character. In an attempt to capture other dimensions of what it means to be the main character, I turn to two additional measures as they apply to European settlers and Native Americans—the two groups mentioned most in these texts.

Patterns of Agency

As defined here, agency has to do with issues such as Who initiated and carried out the actions in a narrative? and Who was a bystander or a victim? Who did the acting, and who was acted upon? I examine these issues from the perspective of what Michael Silverstein (1980) has termed "propositional referentiality." Propositional referentiality plays an essential role in organizing language as a mediational means (Wertsch, 1985) and is concerned with the roles that constituents play within propositions or their linguistic expression, sentences.

For my present analyses, I will focus on two general groupings of propositional referentiality: what I shall term a superordinate category and a subordinate category. Each of these includes subcategories that are usually distinguished in linguistic analyses, but for examining what I am calling agency in narrative they can serve as general headings. In the superordinate category I include noun phrases in the position of (a) subject of an active transitive clause, (b) subject of an intransitive clause, (c) subject of a copula clause, and (d) noun phrase following "by" (either present in surface form or deleted) in a passive transitive clause.

Linguistic analyses concerned with propositional referentiality or grammatical roles within clause structure would typically include only items (a) and (d)under the heading of agency. The broader notion I am employing, however, is aimed at capturing cases in which an individual or group is generally presented as being at the center of action. A noun phrase may be given this status by referring to the initiator of an action, the party that carries out action on another party, or the focus of description. Examples (1), (2), (3), and (4), from texts in this study, are examples of (a), (b), (c), and (d), respectively.

1. *They* [the Indians] taught them [the Pilgrims] how to fish, grow, and fertilize crops, prepare for long hard winters, and to appreciate nature.
2. *The population of white people* grew disproportionately.
3. *The settlers* were an ambitious sort.
4. The Indians, with a different culture, dress, language, religion, etc. were feared by *the newcomers*.

Like the superordinate category, the subordinate category used here does not correspond to any single role of propositional referentiality. Instead, it groups together several grammatical roles, the common thread being that noun phrases in all of them indicate a secondary status of the individual or group mentioned vis-à-vis the individual or group mentioned in the position of a superordinate noun phrase. This secondary status could derive from the fact that the subordinate noun phrase refers to a group that receives the action of the actor (sometimes as a victim), or it could derive from the fact that the group is referred to in a way indicating that it is a secondary and not a main character. The following items were coded as noun phrases in the subordinate category: (e) direct object in a transitive clause (either active or passive), (f) indirect object in a transitive clause (either active or passive), and (g) noun phrases following "with" in the sense of "in collaboration with." Examples (5), (6), and (7), from the subjects' texts, are examples of (e), (f), and (g), respectively.

5. Within a decade or two, he [Columbus] had completely decimated *the entire Arawak Indian tribe.*
6. This enraged the colonies because England refused to give *them* representation in Parliament.
7. The settlers also exploited the Indians by trading goods with *them* that complicated the Indians' way of life.

All noun phrases referring to European settlers or to Native Americans that occurred in superordinate or subordinate positions were coded. Of the noun phrases in the students' texts that referred to the European settlers, 89.1 percent appeared in superordinate position. The corresponding figure for noun phrases that referred to Native Americans was 64 percent. Hence, when European settlers were mentioned, they were almost always given primary status in a clause, a tendency that was markedly less pronounced for Native Americans. Unlike the European settlers, Native Americans were often presented as recipients or victims of action. As already noted, in many cases the appearance of noun phrases in the subordinate position indicated that an individual or group had the status of being acted on by groups mentioned in superordinate noun phrases. For example, consider the following paragraph from one student's text, coded for noun phrases in superordinate ("[sup]") and subordinate ("[sub]") positions:

> However, *the settlers* [sup] did not stay thankful for long. *The Pilgrims* [sup] felt that it was their duty as good Christians to save *these "savages"* [sub] from sin. *The settlers* [sup] also exploited *the Indians* [sub] by trading goods with *them* [sub] that complicated the Indians' way of life. *They* [sup] also took the Indians' land, and hunting grounds. *The settlers* [sup] also used the delicate situations that were between tribal enemies to set *the Indians* [sub] against each other for economic benefit.

Throughout this paragraph, noun phrases referring to European settlers were in a superordinate position and noun phrases referring to Native Americans were in a subordinate position. The resulting picture is one in which the European settlers are represented as being the main force moving the narrative forward. They are the active agents in this passage. In contrast, the Native Americans are not represented as main characters in the same way. Instead, they are represented as recipients or victims of the European settlers' actions. The pattern of propositional referentiality within clauses obviously is quite consistent with, and indeed may be seen as being an essential constitutive factor of, the organization of agency and identification of main characters in the narrative as a whole.

Although the pattern of mentioning Native Americans in the subordinate role was not always as consistent as in the preceding paragraph, it was quite strong across students. One indication of this is the relative tendency of the students to mention Native Americans and European settlers in the subordinate position. The texts of

18 of the 24 subjects included at least one mention of Native Americans or European settlers in the subordinate position. Of these 18 cases, 7 included more references to Native Americans than to European settlers in the subordinate position, 8 included an equal number of references to Native Americans and to European settlers in the subordinate position, but only 3 included more references to European settlers than to Native Americans in the subordinate position. This pattern is particularly striking, given the much greater number of references overall to European settlers (505) than to Native Americans (94).

The general pattern of propositional referentiality, then, is one in which the vast majority of references to European settlers were made in the superordinate position, whereas this tendency was less pronounced in the case of Native Americans. Furthermore, there was a clear tendency for noun phrases in subordinate positions to be used to refer to Native Americans rather than to European settlers.

Patterns of Presupposed Presence

The third measure I use to assess the construction of main characters in the texts produced by the subjects in this study involves *presupposed presence*. The notion of presupposed presence is related to "discourse referentiality" as opposed to "propositional referentiality" (Silverstein, 1980; Wertsch, 1985). This means that it has to do with the relationship between unique, situated utterances and the contexts in which they occur. More specifically, it has to do with how utterances function to presuppose the context of speech in which they occur, on the one hand, or act in a "performative" capacity to create or entail the context, on the other.

The notion of presupposed presence is concerned with the fact that the individuals or groups mentioned in a text can be treated as being more or less present in the speech context and hence assumed to be more or less accessible to speaker and listener (or writer and reader). This is manifested in a speaker's tendency to refer to characters as if their presence is obvious and hence can be assumed. In such cases, there is no need to identify the character by using elaborate, explicit forms. Indeed, a speaker may go so far as to use no explicit surface form at all. In contrast, a speaker may assume that the character is not obvious or is not present in the attention or consciousness (Chafe, 1974) of the interlocutors involved in the speech setting. In such cases, the character will need to be introduced or reintroduced through the use of explicit referring expressions.

There are certain parallels between the notion of presupposed presence and the notions of "given information" (Chafe, 1974, 1976), "old information" (Halliday, 1967), or "psychological subject" (Vygotsky, 1987). In these latter three cases, the basic claim is that information is available either in the "extralinguistic" or "intralinguistic" speech-event context (Wertsch, 1985), and this makes "attentuation" (Chafe, 1976) or "abbreviation" (Vygotsky, 1987) possible, typically in the form of pronominal referring expressions or deletions. The relationship is a "presupposing" one (Silverstein, 1976) in the sense that information is available in the context and can therefore be presupposed when producing utterances. In this sense, the context of the speech event shapes the utterance.

In contrast to this, the relationship between utterance and context is the reverse in instances of presupposed presence. Instead of a presupposing relationship, it is a "creative" (Silverstein, 1985) or "performative" (Silverstein, 1976) one. In such instances, producing utterances creates or re-creates the context. The specific focus in this case is on the assumed presence of certain characters in the speech-event context. Instead of the context shaping the utterance, the focus is on how an utterance shapes the context.

This is not to deny that a precondition for attenuation in instances of presupposed presence is that certain information is available from the extralinguistic and intralinguistic context. If no such information is available, the utterance may be uninterpretable or may appear to be "egocentric" in the sense that Piaget (1955) outlined. However, in many cases such information is equally available for two or more characters in a text, yet attenuation may be much more pronounced in the case of references to one than the other. In such cases, there is a kind of "as if" effect. Certain characters are treated *as if* they are more obvious, more present in the consciousness of the speaker and listener than others, and this treatment is precisely what creates the impression of presupposed presence.

To examine the presupposed presence of various characters in the texts that the subjects produced for this study, two forms of attenuation were analyzed: (a) pronouns (in any position of propositional referentiality) and (b) agent noun-phrase deletions that occurred in passive clauses. Other forms of noun-phrase deletion such as gapping and dropping noun phrases from compound sentences also occurred in the texts, but in many instances it was difficult to be certain of the identity of the referent in such cases. For this reason, the analysis of noun-phrase deletion was limited to the more conservative measure of agent deletion in passive clauses. An example of attenuation in the form of pronominalization is (8), and an example of agent noun-phrase deletion from a passive clause is shown in (9):

8. In short, *they* [settlers from England] were beginning to feel smothered, just as *they* had in England.
9. The situation became worse and worse, and finally the Indians were driven west [i.e., *by European settlers*].

In both the case of pronominal attenuation and the case of agent noun-phrase deletion from passive clauses, there was a strong pattern of presupposed presence for European settlers but a near absence of presupposed presence for Native Americans. There were 93 pronominal references to European settlers and only 4 such pronominal references to Native Americans in the texts. The difference is even more striking in the case of agent-noun phrase deletion from passive clauses. Eighty-nine such deletions occurred when the referents were European settlers, whereas only 1 such deletion occurred in the case when the referent was a Native American.

To some limited extent, these differences can be attributed to differences in the frequency with which European settlers and Native Americans were mentioned in the texts. However, the difference in the use of attenuated reference is much more pronounced than the general difference in frequency of mention. The striking differences in both patterns of attenuation suggest a strong presupposed presence of European settlers in contrast to that of Native Americans. The students producing these texts tended to assign European settlers the role of being much more obviously present than Native Americans in their own and their interlocutors' consciousness and in the speech event contexts in which they were operating. Indeed, in many cases the European settlers were assumed to be so obviously present that there was no need to mention them at all in surface form; their presence could simply be presupposed. In contrast, when mentioning Native Americans, the subjects writing the texts tended to use explicit forms, a practice indicating that the Native Americans were not considered to be so readily present in the speech-event context.

In sum, I have examined the subjects' accounts of the origins of the United States from the perspectives of the events included, the theme, and the construction of main characters (as reflected by frequency of mention, patterns of agency, and patterns of presupposed presence). These measures reflect various facets of what I view as a single, integrated cultural tool in the form of an official narrative that provides "a structure of relationships by which the events contained in the account are endowed with a meaning, by being identified as part of an integrated whole" (White, 1987, p. 9). The facets operate in tandem, mutually reinforcing one another around a central core of meaning based on a circumscribed set of events in which European settlers were the main characters who were engaged in a quest for freedom. The degree to which this narrative form was tightly organized in a coherent meaning system suggests that the cultural tool at issue would provide strong affordances and strong constraints on efforts to produce an account of the origins of the United States. I take up these issues next.

The Mastery and Appropriation of Historical Texts

In my review of how students can know too little or too much about history, I have focused on levels of mastery of a basic cultural tool—the form of an official narrative. While recognizing that it is possible, and often quite important, to analyze how well students and others have mastered a cultural tool, such analyses can be quite limited in that they do not consider several complexities in the relationship between agents and the mediational means they employ. Instead of considering some of the complexities of appropriation, they tend to assume that agents readily accept and passively consume cultural tools. In chapter 2, however, I stressed that mediated action always involves an irreducible tension between a cultural tool and an agent's use of it. In what follows, I turn once again to this irreducible tension to examine the broader picture of mediated action, using the college students' narrative texts about the origins of the United States as an illustration.

Before turning to this issue, I should note that some readers might be asking why it is necessary to invoke the notions of cultural tools and mediated action at all in this discussion. For example, in reviewing how it is possible to know too little or too much about history, why not frame this in standard ways encountered in psychology? Why not just talk about how well students have learned information? What is added by invoking the notion of mediated action? To some degree, answers to these questions can be found in accounts of how cultural tools are produced, but the major response I have concerns the dynamic tension that exists between cultural tools and agents' consumption of them. This notion of tension between agent and cultural tool is one that stands at the center of accounts of mediated action, but it is unlikely to arise in standard analyses that focus on cognitive processes.

The subjects' production of texts about the origins of the United States can be understood from the perspective of Bakhtin's claims about the "special dialogic relations" (1986, p. 105) between the "repeatable" and the "individual, unique, and unrepeatable" poles of an utterance. As I outlined earlier, this special dialogic relation is a particular case of the more general irreducible tension that characterizes mediated action. Essential aspects of these dialogic relations derive from the fact that utterances and the language appropriated to produce them always "belong" to someone. In the illustration I am using, the quest for freedom narrative line is not "neutral and impersonal." Instead, it exists "in other people's concrete contexts, serving other people's intentions" (Bakhtin, 1981, p. 294). As a result, the process of producing texts about the origins of the United States—texts that might otherwise be considered to be products of our own efforts—involves at least two voices: the voice of the cultural tool (the quest for freedom narrative in this case) and the voice of the agent producing utterances in a unique speech situation. In some cases, these two voices may come together in harmony or even seeming unison, and in others a great deal of discord or dissonance may be in evidence. In all cases, the fact that two voices are involved gives rise to one or another form of "multivoicedness."

In what follows I examine two forms of mulivoicedness and explore their implications for interpreting the texts about U.S. history that I have been using as illustrations. The first form of multivoicedness is heteroglossia (outlined earlier), and the second is what I term "means conflict." In my view, any adequate account of historical representation will have to take into consideration the dynamics of at least these forms of multivoicedness. Analyses that focus exclusively either on the cultural tool or on the agents using them will miss an essential dimension of how the past is represented in such cases.

As noted earlier, heteroglossia is a property of any utterance and involves the kind of inherent, irreducible tension that is part of mediated action. In Bakhtin's treatment, heteroglossia is a necessary consequence of the fact that every utterance involves both "reiterative" (reproducible, repeatable) and "nonreiterative" (unique, unrepeatable) elements. In the cases I consider, heteroglossia arises as a consequence of an individual's stance toward the narrative being appropriated to produce a particular account of the past. This stance may range from complete acceptance, on the one hand, to resistance (e.g., through parody) or even outright rejection (cf.

Tulviste & Wertsch, 1994), on the other. The stance involved in a particular performance may reflect a general attitude toward a narrative such as the quest-for-freedom narrative, but it by no means should be assumed to be a fixed property of an agent. Instead, a speaker may manifest different stances toward a particular narrative line used as a cultural tool on different occasions.

The second form of multivoicedness I examine, means conflict, derives from the fact that more than one item from a "stock of stories" (MacIntyre, 1984) may be invoked to produce an account of a single event or action. More specifically, it concerns the fact that in many cases two or more conflicting or contradictory narratives (i.e., serving as mediational means) are appropriated in producing a single text. The use of multiple mediational means can, at least in principle, be a factor that operates independently of the multivoicedness that derives from heteroglossia.

As is the case for any nation-state, there is more than one narrative that may be used as a cultural tool in generating an account of U.S. history. Indeed, authors such as Shklar (1991, p. 8) have argued that "Americans have lived with extreme contradictions for most of their history by being dedicated to political equality as well as to its complete rejection." In her view, "in truth, from the nation's beginnings as an independent republic, Americans were torn by 'glaring inconsistencies between their professed principles of citizenship and their deep-seated desire to exclude certain groups permanently from the privileges of membership.' These tensions constitute the real history of its citizens" (pp. 14–15).[1] The "certain groups" Shklar has in mind are slaves and women, but they also include Native Americans, which comprise the population that will be at the core of my analysis that follows.

The different and often openly contradictory stories invoked as mediational means to make sense of the past of the United States are of course not "neutral and impersonal." Instead, they reflect the perspectives and interests of various groups (see Tanaka, 1994). In Bakhtinian terms, they exist "in [various] people's concrete contexts, serving [various] people's intentions," and hence reflect different voice types, social languages, or world views. Such a view has little room for the assumption that narrative tools are ideologically neutral instruments for speaking and thinking.

When one tries to interpret the texts produced by the college students in my illustration, issues of heteroglossia and means conflict become quite important. Instead of examining how closely subjects hew to the quest-for-freedom narrative theme, I now focus on the kind of special dialogic relations they can have with it. These dialogic relations take on a variety of forms, ranging from relative acceptance and harmony, on the one hand, to resistance and rejection, on the other.

I am particularly interested in how the participants introduced and dealt with information that is not consistent with the quest-for-freedom narrative line. As authors such as Zinn (1980) have pointed out, it is possible to identify narratives about the United States that stand in marked contrast to the quest-for-freedom story that was so prevalent in the students' texts. The one that appeared quite frequently and provided some of the most striking instances of means conflict was the narrative about the European settlers' poor treatment of Native Americans.

Information about the treatment of Native Americans that was potentially inconsistent with the quest-for-freedom theme did not occur at all in 5 of the 23 texts (category 1 texts) organized around this theme. In these cases, one must assume either that the participants were unaware of the sorts of alternative stories that might introduce such contradictions or that they elected not to include them. Given the low likelihood of the former, it is probable that participants did not include such information precisely *because* it would create conflict. Such a course of action is quite consistent with claims about how narrative as a "cognitive instrument" organize an ensemble of interrelationships into an integrated, coherent whole.

Texts in a second category (category 2: 5 cases) included information about Native Americans, but in these cases the information was presented in such a way that it in no way came into conflict with the quest-for-freedom theme. Again, the absence of conflict may have reflected the constraints imposed by narrative form, constraints having to do with a narrative's tendency to grasp together information into an integrated, coherent whole. An example of this sort of text is the following: "The first few months were difficult ones but the Puritans obviously survived and in November when all the crops had been harvested, the Pilgrims with the help of some Indians captured a turkey and started the tradition of Thanksgiving" (from O'Connor, 1991, p. 12). This is the only mention of Native Americas in this subject's narrative. In such cases, means conflict as a form of multivoicedness is not obvious, even though the characters that could give rise to such conflict were mentioned.

One text in category 3 included information about Native Americans that seems to conflict with the quest-for-freedom theme, but the participant made no attempt to resolve this conflict. In this case, the participant introduced the quest-for-freedom theme by stating that the Pilgrims were "religious refugees who were seeking religious freedom from England." He then proceeded to write in his discussion of the American Revolution that "this new territory [the land purchased from France] is where the people of the US forced the native Americans to live. These Indians were ripped out of their homes and sent west. Most of them died before they got there. This continued all the way through to President Andrew Jackson. Now back to the war" (from O'Connor, 1991, pp. 13–14). With "Now back to the war," the participant closed off his discussion of the topic at hand and returned to a topic that had been previously introduced. He made no further mention of Native Americans in his story, and there is no apparent attempt to reconcile the very different perspectives of two conflicting narratives about the early period of U.S. history.

I label texts in a fourth category (category 4: 2 cases) as instances of "resolution by plot structure." In these cases, participants included information that was potentially inconsistent with the quest-for-freedom theme, but they organized this information in such a way that the inconsistency was minimized. Specifically, their mention of Native Americans came *before* any mention of the quest-for-freedom theme. One participant began her text as follows:

> For thousands of years, native Americans lived peacefully in my country. Then, in 1492, Christopher Columbus, an explorer looking for wealth, went astray in search for India and landed in what we now call North America. . . . He returned to Spain to tell them of his discovery. Soon, there was another colony in Plymouth, MA which was established in 1620. *Through disease and warfare, the native Americans died, were killed or fled to the western portion of the country.* (Emphasis added; from O'Connor, 1991, p. 14)

This participant introduced the quest-for-freedom theme only *after* this segment of her narrative, and she never returned to any mention of Native Americans.

For the two participants who used this strategy to resolve inconsistency, the tension between the quest for freedom and the deprivation of others of their freedom is seemingly resolved, or at least minimized, by bringing in the theme of freedom only after the potentially conflicting story line ends. In these cases, then, the linear organization of the narrative—that is, its plot or "syuzhet" (Tomashevskii, 1965)—serves an important function.

A fifth category of texts (category 5: 2 cases) can be labeled as instances of "resolution by attribution to characters." In these cases, the inconsistency between the quest-for-freedom theme and the characters' treatment of Native Americans was resolved by attributing temporary and seemingly out-of-character mental states or motives to the characters. For example, one participant wrote:

> Seeing the success of the first settlers, many more people wished to free themselves from the religious bonds of the king. These settlers mostly came to the Northern section of what is now the United States.
>
> The Pilgrims led hard lives. The weather conditions of the "New World" were not much like what they were used to. The winters were very cold, and a lot of snow fell. The weather also prevented the settlers from growing the crops that they were accustomed to.
>
> Thank God for the Indians! For with their great help and knowledge, the Indians saved the lives of many settlers and made it possible for other settlers to come to the "New World."
>
> However, *the settlers did not stay thankful for long.* The Pilgrims felt that it was their duty to save these "savages" from sin. The settlers also exploited the Indians by trading goods with them that complicated the Indians' way of life. They also took the Indians' land, and hunting grounds. The settlers also used the delicate situations that were between tribal enemies to set the Indians against each other for economic benefit.
>
> The situation soon became worse and worse, and soon the Indians were driven west.
>
> During the time of strife with the Indians, the settlers were trying to free themselves from the king's rule. (Emphasis added; from O'Connor, 1991, pp. 15–16)

In contrast to students in the previous group, students in this group introduced the issue of how Native Americans were treated after the quest-for-freedom theme had been introduced. This left them with the problem of reconciling two inconsistent stories—the continued striving of a group of people for freedom, on the one hand, and the actions by these same people that deprived another group of its freedom, on the other.

The participants seemed to attempt to resolve this tension by introducing a change in the mental state of the protagonists in their narratives from one of gratitude toward the Native Americans to one of hostility. Information about this change of mental state was introduced in such a way that it served to bracket information about topics such as the appropriation of land, economic exploitation, and religious intolerance. These hostile actions on the part of the settlers were represented in the narrative as a temporary digression from the main story line and as being temporary and out of character for the settlers.

Further support for this interpretation can be found in other parts of these subjects' texts. For example, the excerpt above included the phrase "having driven the Indians west," which seems to have provided the narrator with a way to switch back to what was presumably the characters' original and normal motivational state, that of striving for freedom.

The four categories of texts I have outlined so far that include references to Native Americans (i.e., categories 2–5) all involve at least a potential form of means conflict. In the case of category 2, this conflict does not emerge because Native Americans are presented as having only cordial relations with the European settlers. In the cases of categories 3, 4, and 5, there is evidence that the participants recognized the potential for means conflict between the quest-for-freedom narrative and other narratives about the treatment of Native Americans, but they organized their texts in various ways so that this conflict was avoided or at least minimized. In terms of the notions put forth earlier, categories 3, 4, and 5 involved potential means conflict, but there was little evidence that those producing the texts pursued the implications of this conflict. It is almost as if multivoicedness in the form of means conflict arose for these participants in spite of themselves, but they sought to minimize or avoid it.

The remaining two categories I consider involve a much greater degree of heteroglossia in the form of resistance to the quest-for-freedom narrative. As will become evident, this narrative still provided the basic framework for the texts, but the authors played a more active role in producing them. This made it possible for subjects to use a mediational means without accepting it in its totality. The users were able to resist "from within" even as they continued to invoke the same basic narrative tool.

I label texts in category 6 (4 cases) as instances of "resolution by commentary." In these cases, the participants commented directly on the incongruity produced by means conflict. For instance, one participant wrote:

> The Pilgrims came here for freedom—to get away from the Church of England. America was like a haven for them; it was a place where they could live as they pleased. But, like Columbus, they encountered Indians also. And also like Columbus, they treated them very poorly. *It's sadly ironic that the Pilgrims left England so they could be free but when they got here, they inflicted their views on the*

Indians. It's unfortunate, and unfair, that that happened. (Emphasis added; from O'Connor, 1991, pp. 17–18)

This participant's explicit commentary that it is "sadly ironic," "unfortunate," and "unfair" that people in the quest-for-freedom deprived others of their freedom, property, and lives distinguishes her text from those in any of the previous five categories. While still relying primarily on the same basic item from a stock of stories, she temporarily steps outside of this framework to make an explicitly critical comment. A new voice—the voice of a critical commentator—emerges alongside the voice of someone using the quest-for-freedom narrative and makes an explicit criticism about the conflict between this and other items from the stock stories that might be invoked to represent the past.

The final category of texts I outline (category 7: 1 case) can be labeled "satiric resolution." In this case, the subject used the basic quest-for-freedom narrative but in a satirical, if not cynical, way. There are multiple indications that he viewed the quest-for-freedom text as a story toward which he could take a critical, resisting stance, but in contrast to cases involving resolution through commentary, his resistance was not manifested in overt comments about means conflict:

> *Long ago in England*, there was a group of people who became tired with their lack of freedom concerning such issues as religion, tea tax, and so forth. They decided that they did not want to be English any longer. It seems that some of them had some knowledge about what was called the new world, *a world with large amounts of land and* no *inhabitants* ["no" italicized in the original]. So rather than revolt against the ruling establishment, they set out to create their own establishment, where they would have the freedom they so greatly desired.
>
> Their pilgrimage to the new world began as they set off to sea in a boat they called the Mayflower. On they sailed until they had reached the land which Columbus had stumbled upon a hundred and some years ago. These pilgrims, as they were—or at least now are—called landed on Plymouth Rock, and planted their feet on what was to become their land of the free.
>
> *Along their journey to freedom, however, there were a few minor difficulties. The first problem they encountered was that the land* WAS *inhabited after all* ["was" italicized in the original]. But seeing as how these natives were clearly far too primitive to match the battling skills of our pilgrims, *these pilgrims sat down to a nice meal of turkey and cranberries with the natives, and then killed them.*
>
> After they had settled their new homes—*having cleared their desired land of things like trees and natives*—they ran into their

next problem: the English had followed them, and wanted to rule the new world as well as the old! So they fought and fought. And eventually, the pilgrims were triumphant. They sent the English back and began to establish the land of freedom.

Our pilgrims reveled in their new freedom, and chose their own religions, and had a wonderful life. Their journey towards freedom was almost complete, until one day a boat from Africa arrived, and so they were confronted with their third obstacle on their way to creating the land of the free. (Emphasis added; from O'Connor, 1991, pp. 18–19)

This participant began his text with a phrase characteristic of fairy tales, thus indicating from the outset that what followed was not to be considered a straightforward historical account. The forms of resistance he employed included: (1) indicating his attitude toward the events he was relating by stressing the contrast between the generally accepted interpretation of the situation ("a world with large amounts of land and *no* inhabitants") and what he took to be the situation ("the land *WAS* inhabited after all"); (2) understating the situation ("a few minor difficulties"); and (3) juxtaposing two events involving Native Americans that are normally taken as separate ("these pilgrims sat down to a nice meal of turkey and cranberries with the natives, and then killed them"). He went on to establish the Native Americans as no more important to the settlers than physical obstructions that had to be removed ("having cleared their desired lands of things like trees and natives"). Thus, throughout his text the participant used various ways to resist the quest-for-freedom narrative and to incorporate various elements of alternative, conflicting narratives.

In this chapter, I have outlined a few of the implications that follow from viewing narratives as cultural tools. I have limited my focus to historical narratives and to the ways in which they are mastered and used by laypeople, but this still leaves open a vast array of issues, only some of which I have addressed. The starting point for all the analyses presented in this chapter is the special properties of narrative as a mediational means. Borrowing from Mink (1978, p. 144), my central point has been that "the cognitive function of narrative form . . . is not just to relate a succession of events but to body forth an ensemble of interrelationships of many different kinds as a single whole." It is this tendency of narrative to "grasp together" (Mink, 1972, p. 736) diverse elements such as "agents, goals, means, interactions, circumstances, unexpected results, etc." that is at the core of my treatment of narratives as cultural tools.

As my review of the research of Beck and her colleagues suggests, elementary school students often have a great deal of difficulty grasping together the diverse elements that go into historical narratives, at least those about the Revolutionary period in U.S. history. Many of the students in her studies found it next to impossible to understand, let alone remember, the kinds of narratives they encountered in elementary school history textbooks and classes. Hence I characterized their state as "knowing too little."

In contrast to this case of knowing too little, I characterized the university students in the illustrations I provided as "knowing too much." What they specifically know too much about is the quest-for-freedom narrative of the origins of the United States. My claim is not that these students knew too much about a variety of narrative accounts of the origins of the United States or that they even knew the quest-for-freedom narrative in all that much detail. However, they did seem to know this narrative in such a way that it served quite effectively to "grasp together" a set of events, motivations, and characters in a powerful way. The various analyses of events, theme, and main characters that I outlined provided several perspectives from which one can view the nature of the quest-for-freedom narrative that virtually all the subjects in this study appropriated in generating their texts. The general conclusion to be derived from these analyses is that several factors operate in tandem to create a relatively rigid and tightly scripted cultural tool. This is a cultural tool that offers affordances and, perhaps more important, constraints on what individuals using it are likely to generate in the way of an account of the origins of the United States.

The kinds of constraints I have in mind come into focus as one considers the various ways in which the irreducible tension between cultural tool and an agent's use of that tool may be played out in the case of the quest-for-freedom narrative. In my review of the various forms that multivoicedness can take in this case, I emphasized the range of possibilities that exists for appropriating this narrative tool. Some students generated texts that resemble a basic quest-for-freedom narrative and that show relatively little effect of heteroglossia and means conflict. At the other end of this range are texts that clearly reflect subjects' struggles that derived from means conflict and from heteroglossia. Such struggle is quite evident in cases of resolution by commentary and satiric resolution.

While I do not wish to minimize the range of possibilities subjects in this study demonstrated for generating an account of the origins of the United States, one of the most striking facts about their texts is that *all of them were fundamentally grounded in the quest-for-freedom narrative tool*. No matter how much or how little the subjects seemed to accept and agree with this narrative tool, they all used it in one way or another. This is especially noteworthy in the case of subjects whose texts reflect resolution by commentary or satiric resolution. In one way or another, these subjects conveyed that they were resisting the quest-for-freedom narrative, yet in the end they still employed it. In fact, no student even attempted to employ another narrative tool in any extended way.

The obvious question that arises in such cases is, Why did these students use this cultural tool when they had such obvious arguments with it? Indeed, upon reading these texts, one is almost tempted to ask the students who produced them, "If you really disagree with this account of the United States, why didn't you produce something completely different?" In the next two chapters, I address this question in more detail. For now, let me simply note that the subjects did appropriate this cultural tool and stress that, as a result, they were highly constrained in what they could say. The individuals have used the cultural tools they have been given, even though they seem to have difficulties with the ways in which these cultural tools shape their own narratives. In such cases, individuals may try to resist the ways in which such cultural tools shape their actions, but they are often highly constrained in the forms that such resistance can take.

Note

1. The work quoted by Shklar is J. H. Kettner's *The Development of American Citizenship, 1608–1807* (Chapel Hill: University of North Carolina Press, 1978), p. 288.

❅ 4 ❅

Mediated Action in Social Space

Most of the illustrations of mediated action I have used up to this point have involved agents acting in apparent isolation: their actions (e.g., pole vaulting, multiplication, recounting the past) have not involved social interaction with others. This isolation may be viewed as being only apparent, however, in that the agents always employ cultural tools provided by particular sociocultural settings.

The fact that one is tempted to say that one and the same instance of mediated action both is and is not socially situated reflects the fact that two notions of "social" are at work here. One sense of social that has to do with whether one or more than one individual in the immediate context participates in the action. I use the terms "social interactional" and "intermental" (see below) when dealing with phenomena at this level of analysis. These terms contrast with "individual" and "intramental," respectively A second sense of social has to do with the sociocultural situatedness of human action, something that derives from the fact that mediational means are part of any cultural, historical, and institutional setting. I continue to use the term "sociocultural" when dealing with this level of analysis. As I have been arguing throughout, virtually all human action, be it on the individual or social interactional plane, is socioculturally situated; even when an individual sits in solitude and contemplates something, she is socioculturally situated by virtue of the mediational means she employs.

109

The distinction between social interactional and individual processes that I wish to examine is grounded in Vygotsky's account of "intermental"[1] and "intramental" functioning. One of the places where he outlined these notions most clearly was in formulating his "general genetic law of cultural development":

> Any function in the child's cultural development appears twice, or on two planes. First it appears on the social plane, and then on the psychological plane. First it appears between people as an interpsychological category, and then within the child as an intrapsychological category. This is equally true with regard to voluntary attention, logical memory, the formation of concepts, and the development of volition. . . . It goes without saying that internalization transforms the process itself and changes its structure and functions. Social relations or relations among people genetically underlie all higher functions and their relationships. (1981b, p. 163)

Essential to Vygotsky's formulation of the intermental and intramental planes is that they are inherently related. Indeed, the boundaries between social and individual functioning are quite permeable in his account, and his emphasis was on the transformations between intermental and intramental processes rather than on the gulf that separates them: "[Higher mental functions'] composition, genetic structure, and means of action [forms of mediation]—in a word, their whole nature—is social. Even when we turn to [internal] mental processes, their nature remains quasi-social. In their own private sphere, human beings retain the functions of social interaction" 1981b, p. 164). This statement does not assume that higher mental functioning in the individual is a direct and simple copy of socially organized processes; the point Vygotsky made in his formulation of the general genetic law of cultural development about transformations in internalization warns against any such view. However, it does mean that there is a close connection, grounded in genetic transformations, between the specific structures and processes of intermental and intramental functioning.

Hence, from Vygotsky's perspective, intramental functioning is social not only in the sense that it is socioculturally situated but also in the sense that it "retain[s] the functions of social interaction." For example, many forms of problem solving on the individual level are viewed as being inherently dialogic due to the fact that they derive from participation in dialogic encounters on the intermental plane (Wertsch, 1980, 1985). The key to understanding Vygotsky's claim here, as is the case at many points in his writings, is to be found in his analysis of mediational means. From his perspective, the forms of dialogic speech that mediate intermental processes are taken over to form the intramental plane of functioning.

The close relationship, grounded in mediational means, that Vygotsky saw between the intermental and intramental planes of functioning is also reflected in his use of the term "mental function." When used by him, this term applies equally well to social interaction and to individual processes. One could restate Vygotsky's general genetic law by saying that *one and the same* "function in the child's cultural development appears twice, on two planes." From this perspective, it is as appropriate to assign to groups as well as to individuals terms such as "think," "attend," and "remember." As Middleton 1987) has noted, this is a line of reasoning that was being pursued by Bartlett (1932) in England at the same time that Vygotsky was writing, and today it is a point that is being revisited by investigators who have undertaken studies of "social memory" (cf. *Quarterly newsletter of the Laboratory of Comparative Human Cognition*, 1987), "socially shared cognition" (Resnick, Levine, & Teasley, 1991), and "distributed cognition" (Salomon, 1993). Indeed, some of these recent studies go beyond Vygotsky's claims in their emphasis on intermental functioning as a stable and point rather than a way station to the intramental plane. For example, these claims have been developed recently in cognitive science by Hutchins (1995a).

Intersubjectivity and Alterity in Social Interaction

To explore the implications of Vygotsky's claims about intermental functioning, it is essential to specify the nature of the social processes involved. I attempt to do this by outlining two opposing tendencies that may be seen as characterizing social interaction: "intersubjectivity" and "alterity." In any particular episode of social interaction, the relative importance of these two tendencies may vary, but both are always at work. Hence, the challenge is to "live in the middle" (Holquist, 1994) and recognize how these two forces are part of an integrated, dynamic picture. Carrying this out is often quite difficult, something that is reflected by the fact that accounts of social interaction frequently succumb to the temptation to focus exclusively on one or the other tendency.

As understood here, intersubjectivity concerns the degree to which interlocutors in a communicative situation share a perspective. Ragnar Rommetveit has outlined intersubjectivity in the following terms:

> The basic problem of human intersubjectivity becomes . . . a question concerning in what sense and under what conditions two persons who engage in a dialogue can transcend their different private worlds. And the linguistic basis for this enterprise, I shall argue, is not a fixed repertory of shared "literal" meanings, but very general and partially negotiated drafts of contracts concerning categorization and attribution inherent in ordinary language. (1979d, p. 7)

In Rommetveit's account, what any particular agent sees going on in a situation is private. However,

> it can be talked about and hence—at least under certain conditions and in some cases—become a temporarily shared social reality. The solitary observer may thus try to transform his "private" outlook on the situation into a social reality simply by telling some other person about it. Once the other person accepts the invitation to listen and engage in a dialogue, he leaves behind whatever his preoccupations might have been the moment "silence was transformed into speech." . . . From that moment on the two of them are jointly committed to a temporarily shared social world, established and continually modified by acts of communication. (1979a, p. 10)

Rommetveit's focus on the "architecture of intersubjectivity" (1979c) might seem to suggest that he sees total or pure intersubjectivity as being possible, but in actuality he rejects such a possibility. Indeed, he views pure intersubjectivity as "*a convenient fiction which allows scholars of human communication to pursue their trade with scientific rigour, formal elegance, and academic success while evading practically urgent and basic existential issues of human intersubjectivity*" (1979b, p. 148, emphasis in the original). In Rommetveit's view, pure intersubjectivity is a kind of rationalist dream grounded in the assumption that it is possible to share and transmit "a fixed repertory of shared 'literal' meanings" (1979d, p. 12).

Rommetveit (1979c, 1988) and his colleagues (e.g., Linell, 1982, 1988) have developed compelling critiques of analyses that focus on the transmission of literal meaning and that assume pure intersubjectivity is possible. In actuality, their critique is concerned more with the role that intersubjectivity plays in an analytic strategy than with the notion itself. The point is not to avoid the notion of intersubjectivity but to avoid viewing human communication from the perspective of how it fails to measure up to the false ideal of pure intersubjectivity. Indeed, Rommetveit's analysis suggests that intersubjectivity should be viewed as a tendency that characterizes human communication—a tendency that operates in dynamic tension with other, often opposing tendencies. This is an approach consistent with ideas outlined by Yuri Lotman (1988) in his analysis of the "functional dualism" of "texts."[2]

The first of the two textual functions Lotman envisioned under this heading is associated with intersubjectivity and can be termed the "univocal" function. It focuses on how it is possible to "convey meanings adequately" (1988, p. 34). According to Lotman, "this function is fulfilled best when the codes of the speaker and the listener most completely coincide and, consequently, when the text has the maximum degree of univocality." From Rommetveit's perspective, it is essential to keep in mind that such conditions seldom, if ever, exist in perfect form in human communication. In a similar vein, Lotman noted that "the ideal boundary mechanism for such an operation would be an artificial language and a text in an artificial language."

Like Rommetveit, Lotman saw major limitations in focusing on artificial languages when trying to understand human communication. Among other things, he noted that such languages do not model "language as such, but one of its functions—the ability to transmit a message adequately" (1990, p. 13). In his view, such a focus introduces a powerful terministic screen into the analysis, a screen that focuses our attention on language as a means for transmitting information and filters out other possibilities, especially the "poetic" uses of language:

> From the one position the informational point of view (using "informational" in the narrow sense) represents language as a machine for transmitting invariant messages, and poetic language is then regarded as a small and, generally speaking, abnormal corner of this system. According to this approach poetic language is seen merely as natural language with an overlay of supplementary restrictions and hence a significantly reduced informational capacity. (p. 17)

Although Rommetveit did not focus on the poetic function of language as such, the parallels between his cautionary note about focusing on "a fixed repertory of shared 'literal' meanings" (1979a, p. 7) and Lotman's comments about treating language as "a machine for transmitting invariant messages" are clear.

A related parallel between the lines of reasoning developed by Rommetveit and Lotman can be found in their views about the origins of accounts that focus on the univocal, information-transmission function of language. Rommetveit's critique of *"Habermas' promised land of 'pure intersubjectivity'"* (1979d, p. 148; emphasis in original) focuses on the rationalist ideal of "complete symmetry in the distrubution of assertion and disputation, revelation and hiding, prescription and following, among the partners of communication" (Habermas, 1970, p. 143). Lotman traced the roots of the idea of information transmission to similar rationalist and positivistic origins. For example, he argued that one of the principle founders of the information-transmission view of language was Ferdinand de Saussure, who "clearly saw the [univocal] function as the main principle of language" (Lotman, 1990, p. 17). In Lotman's view, this is reflected in

> the precision of his oppositions, his emphasis on the universal significance of the principle of arbitrariness in the relation of signified to signifier, and so on. Behind Saussure we can sense the culture of the nineteenth century with its faith in positivistic science, its conviction that knowledge is good and ignorance an absolute evil, its aims at universal literacy, the novels of Zola and the Goncourts.

In sum, an exclusive focus on the transmission of literal meaning and pure intersubjectivity runs the risk of forcing investigators to view essential aspects of human communication as the "dynamic residuals" (Rommetveit, 1979b) that somehow escape a rationalist analysis. Both Rommetveit and Lotman viewed it as essential not to ground an analysis in the univocal function and then characterize other aspects of human communication in terms of "negative rationalism" (Rommetveit, 1979b)—the failure to live up to the tenets of rationality. Indeed, the price of taking the univocal function to be "the only function, or even the basic one," is that one is confronted with "a whole number of paradoxes" (Lotman, 1990, p. 12). The alternative outlined by Lotman and followed here is to recognize the role of the univocal function and intersubjectivity in human communication but at the same time to incorporate these notions into a system of dynamic tensions involving another functional tendency.

This other tendency can be termed the "dialogic function," a function that is closely tied to Bakhtin's notion of "alterity" (Bakhtin, 1979; Clark & Holquist, 1984; Todorov, 1984). In contrast to the univocal function of a text—a function that "requires maximal semiotic ordering and structural uniformity of the media used in the process of reception and transmission" (Lotman, 1988, p. 41)—the dialogic function of text is grounded in the kind of multivoicedness that so concerned Bakhtin. According to Lotman:

> The second function of text is to generate new meanings. In this respect a text ceases to be a passive link in conveying some constant information between input (sender) and output (receiver). Whereas in the first case a difference between the message at the input and that at the output of an information circuit can occur only as a result of a defect in the communications channel, and is to be attributed to the technical imperfections of this sytem, in the second case such a difference is the very essence of a text's function as a "thinking device." What from the first standpoint is a defect, from the second is a norm, and vice versa. (1988, pp. 36–37)

In contrast to the univocal function, which tends toward a single, shared, homogeneous perspective comprising intersubjectivity, the dialogic function tends toward dynamism, heterogeneity, and conflict among voices. Instead of trying to "receive" meanings that reside in speakers' utterances as envisioned by the "conduit metaphor" (Reddy, 1979), the focus is on how an interlocutor might use texts as thinking devices and respond to them in such a way that new meanings are generated.

Lotman's analysis implies that communication models that focus solely on the transmission of messages cannot be amended in any simple way to deal with the dialogic organization of texts. Following the common practice of making arrows in a transmission model bidirectional might appear to address this issue, but it does nothing to resolve the fact that a single, univocal message is still presupposed as the underlying process. In Lotman's view, such a presupposition is not tenable because "the main structural attribute of a text in this second function is its internal heterogeneity" (1988, p. 37). The kind of heterogeneity he had in mind is a heterogeneity of different perspectives, or "voices" (Wertsch, 1991), and it gives rise to an image of "inter-animation" (Bakhtin, 1984) and rhetorical encounter (Billig, 1987):

> in its second function a text is not a passive receptacle, or bearer of some content placed in it from without, but a generator. The essence of the process of generation, however, is not only an evolution but also, to a considerable extent, an interaction between structures. Their interaction in the closed world of a text becomes an active cultural factor as a working semiotic system. A text of this type is always richer than any particular language and cannot be put together automatically from it. A text is a semiotic space in which languages interact, interfere, and organize themselves hierarchically. (Lotman, 1988, p. 37)

Lotman emphasized that both the univocal and dialogic functions of text can be found in any sociocultural setting, but one or the other dominates in certain areas of activity or in general during certain periods of history. For example, he argued that in some sociocultural settings the univocal function takes on particular importance:

> The mechanism of identification, the elimination of differences and the raising of a text to the status of a standard, does not just serve as a principle guaranteeing that a message will be adequately received in a system of communication: no less important is its function of providing a common memory for the group, of transforming it from an unstructured crowd into "une personne morale," to use Rousseau's expression. This function is especially important in nonliterate cultures and in cultures with a dominant mythological consciousness, but it tends also to be present to some degree in any culture. (1988, p. 35)

In accordance with his notions about functional dualism, however, Lotman argued that even in such cases where great weight is given to the univocal function the dialogic function of texts continues to exert a countervailing force.

The notion of alterity comes clearly into focus in connection with Lotman's account of the dialogic function. Like appropriation, alterity is a notion that derives from Bakhtin's writings and concerns the distinction between self and other. In this case, the Russian term is *drugost'*. As Clark and Holquist (1984, pp. 63–66) note, this term "hints at the relationship between the words for 'friend' (*drug*) and 'other' (*drugoj*), where -*oj* is the standard adjectival marker added to the root *drug*. This shading suggests the positive values of the other in Bakhtin's thinking." In Bakhtin's analysis, alterity is a phenomenon to be accepted, positively described, and celebrated rather than associated with some kind of inadequacy or failing, as it might be viewed from a perspective concerned with the univocal function, the transmission of literal meanings, and pure intersubjectivity. For Bakhtin:

> To be means to be for the other, and through him, for oneself. Man has no internal sovereign territory; he is all and always on the boundary; looking within himself, he looks *in the eyes of the other* or *through the eyes of the other*. . . . I cannot do without the other; I cannot become myself without the other; I must find myself in the other, finding the other in me (in mutual reflection and perception). (1979, p. 312)

According to Clark and Holquist (1984, p. 65), Bakhtin "conceives of otherness as the ground of all existence and of dialogue as the primal structure of any particular existence, representing a constant exchange between what is already and what is not yet." From a Bakhtinian perspective, dialogue takes on many forms (Clark & Holquist, 1984; Wertsch, 1991), the basic principle being that it involves the dynamic between one voice and another. For example, this is evident in Bakhtin's account of how we understand the utterances of others, a process that would seem to be closely tied to intersubjectivity:

> The fact is that when the listener perceives and understands the meaning (the language meaning) of speech, he simultaneously takes an active, responsive attitude toward it. He either agrees or disagrees with it (completely or partially), augments it, applies it, prepares for its execution, and so on. And the listener adopts this responsive attitude for the entire duration of the process of listening and understanding, from the very beginning—sometimes literally from the speaker's first word. Any understanding of live speech, a live utterance, is inherently responsive, although the degree of this activity varies extremely. Any understanding is imbued with response and necessarily elicits it in one form or another: the listener becomes the speaker. A passive understanding of the meaning of perceived speech is only an abstract aspect of the actual whole of active responsive understanding, which is then actualized in a subsequent response that is actually articulated. (1986, p. 68)

The fact that Bakhtin allowed for "passive understanding" of an utterance, although viewing it as "only an abstract aspect of the actual whole," suggests that there was room for the univocal function in the picture of human communication he outlined. This search for a way to recognize the simultaneous operation of more than one function was what Lotman was seeking in his account of functional dualism.

The general point to be made about intersubjectivity and alterity, then, is not that communication is best understood in terms of one or the other in isolation. Instead, virtually every text is viewed as involving *both* univocal, information-transmission characteristics, and hence intersubjectivity, as well as dialogic, thought-generating tendencies, and hence alterity.

Intersubjectivity and Alterity in Studies of Intermental Functioning

Several attempts have been made in developmental psychology and related disciplines to utilize notions of intersubjectivity and alterity in analyses of intermental functioning. In general, the first phase of this research focused on intersubjectivity, and this research has been subjected to critiques calling for greater attention to be paid to alterity. The studies I have in mind focused on the emergence of inter-subjectivity in adult–child interaction. For example, Wertsch (1979) examined adult–child intermental functioning in terms of varying levels of intersubjectivity as part of an attempt to extend some of Vygotsky's (1987) ideas about the "zone of proximal development," and Rogoff (1990) explored issues of intersubjectivity in ontogenesis, tracing it back to the earliest phases of infants' lives.

From this perspective, intersubjectivity is viewed as a kind of metric for examining intermental functioning between adults and young children, and increasing levels of intersubjectivity are associated with higher levels of intramental functioning in children. Authors such as Stern (1985) and Trevarthen (1979) have argued that certain forms of shared meaning or affective tone may be observed almost from birth, thus providing necessary but not sufficient foundations for further development. Other authors (e.g., Wertsch, 1984) have focused on the developmental accomplishments made by children through socialization at later stages. Authors concerned with this latter set of issues have focused on the fact that it is sometimes unclear that children understand even quite basic aspects of the setting in the same way as adults, and increases in age and experience with particular task environments are associated with greater intersubjectivity between adult and child. Rogoff and her colleagues (Rogoff, 1990; Rogoff, Malkin, & Gilbride, 1984) have combined the two views, arguing that intersubjectivity is both a prerequisite of communication, which occurs between caregiver and infant in early infancy, and is negotiated in joint activity between adult and child.

While few would dispute that increasing intersubjectivity is one dimension along which children's development occurs, several investigators have begun to argue that research focusing on this issue is missing some essential aspects of interaction and change. As Matusov (1996, p. 26) has argued, a single-minded focus on intersubjectivity, where intersubjectivity is understood as sharing common understanding, may "limit researchers to study only consensus-oriented activities and to focus on processes of unification of the participants' subjectivities." In a similar vein, Smolka, de Goes, and Pino (1995) have argued that some of the most important developmental landmarks for children may arise through conflict rather than consensus.

As Goodnow (1990) has noted, this is a point on which the approach taken by "social Genevans" such as Doise and Mugny (1984) and Perret-Clermont (1980) has differed from Vygotskian analyses. A basic tenet of the social Genevans is that "the discrepancy or conflict that best sparks cognitive development takes a social form . . . the discrepancy one responds to most strongly is a difference in opinion or perspective between one's own view and that of another" (Goodnow, 1990, p. 278). In contrast, Vygotskian-based accounts "contain a strong emphasis on social interactions, especially those where the more and the less expert combine to work out a shared definition of a situation and to move the novice from a state in which performance can proceed only with help to a state in which performance can be carried through unaided" (p. 279). In the terminology used throughout this chapter, one could say that social Genevan and some other neo-Piagetian approaches focus on alterity, whereas Vygotskian accounts of intermental functioning have tended to focus on intersubjectivity.

Intersubjectivity and Alterity in Instructional Discourse

One form of intermental functioning that has received a great deal of attention since the early 1970s is instructional discourse (e.g., Cazden, 1988; Flanders, 1970; Mehan, 1979; Wortham, 1994). Understanding such discourse is viewed as central to understanding why some forms of instruction are effective and others are not, but research on this issue has so far yielded only partial and often conflicting results. One reason for the conflicting results is the failure to appreciate the power of the mediational means involved. Mediational means are often viewed as simply reflecting underlying psychological and social processes, not as having a central role in shaping discourse. In what follows, I attempt to outline an alternative picture that emerges when cultural tools and mediated action are made the focus of the analysis.

A complete account of the mediational means that shape classroom discourse might include analyses of textbooks, audiovisual aids, calculators, science equipment, the physical layout of the classroom, and so forth. My focus will be on a much narrower set of issues—namely, the spoken language used by teachers and students. In particular, I return to the issue of how speech genres (Bakhtin, 1986; Wertsch, 1991) shape discourse. The focus in what follows will be on the "typical situations of speech communication, typical themes, and . . . particular contacts between the *meanings* of words" (Bakhtin, 1986, p. 87) that make up classroom discourse.

Although Bakhtin (1986) outlined a fairly extensive account of speech genres, he provided relatively little detail about what defines and differentiates specific genres. Instead, he tended to provide suggestive lists such as "everyday genres of greetings, farewell, congratulations, all kinds of wishes, information about health, business, and so forth" (1986, p. 79). This list appears in the context of some general comments Bakhtin made about how some speech genres are fairly standard and rigid, whereas others, such as table conversation and intimate conversations within the family, are "freer and more creative" (p. 80).

Studies of classroom discourse have yielded some general evidence that suggests the existence of fairly standard and rigid speech genres. One indication of this is that teachers in elementary school and high school classrooms are consistently reported as doing the majority of the talking. Investigations of a wide range of classroom settings at various grade levels generally report that teachers' speech accounts for between two-thirds and three-fourths of the utterances in the classroom. In some cases, much of this talk concerns discipline and "classroom management," but even during segments of discourse clearly intended to be instructional, teachers' speech typically accounts for the majority of the utterances.

In addition to documenting general quantitative trends, investigators have delved into the qualitative aspects of instructional discourse. One of the important sets of distinctions used to examine the specific form, as opposed to the general amount, of teacher speech is that among "authentic questions," "quasi-authentic questions," and "test questions" (Nystrand, 1997, p. 38):

> Authentic questions are questions for which the asker has not prespecified an answer. . . . Dialogically, authentic teacher questions signal to students the teacher's interest in what they think and know and not just whether they can report what someone else thinks or has said. Authentic questions invite students to contribute something new to the discussion that can change or modify it in some way.
>
> By contrast, a *test question* allows students no control over the flow of the discussion. Because authentic questions allow an indeterminate number of acceptable answers and open the floor to students' ideas, they work dialogically. . . . a test question allows only one possible right answer, and is hence monologic (in Lotman's terms, univocal).

The use of test questions "correspond[s] to [a] typical situation of speech communication" (Bakhtin, 1986, p. 87)—namely, recitation as a form of classroom discourse. In a study of the discourse of eighth- and ninth-grade writing classrooms, Nystrand (1997, p. 44), reports that "in virtually all the classes, the teacher asked nearly all the questions; few about literature were authentic, and equally few followed up on student responses." Having made these points, Nystrand goes on to caution that "authentic questions, discussion, small-group work, and interaction, though important, do not categorically produce learning" (p. 72). Much depends on the larger setting in which such practices occur. However, Nystrand's findings clearly suggest that the practice of having teachers ask almost all the questions and the absence of authentic questions are not desirable from the standpoint of student learning. In Nystrand's view, such practices contribute to a setting that does not assign "significant and serious epistemic roles to students that the students themselves can value" (p. 72).

The kind of interaction criticized by Nystrand has been the subject of a major ethnographic study of an elementary school classroom by Mehan (1979). A great deal of the interaction Mehan observed in a combined first-, second-, and third-grade classroom over the course of a year occurred in a quite standard, scripted from involving a teacher's "initiation" (e.g., "What is the capital of the United States?") followed by a student's "reply" (e.g., "Washington, D.C.") followed in turn by the teacher's "evaluation" (e.g., "Good."). A corpus of interaction Mehan examined from nine lessons revealed that "the three-part sequential pattern predominates in teacher-initiated interaction" (p. 54).

Heavy reliance on the initiation-reply-evaluation (I-R-E) sequence reflects several essential assumptions on the part of the teachers and pupils who participate in classroom discourse. The first assumption is that most questions in classroom discourse should be asked by teachers. The heavy predominance of teacher speech in general and teacher questions in particular in several studies reflects the power of this underlying assumption.

The second assumption concerns the efficacy of the "instructional questions" (Nystrand's test questions) involved. Their heavy use suggests that test questions are generally viewed as serving a powerful and productive role in instruction. This form of utterance seems to be used very widely in American classroom discourse, and it is often found in parent–child interaction at home, at least in the case of middle-class families. However, as Heath (1983) has noted, test questions are extremely rare in the parent–child interactions found among certain groups, an observation that may have major implications of why children from these groups encounter so much difficulty in mastering the forms of speaking and thinking required to succeed in school.

The third assumption has to do with the special kind of relationship between teacher and pupil. This is an asymmetric relationship in which teachers have the right (indeed the responsibility) to ask instructional questions and pupils have the obligation to answer them, but not vice versa. In terms of the properties of mediated action outlined in chapter 2, this means that test questions and I-R-E sequences as cultural tools are associated with a particular organization of power and authority, an organization reflected in the fact that students are not given "significant and serious epistemic roles" (Nystrand, 1997, p. 72). To say this of course is not to suggest that anyone can invoke a speech genre involving test questions and automatically obtain power and authority as a result. It is to say, however, that if interlocutors engage in a "language game" (Wittgenstein, 1972) organized around this speech genre, they tacitly agree to a particular arrangement of power and authority. In some cases, misunderstanding or disagreements about the speech genre being used may arise, and in those cases conflict may emerge. For example, one interlocutor might resist another's attempt to use test questions by saying something like, "Who do you think you are, a teacher?"

The possibility for conflict in such cases reflects the more general point that the "particular contacts between the *meanings* of words and actual concrete reality under certain typical circumstances" (Bakhtin, 1986, p. 87) may take various forms. On the one hand, utterances must occur in some already existing context and as a result have certain presuppositions. Notions such as "given information" (Chafe, 1974, 1976; Clark & Haviland, 1977; Halliday, 1967) and "psychological subject" (Vygotsky, 1987) are grounded in this observation. On the other hand, making an utterance defines or transforms this context in some way. This is the "performative" or "creative" dimension of speaking analyzed by theorists such as Austin (1975) and Silverstein (1976, 1985). The point is that using utterances clearly associated with particular speech genres may reflect an existing, agreed-upon speech situation *or* it may constitute a "bid" (Rommetveit, 1974) to define the speech situation in a particular way. In the case of conflict just outlined, the bid was contested rather than accepted and presupposed.

A fourth point to make about a speech genre grounded in test questions concerns the assumptions about the mastery, possession, and communication of knowledge it presupposes. Specifically, test questions and I-R-E sequences presuppose that individuals "have" some bit of knowledge or information. Furthermore, this information is typically assumed to exist in the form of some kind of internal representation, and the task is to display it in an external, public form when the teacher makes a request for it. From the perspective of Lotman's account of functional dualism, the use of test questions reflects a set of assumptions about the univocal function of language. If students cannot respond appropriately to test questions the normal assumption is that something went awry in the accurate transmission or reception of information that occurred earlier; language had not lived up to its "ability to transmit a message adequately" (Lotman, 1990, p. 13). Furthermore, it is the nature of the I-R-E sequence to treat neither the initiation question by the teacher nor the reply by the student as a thinking device. Students who are not given a significant and serious epistemic role are not invited to respond to a teacher's question such as "What is the capital of France?" by saying, "That is a question that I find very interesting." Conversely, in the I-R-E sequence the student's reply is never considered a thinking device for further discussion. Instead, it is either evaluated as correct or incorrect, and the recitation moves on.

One of the most striking facts about speech genres involving test questions and I-R-E sequences is their resistance to change in the face of extended criticism. Investigators such as Nystrand (1993) have documented on a broad scale what other observers have suspected for decades—namely, that inauthentic or test questions seem to have little positive impact on students' learning and achievement. Indeed, Nystrand found that even a very small number of authentic questions is associated with positive student outcomes, whereas massive amounts of test questions in the absence of authentic questions have no such impact. If all this is true, why do test questions continue to be so pervasive in classroom discourse? In my view, the key to understanding this has to do with the claim I outlined in chapter 2—that mediated action typically has multiple simultaneous goals. The point here is the test questions are not without a function, but the function they serve—which has to do with creating and maintaining the relations of power and authority in classrooms—does not foster academic achievement. In this connection, for example, Lemke (1990) has argued that in some cases the use of a series of test questions makes it possible for a teacher to maintain the floor and cover the same material that would be covered in a traditional lecture format but to appear to be interactive in the process.

Given the demands of a sociocultural setting shaped by forces such as standardized curricula and achievement testing, the temptation to rely heavily on test questions is quite understandable. Indeed, from this perspective they must be viewed as being quite appropriate and adaptive. What this means from the perspective of student's academic achievement, however, is that the most effective speech genres might not be employed. As I argued in chapter 2, it is often the case that cultural tools that have emerged in response to pressures in one context or domain of action are made to do "double duty" by being used in another form of mediated action. The pervasive use of a recitation speech genre to instruct students may be taken as a case in point. It also reflects, however, the pattern that many forms of mediated action have of serving multiple simultaneous goals. In the sociocultural setting in which they operate, teachers are charged with the simultaneous goals of maintaining an institutional order *and* fostering student learning (as well as other tasks too numerous to mention). As a result, it is not to much the case that the teachers studied by Nystrand or Mehan are simply using the wrong cultural tool for the task at hand; instead, they are responding to multiple simultaneous demands, and the challenge is to employ speech genres that can respond most appropriately.

Reciprocal Teaching as Instructional Discourse

Since the early 1990s, a great deal of attention has been given to the issue of how students could be given the kind of "significant and serious epistemic roles" that Nystrand (1997) has argued are missing in so many settings of classroom discourse. One practice that has received a great deal of attention under this heading is "reciprocal teaching." Reciprocal teaching was originally developed by Palincsar and Brown (1984, 1988) in an effort to help middle-school students who are able to decode written texts but have serious difficulties understanding and remembering them. As Palincsar (quoted in Bruer, 1993, p. 205) has noted, many teachers view such students as presenting some of the most baffling problems they encounter. In developing the techniques of reciprocal teaching, Palincsar and Brown drew on an existing body of research about reasoning and reading to outline a set of strategies required for effective comprehension. They then devised a procedure for encouraging students to master and appropriate these strategies. In addition to demonstrating the effectiveness of these procedures for middle-school students with reading comprehension problems, Palincsar, Brown, and Campione (1993) and other investigators have recently expanded the application of reciprocal teaching to children of other ages and abilities.

In summarizing the impressive results from over a decade of research in reciprocal teaching, Palincsar et al. (1993, p. 45) write:

> Most research on reciprocal teaching has been conducted in the area of reading and listening comprehension instruction by general, remedial, and special educators. Generally, the instruction has been conducted in small groups (averaging six to eight). Students entering these studies scored approximately 30% correct on independent measures of text comprehension and participated in the intervention for a minimum of 25 instructional days. The criterion was applied to determine success was the attainment of an independent score of 75 to 80% correct on four or five consecutively administered measures of comprehension, assessing recall of text, ability to draw inferences, ability to state the gist of material read, and application of knowledge acquired from the text to a novel situation. Using this criterion, approximately 80% of both the primary and middle school students were judged successful. Furthermore, these gains were observed to be maintained for up to six months to a year following instruction. (Brown & Palincsar, 1982; Palincsar & Brown, 1984, 1989)

When reviewing such results, one must remember that they often concern students who have traditionally done extremely poorly in instructional settings and have been extremely resistant to successful intervention by teachers and researchers. The success reciprocal teaching has had with these populations has led Bruer (1993, p. 2) to call it the "educational equivalent of polio vaccine."

In reciprocal teaching, students as well as teachers take on the role of guiding other members of a group through the processes required to understand texts (usually written texts). The discussions are not open ended but are organized around a set of strategies used by expert readers. Forms of dialogue based on these strategies are first modeled by a teacher, and then the teacher coaches students as they take these over in group discussion settings. The students are introduced to their role of dialogue leader through explicit instruction about appropriate strategic directives, through imitating the teachers' modeled activities, and through feedback from the teacher about their attempts to lead the discussion, but in all cases the goal is to have students take on the active role of posing questions about the text to others.

Consider a reciprocal teaching session concerned with a text about how salt is produced. The students in this session were seventh graders, all of whom had been identified as being poor comprehenders.

By the time this session occurred, however, they had had extensive experience in reciprocal teaching, and as a result the form of dialogue in which they engaged was quite well organized and to the point, standing in marked contrast to the kinds of interchanges they had produced earlier. The two students ("C" and "A") involved in this session first read the text and then engaged in a reciprocal teaching dialogue, receiving occasional feedback from the teacher ("T"):

c: Name three different basic methods how salt is produced.
a: Evaporation, mining, evaporation . . . artificial heat evaporation.
c: Correct, very good. My summary on this paragraph is about ways that salt is being produced.
t: Very good. Could you select the next teacher? (Palincsar & Brown, 1984, p. 162)

In this case, the instruction, modeling, and feedback provided by the teacher was minimal, primarily because the dialogue occurred after many sessions of reciprocal teaching and the students had largely mastered the procedure. In earlier sessions, the teacher had to provide a great deal of support, and even when she did so students seemed to find it quite difficult to see the point of the dialogue and carry it on effectively. This reflects the general pattern noted by Palincsar and Brown (1984, p. 135): "unclear questions and detailed summaries predominated in the early sessions, while main idea questions and summaries were most common in the later sessions."

The specific strategies on which reciprocal teaching is based derive from research conducted by Brown (1980) and others on the kinds of procedures used by individuals in effective reading and reasoning. On the basis of this research, reciprocal teaching focuses on the strategies of "questioning," "summarizing," "clarifying," and "predicting."

> The dialogue leader (adult or child) begins the discussion by *asking questions* about the context of the text. The group discusses these questions, raises additional questions, and, in the case of disagreement or misunderstanding, rereads the text. Whereas the questions are used to stimulate discussion, *summarizing* is used to identify the gist of what has been read and discussed and to prepare the group to proceed to the next portion of the text. Once again, there is discussion for the purpose of achieving consensus regarding the summary. The third strategy, *clarification*, is used opportunistically for the purpose of restoring meaning when a concept, word, or phrase has been misunderstood or is unfamiliar to some-

one in the group. Finally, the discussion leader provides the opportunity for *predictions* regarding upcoming content. Group members generate their predictions based on their prior knowledge of the content of the text as well as clues provided in the text itself (e.g., embedded questions). (Palincsar et al., 1993, pp. 43–44)

Strategies such as the ones mentioned here have long been identified as being key to effective reading and are striking by their absence in students who have problems comprehending and remembering textual material. The issue that has vexed researchers and practitioners has not been identifying these steps but introducing poor comprehenders to them in such a way that these students take them over and use them actively. Palincsar and Brown (1984) approached this problem by identifying effective comprehension strategies on the intramental plane of functioning, transforming these strategies into a specific form of intermental functioning, and engaging poor comprehenders in such functioning, thereby giving rise to appropriate changes in their intramental processes.

The results of following this strategy have been quite striking. In addition to major transformations in intermental functioning, investigators have been able to document impressive and lasting improvement in students' intramental functioning, even after their participation in reciprocal teaching ceased. Palincsar and Brown (1984, p. 125) have documented this through a series of assessments conducted during and after reciprocal teaching:

Each day, before (baseline), during, and after (maintenance) training, the students took an unassisted assessment, where they read a novel passage and answered ten comprehension questions on it from memory. From their baseline performance of 15% correct, they improved during training to accuracy levels of 85%, levels they maintained when the intervention was terminated. Even after a 6-month delay, the students averaged 60% correct without help, and it took only 1 day of renewed reciprocal teaching to return them to the 85% level achieved during training.

From the perspective of mediated action, reciprocal teaching may be viewed as a procedure *re-mediates* the action of poor readers. it provides them with new items in their "cultural tool kit" (Wertsch, 1991). In this connection, there is strong evidence that the students had not only mastered but appropriated the procedures of reciprocal teaching. Specifically, the fact that they spontaneously used the strategies included in reciprocal teaching in their own intramental functioning six months after their last reciprocal teaching session suggests that the "situation definition" (Wertsch, 1984) of a reading comprehension task that they spontaneously used is grounded in these strategies.

Understanding why poor readers do not initially acquire the cultural tools required for effective reading in the way that good readers do is beyond the scope of what I have to say. Instead, I continue to focus on some of the concrete processes involved in reciprocal teaching and why they seem to have their impact. The first point to make in this respect is that much of reciprocal teaching's success is directly tied to its reorganization of "participant structure" (Phillips, 1972; Herrenkohl, 1995) of the activity. The organization of the participants' rights, roles, and responsibilities in reciprocal teaching settings (Herrenkohl & Wertsch, in press) is quite different from that in typical classroom discourse. In particular, the level of engagement and the power and authority given to students in reciprocal teaching seem to be crucial.

Palincsar and her colleagues (Palincsar & Brown, 1984; Palincsar et al., 1993) have examined this dimension of reciprocal teaching by comparing it to other procedures that would seem to offer the same cognitive benefits but leave the participant structure fundamentally unchanged. For example, in one study Palincsar and Brown (1984) employed a "locating information" (LI) procedure with a control group of students. This is based on a procedure widely used by teachers of remedial reading, to help students cope with questions on texts they have just read:

> The students are shown where in the text the answer to a text-explicit question can be found. The teacher demonstrates how to combine across separate sections of text to answer a text-implicit question, and the students are shown how to use their prior knowledge to answer a script-implicit question.
>
> After reading the assessment passages independently (help was given if they couldn't understand anything), the student and teacher answered the questions together with the text in front of them. The student attempted to answer. The teacher praised correct responses; following incorrect responses, she guided the student back into the passage to the appropriate paragraph where the answer could be found. If necessary, the line(s) where the answer could be found was given, as well as prompts to help the students find the answer. During the procedure, the students were being taught that the answers to the questions could be found with a little work with the text and their prior knowledge, a proposition that they greeted with some surprise! Answers to questions were discussed and mutually agreed

upon by student and investigator. On the following assessment pas-
sages, the students worked unaided and answered questions from
memory, just as in the Reciprocal Teaching group. (p. 132)

Palincsar and Brown (1984) report that, relative to reciprocal
teaching, the LI procedure had little effect on students' reading comprehension levels. Whereas the comprehension levels of students
participating in reciprocal teaching improved quite significantly,
reaching those of average readers, the comprehension levels of the
students participating in the locating information intervention (also
poor comprehenders) did not improve significantly. Indeed, comprehension levels of participants in the LI procedure failed to differ significantly from those of another group of poor comprehenders who
were simply tested and retested over the course of the study.

What this strongly suggests is that it is not the *type* of question
that influences students' learning but the fact that *students ask
them*—that is, the participant structure in which these questions are
embedded influences students' learning significantly. The questions
involved in the LI procedure, and indeed many questions posed by
teachers in normal classroom discourse, are quite similar to those
found in reciprocal teaching, but in many cases they clearly do not
have the same impact. There seems to be something very powerful,
then, about the *students'* taking one the role of posing, as opposed to
merely answering, questions in reciprocal teaching.

To use terminology introduced earlier in this chapter, the novel
participant structure introduced by reciprocal teaching involves new
forms of alterity. When participating in reciprocal teaching, students
are required to speak from a perspective that calls on them to ask
appropriate questions and to recognize and assess appropriate responses, a perspective that differs markedly from that required in
speech genres organized around test questions and I-R-E sequences.
The density and simultaneity of multiple perspectives involved in
reciprocal teaching are simply not encountered when students respond to others' test questions. This suggests a particular application to Bakhtin's account of alterity, an account in which he asserted
that "I cannot do without the other; I cannot become myself without the other; I must find myself in the other, finding the other in
me (in mutual reflection and perception)" (1979, p. 312). By participating in reciprocal teaching, students become themselves with the
other in a particular and a particularly beneficial way.

This is not to suggest that test questions and I-R-E sequences are
concerned solely with the univocal function of texts and with

intersubjectivity whereas reciprocal teaching is concerned solely with the dialogic function of tests and with alterity. Even though Nystrand (1997) characterizes inauthentic, test questions in terms of a mono-logic form of discourse, he recognizes the dialogic processes they involve. Conversely, even though reciprocal teaching can be characterized as involving a denser and more productive form of alterity than other types of classroom discourse, the univocal function and intersubjectivity are still involved. Specifically, what the students participating in reciprocal teaching may be said to achieve is a higher level of intersubjectivity with their teachers about appropriate strategic questions to pose when reading a text. On the other hand, however, this higher level of intersubjectivity is concerned with an inherently dialogic process. Instead of assuming that understanding a text is a process of passively receiving transmitted information, this practice assumes that reading involves active, dialogic engagement.

A little-investigated fact about reciprocal teaching is that it often takes upward of five sessions for students to use the technique effectively. One possible reason for this is that the form of alterity is strikingly different from that usually encountered in classroom discourse. Palincsar and Brown (1984) report that, in the initial sessions students, often have little or no idea of the appropriate directives to use. In these sessions, the teacher often must intervene up to the point of providing the specific utterances to be copied verbatim by students as models for what they say to others. For example, Palincsar and Brown (1984) report the following interchange between a teacher and a seventh grader, Charles, who had poor comprehension (IQ = 70, reading comprehension grade equivalent = third grade). This was from Charles's first reciprocal teaching session and was about a paragraph on water moccasins and other snakes:

c: What is found in the southeastern snakes, also the copperhead, rattlesnakes, vipers—they have. I'm not doing this right.
t: All right. Do you want to know about the pit viper?
c: Yeah.
t: What would be a good question about the pit vipers that starts with the word "why"?
c: (No response)
t: How about, "Why are the snakes called pit vipers?"
c: Why do they want to know that they are called pit vipers?
t: Try it again.
c: Why do they, pit vipers in a pit?
t: How about, "Why do they call the snakes pit vipers?"

c: Why do they call the snakes pit vipers?

t: There you go! Good for you. (Palincsar & Brown, 1984, p. 138)

In this interchange, it is apparent that Charles had very little understanding of how to go about the kind of strategic questioning envisioned by Palincsar and Brown (1984). He clearly did not know what directive to pose, and the procedure was so alien to him that he had great difficulty repeating the teacher's suggested utterances, let alone producing appropriate ones on his own. When analyzed from the perspective of mediated action, these points are quite interesting. They provide yet another illustration of the irreducible tension between agent and cultural tool inherent in mediated action. As Charles's problems with the questions demonstrate, cultural tools in and of themselves are relatively meaningless in the absence of competent use by an agent. Some minimal degree of mastery by an agent is required before these tools can really begin to be a part of mediated action on the intramental plane. Of course, such mediated action can occur on the intermental plane, but only with a good deal of "scaffolding" (Wood, Bruner, & Ross, 1976) or "other-regulation" (Wertsch, Minick, & Arns, 1984).

This illustration also reinforces the point that speech genres, not other units of language, are the relevant cultural tools at issue. There is no suggestion here that Charles did not understand the English words and sentences used by the teacher. Instead, his problems stemmed from an inability to recognize and use a speech genre or general pattern of utterances, a pattern that "correspond[s] to typical situations of speech communication, typical themes, and, consequently, also to particular contacts between the *meanings* of words and actual concrete reality under certain typical circumstances" (Bakhtin, 1986, p. 87).

The type of situation and theme involved in this example is what defines reciprocal teaching. Charles did not yet have "a sense of the speech whole" (Bakhtin, 1979, p. 79) that characterizes reciprocal teaching, and as a result he had extreme difficulty in participating in the procedure at this point. Indeed, when Charles finally asked, "Why do they call the snakes pit vipers?" it would seem reasonable to give primary credit for this utterance to the cultural tool and the teacher rather than to Charles as an agent. After all, he was simply reusing a form that had just been supplied to him. If every utterance involves at least two voices (Wertsch, 1991), then it would seem that one voice (that of the discourse form of reciprocal teaching) is doing the bulk of the talking in this case.

All this is not to say, however, that Charles's participation as an agent in reciprocal teaching was unimportant or useless. Such an interpretation could easily be derived from too exclusive a focus on the agent in isolation, and it would overlook two important points about this form of mediated action. First, even if the cultural tool is primarily responsible for shaping an utterance, this utterance may continue to play a role in dialogic encounters with others. The utterance that Charles eventually produced through the teacher's prompts and modeling was one to which other students then replied, and he was thereby drawn into a dialogic exchange.

Second, using the words of others, even when they seem to be very poorly understood, can have an important influence on the agent using them in the longer run. Charles's ability to produce appropriate directives to others improved markedly over the first several days of his participation in reciprocal teaching. This improvement came about through the kinds of teacher prompts reflected in the previous passage. For example, on the seventh day of reciprocal teaching the following interchange occurred in connection with a passage about the Venus flytrap:

> c: What is the most interesting of the insect eating plants, and where do the plants live at?
> t: Two excellent questions! They are both clear and important questions. Ask us one at a time now.

There is a striking difference between this interchange and the one from the first day, in which Charles understood practically nothing about the desired speech genre. Such progress in mastering strategic directives is not always characteristic of the first seven days of reciprocal teaching, but the difference between this interchange and the one reported earlier is indicative of the general kind of transformation students undergo.

The process of mastering the strategic directives involved in reciprocal teaching can be usefully understood as an instance of "performance before competence," to use Cazden's (1981) felicitous expression. Consistent with this view is the idea that development often occurs through using a cultural tool *before* an agent fully understands what this cultural tool is or how it works. Such an interpretation contrasts with the standard assumption that an agent must understand what she is doing before she can do it. As I have argued elsewhere (Wertsch, 1985), Vygotsky outlined a developmental dynamic in which a child or other learner may arrive at a level of consciousness and control of a form of mediated action as a result of, and hence only *after*, having carried out that action for some time. In his analysis of how a young child's act of reaching can be transformed into the act of pointing through social interaction with an adult, Vygotsky (1981b, p. 161) asserted that "the child is the last to become conscious of the gesture," and he made similar arguments in connection with the mastery of word meaning. In this sense, mediational means play an essential role in creating a leading edge of development.

From the perspective of mediated action, the materiality of mediational means plays an essential role in making the developmental dynamic envisioned here possible. Only because a material form was involved and could be imitated could Charles gain entry into the processes at the heart of reciprocal teaching. In the absence of a mechanism for conveying meaning directly (i.e., in an unmediated fashion) to Charles, a material form must be involved. In his case, this form was nearly the only point of contact he had with the speech genre and with others. To be sure, he was operating at a very low level of intersubjectivity with the teacher in his initial attempts, but this intersubjectivity was possible thanks to the material signs they could employ. Furthermore, he was involved at a very low level of alterity with his interlocutor in his first attempts, but he engaged in this initial level of alterity by relying on the materiality of the mediational means being employed. There seems to be something essential about handling, or in this case, "mouthing," a material form that provides the basis for attaining future levels of intersubjectivity, alterity, and mastery.

In their analyses of reciprocal teaching, Palincsar and her colleagues have focused primarily on intramental outcomes and have paid relatively little attention to the concrete forms of intermental functioning that give rise to it. As is evident from the examples I have reported, these investigators do provide some extensive anecdotal reports that are quite informative. However, their main analytic focus has not been on intermental issues.

Motivated in part by a desire to know more about the kinds of intermental processes involved in reciprocal teaching, Herrenkohl (1995) undertook a study of a form of instruction loosely modeled on this procedure. This study examined student engagement in the context of two fourth-grade science classrooms ("class 1" and "class 2") in a large urban elementary school in New England. Both classes had the same teacher, and twelve students were assigned to each using matched-pairs procedure. As a result, the classes did not differ with respect to the teacher involved, nor did they differ significantly with regard to sex, race, or standardized test scores. The same set of lessons about balance beams was used in each group. The objective was to involve students in substantial discussions regarding their explanations about phenomena related to the balance and building activities.

Lessons in both class 1 and class 2 were organized into three parts: whole-class introductory comments, small-group activities, and whole-class reporting sessions (i.e., students reported about their small-group activities to the whole class). Each of these activities occurred each day of the study. Students worked in groups of four to complete their small-group activities. Two students in each small group were assigned the role of "reporter," while the other two students acted as "scribes." The reporters were responsible for presenting their group's activity orally to the whole class, while the scribes were responsible for organizing relevant information that could be used by the reporters during the reporting session. These roles rotated so that all small-group members had a chance to be reporters and scribes.

At the beginning of the intervention, students in both classes were introduced to three strategic steps to guide them in producing explanations of scientific phenomena. These steps were: (1) predicting and theorizing, (2) summarizing findings, and (3) coordinating predictions and theories with existing evidence (i.e., with findings). From the perspective of mediated action, these steps constitute cultural tools in the form of patterns of speaking, or speech genres. The goal was to encourage students to use these patterns of speaking in social interactions and eventually to master and appropriate them on the intramental plane as well.

The major difference that distinguished class 1 from class 2 was in the participant structure. During the reporting segment of the daily procedure, students in class 2 were each assigned an "audience role" that corresponded to one of the three steps. Thus, some audience members were responsible for checking the group reports for predictions and theories, others were responsible for the summary of findings, and still others were responsible for determining if the reporters discussed the relationship between their group's predictions and findings. In class 1, no special roles were given to the audience members. Since all students were familiar with reporting sessions in their regular science classrooms, it was assumed that, without specific role assignments, students in class 1 would behave in a manner that was consistent with their prior experience in this setting (see Herrenkohl & Guerra, 1996, for further discussion of methods). The three audience roles used in class 2 constitute another participant structure and provide a loose parallel with the strategies mentioned by Palincsar and her colleagues. Among other things, this again means that students were given some power and authority as speakers that they normally do not have in classroom discourse. the kinds of audience roles given to the students in this study are virtually never given to students when responding to teachers.

Analyses of transcribed classroom discussions during the whole-class reporting time revealed that class 1 and class 2 were similar in that the interaction in both was quite different from the standard I-R-E patterns reported by Mehan (1979) and others. There were, however, significant differences between class 1 and class 2. Students in class 2, who took up audience roles associated with the three strategic steps, were much more engaged in discussion and in building scientific explanations than were students in class 1. Herrenkohl (1995, p. 104) reports that,

> Overall, students in [class 2] were more engaged with the cognitive content and the members of their class. Specifically, students in [class 2] spoke for a greater percentage of class time than students in [class 1]. A trend in [class 2] suggested that students continued to take over more of the responsibility for speaking as the training progressed. This trend was not found in [class 1]. Students in [class 2] also asked more questions of the reporters than students in [class 1]. Lastly, students in [class 2] initiated significantly more engagement episodes than students in [class 1]. All of these findings support the conclusion that [class 2] students were more engaged in the training sessions than students in [class 1].

Table 5.1 presents the number of questions that class 1 and class 2 students directed to reporters over the course of the study. Again, reporters were students who were assigned the role of reporting about their small-group activities to the whole class at the end of each day's session. Different children took on this responsibility on different days in class 1 and class 2. Class 2 students who were audience members also took on the responsibility for checking reports of predictions and theories, summarizing findings, and coordinating predictions and theories with evidence. As Table 5.1 shows, virtually all the questions directed to reporters in class 1 were from the teacher. In contrast, in class 2 the students, rather than the teacher, were responsible for a large majority of the questions. Although some students in class 2 asked many more questions than others, every one of the students in class 2 asked more questions than any student in class 1.

Students in class 1 certainly were never told by the teacher, researcher, or anyone else that they could not ask questions. However,

Table 5.1   Number of Questions Directed
to the Reporters by Students in Class 1 and
Class 2

Class 1 Students	Questions	Class 2 Students	Questions
Zeree	0	Rosie	29
Salvador	0	Tammy	16
Jeanie	0	Olivia	24
Susan	1	Denise	19
Peter	1	Emma	3
James	0	Steven	22
Kathy	0	Raul	39
Carrie	0	Carson	2
Billy	0	Dai	11
Nam	0	Rich	15
Julie	1	Qing	41
Carl	0	Christie	5
Teacher	368	Teacher	117
Total	371	Total	343

in line with standard classroom discourse patterns, they virtually never did. The absence of questions on the part of class 1 students is especially striking, given their familiarity with the three strategic steps that guided the oral reporting sessions. It suggests that there is a "social gravity" (Gee, 1991) that operates against substantial student involvement in the whole-class reporting sessions characteristic of class 2. The absence of students' questions in class 1 might reflect, at least in part, a general need to maintain order and discipline in classroom settings (Schrag, 1988). By the time students reach fourth grade, they are well aware of this standard "rule" of teacher control and responsibility within the classroom. It appears that without specific procedures for encouraging them to participate (i.e., assigning them to audience roles for checking each report for the three strategic steps), students simply allow the teacher to adopt the role of questioner. As a result, being a reporter in class 1 gave students access to questions directed to them by the teacher. Such individual attention from the teacher to reporters was not as characteristic of class 2. In contrast, audience members in class 2 were encouraged, or even required, to be more engaged and responsible for their own and others' understandings.

In sum, the major form of participation and engagement was strikingly different for the two groups. In class 1, it involved group reporters interacting with the teacher, while in Class 2 it involved students as well as the teacher interacting with the reporters. Hence, the audience roles given to class 2 students encouraged them to appropriate an important cultural tool—posing questions to others in a public forum. These roles would seem to be effective in encouraging further appropriation as well as mastery of cultural tools associated with effective scientific reasoning in schools.

The findings from Herrenkohl's study as well as the results of analyses of reciprocal teaching raise some interesting points about mastery and appropriation. Both sets of studies demonstrate that it is possible for students to engage in dialogic encounters with written texts and with others in ways that are fairly unusual in typical academic discourse. Furthermore, both studies suggest that it takes several sessions for students to enter into this engagement in a consistent and confident manner. From the perspective of mediated action, this means that in both cases students eventually came to use a set of cultural tools without the need of continuing outside support, or "scaffolding" (Wood, Bruner, & Ross, 1976), on the intermental plane (e.g., teachers' modeling, coaching).

As I noted earlier, the possibility of entering into the form of intermental functioning characteristic of reciprocal teaching relies on the materiality of the mediational means employed. At early stages of the procedure, students often had little or no mastery of these mediational means, but only by using these means could they join the dialogue and master it. The phenomenon of performance before competence is in certain respects counterintuitive, but it seems to be quite important.

The fact that the students, acting independently six months after their last session of reciprocal teaching, continued to employ the new cultural tools introduced by this procedure suggests that they had appropriated as well as mastered these tools. They had made these cultural tools their own and spontaneously employed them at this point in intramental functioning. Similar anecdotal evidence is reported by Herrenkohl (1995) about the students who participated in class 2. Teachers and other adult observers commented that these students were more likely to actively engage in others' presentations by asking probing questions about what had been said.

Such observations and findings raise interesting questions about the nature of appropriation. The way I defined this notion in chapter 2 involves a contrast with mastery, which means that it is possible, at least in principle, to master a cultural tool but not to appropriate it. Perhaps for this reason, or perhaps due to the connotations of "appropriation," the term suggests some kind of reflective, voluntary decision on the part of an independent agent. In the case of question-asking procedures in reciprocal teaching and in Herrenkohl's study, however, it seems that the students were drawn into appropriating a cultural tool with little such reflection or volition. In both cases, students took on particular roles and particular relationships with cultural tools while participating in intermental functioning that had been strategically arranged by teachers and researchers, and they thereby came to use certain cultural tools in a relatively automatic and nonreflective way.

It is certainly possible that at some point in the future any or all of these students might engage in conscious reflection for some reason and may reject the cultural tool they had come to utilize. However, the results reported here suggest that, at least initially, the students seem to have appropriated, and not just to have mastered, the cultural tool that had been given to them without reflecting on it. One might be tempted to speak of the manipulation of appropriation in such cases, but it would seem that most instances of appropriation have this character and should not be viewed as devious.

In this chapter, I have outlined some ways that appropriation of cultural tools is tied to particular forms of intermental functioning. I have harnessed notions of intersubjectivity, alterity, and participant structure to understand intermental functioning of the sort Vygotsky (1978) envisioned occurring in the "zone of proximal development," and I have examined how such intermental functioning may or may not result in desired patterns of appropriation. The terms I have used and the issues I have examined are by no means new—something that is obvious, given my heavy reliance on Vygotsky, Bakhtin, and others. It is also worth noting an important parallel, at least at a general level, between the line of reasoning I have pursued and that developed by another figure whose writings have heavily influenced sociocultural studies, John Dewey. As Valsiner (1997) has noted, Dewey even used similar terms when dealing with the relationship between person and context. Dewey argued that "by doing his share in the associated activity, the individual appropriates the purpose which actuates it, becoming familiar with its methods and subject matters, acquires needed skill, and is saturated with its emotional spirit" (1980, p. 26). This quotation provides a reminder that appropriation is an important issue that has concerned a variety of theorists for some time, and it is for this reason that I take it up in greater detail in the chapters that follow.

Notes

1. Following the practice of Minick (Vygotsky, 1987), I employ the terms "intermental" and "intramental" as translations of "interpsikhicheskii" and "intrapsikhicheskii," respectively. This is more consistent with other translations of the term "psikhicheskii" and "mental" in Wertsch (1981) and elsewhere, but it is a shift away from translation practices followed in Wertsch (1981) and Vygotsky (1978) where the terms "interpsychological" (vs. "intermental") and "intrapsychological" (vs. "intramental") were used.

2. As used by scholars such as Lotman, a text is any semiotic corpus that has significance. It may be verbal (e.g., a single utterance, a book-length treatise) or nonverbal (e.g., a painting, a costume). My focus will be on verbal texts, especially ones that are spoken in the flow of intermental functioning.

✳ 5 ✳

Appropriation and Resistance

In chapter 1, I outlined some of the pitfalls of methodological individualism and how sociocultural research seeks to avoid them. In that same context, I suggested that one of the potential dangers of sociocultural research is social reductionism, or the assumption that it is possible to reduce accounts of human action to social forces alone. In the terminology of Burke's pentad, social reductionism amounts to focusing exclusively on the scene and failing to take the agent into account.

My comments about mediated action in the previous chapters have been motivated by a desire to avoid both forms of reductionism, to "live in the middle," as Holquist (1994) has put it. With regard to mediated action, this means maintaining a focus on the irreducible tension between agent and mediational means, and much of what I have had to say in previous chapters had to do with this. In addition, there is at least one other kind of middle to occupy when trying to analyze mediational means. As I suggested in chapter 2, it is important to know where cultural tools come from as well as to know how they are used. For example, it is not unusual for a cultural tool to have emerged as a spin-off of some process, and in almost all cases there are historical contingencies that shape a mediational means in unintended ways. In the terminology I employ here, I speak of these issues under the heading of "production" of mediational means, and I try to link an analysis of production with an analysis of the "consumption" of mediational means. I argue that these two processes are often intricately related. In particular, forces that go into the production of a cultural tool often play a major role in determining how it will be used.

In chapter 3, I outlined some additional cases in which the importance of the production of mediational means was quite apparent. I suggested there that cultural tools such as narratives from official history can have great power in shaping our understanding about the past, even when we question and try to resist these cultural tools. To my mind, the most striking finding from the study of American college students' accounts of the origins of the United States is that even though several of the students were quite critical of the official quest-for-freedom narrative, every one of their accounts was constructed around it.

In the case of the quest-for-freedom narrative, it is not difficult to identify some of the forces of production. In his review of American history textbooks produced in the twentieth century FitzGerald (1979, p. 47) has noted:

> History textbooks for elementary and secondary schools are not like other kinds of histories. They serve a different function, and they have their own traditions, which continue independent of academic history writing. In the first place, they are essentially nationalistic histories. The first American-history text was written after the American Revolution, and because of it; and most texts are still accounts of the nation-state. In the second place, they are written not to explore but to instruct—to tell children what their elders want them to know about their country. This information is not necessarily what anyone considers the truth of things. Like time capsules, the texts contain the truths selected for posterity.

In the case of producing an American history textbook for elementary and secondary schools, then, many forces are at work in addition to contributions from academic research. Although history textbooks in the United States are produced by private companies, these companies must be very sensitive to the political winds of nationalism and patriotism if they wish to be successful in marketing their product to a broad audience. For example, in 1979 FitzGerald wrote that "the publishers were . . . mindful of the Texas State House of Representatives, which—in a state that already required a loyalty oath from all textbook writers—approved a resolution urging that 'the American history courses in the public school emphasize in the textbooks our glowing and throbbing history of hearts and souls inspired by wonderful American principles and traditions'" (1979, p. 38). Although these comments were made nearly two decades ago, the production of history textbooks has always involved forces of nationalism and patriotism, forces that clearly continue to play a role and can be expected to do so in the future.

To many, it would appear to be easier to appreciate the power of history texts in shaping human consciousness and action in totalitarian or near totalitarian states rather than accept that this is also true of our democratic state. In Orwell's *Nineteen Eighty-four* we see an ominous vision of this process being played out. Indeed, studies by Łuczyński (1997) suggest that highly controlled official histories in places like Poland were effective in shaping what people knew and believed about the past—even after the Soviet era. However, this picture is complicated by the fact that in places like Poland (Łuczyński, 1997), Estonia (Ahonen, 1992, 1997; Tulviste & Wertsch, 1994), and Russia (Wertsch & Rozin, in press) there were quite powerful, quasi-institutionalized forms of "unofficial history" that made resistance to the official versions during the Soviet era more possible. The result, which may at first glance appear to be ironic, was that in many cases people living in the Soviet bloc had more effective ways to circumvent the power of official history to shape their account of the past than do people living in the United States. One of the reasons for this is probably that history has generally been less contested and politicized in the United States than in the former Soviet bloc and hence less discussed and resisted. Whatever the cause, the point is that the production of official history in the form of cultural tools such as textbooks, films, and the media can have a powerful impact on how people represent their past, but a complete analysis must take into account the consumption as well as the production of these cultural tools.

Thus to recognize the power that the production of cultural tools has is not to assume that the study of production alone can provide an adequate account of what people know or believe. While few authors would explicitly espouse this, it is possible to find many instances of studies grounded in this assumption. For example, since the 1970s, there have been numerous analyses of the depiction of violence on television. Many of these analyses are quite detailed and informative and, more important for my present purposes, are implicitly assumed to provide direct insight into what adults and children (especially the latter) think, believe, and are likely to do.

In one of these studies, Gerbner, Gross, Signorielli, Morgan, and Jackson-Beeck (1979, pp. 177–178) set the theoretical stage for their study in the following terms:

Traditionally, the only acceptable extra-familial storytellers were those certified by religious institutions. With the growth of educational institutions, also originally religious, a new group of storytellers interceded between children and the world.

The emergence of mass media fundamentally altered the picture. Children were increasingly open to influences which parents, priests, and teachers could not monitor or control. Beginning with the widespread availability of printed materials for the literate, enlarged by the availability of movies and radio, and culminating with the omnipresence of television, the opportunities for children to directly consume mass-produced stories have rivaled traditional methods of instruction about the world.

Gerbner et al. go on to report that the amount of violence depicted on television was steadily increasing and that this was correlated with increasingly negative perceptions of the world: "The most significant and recurring conclusion of our long-range study is that one correlate of television viewing is a heightened and unequal sense of danger and risk in a mean and selfish world" (p. 196).

The findings reported by researchers such as Gerbner et al. are striking, and I have no desire to argue against their basic recommendations about reducing the amount of violence depicted on television. However, from the perspective of mediated action, their analyses focus almost exclusively on production and have relatively little to say about consumption. To some, this might be taken to imply that such consumption is unproblematic and uncontested. Anyone operating on such an assumption is likely to miss an important component of the process of how human consciousness is shaped by cultural tools and hence by the sociocultural setting more generally. In particular, they are likely to miss the complex dynamic involved in the irreducible tension between agent and cultural tool.

For the most part, my analyses of this tension have focused on how agents accept (reflectively or otherwise) cultural tools and use them. It turns out, however, that the relationship between agent and mediational means is often more complex and less benign. Cultural tools are not always facilitators of mediated action, and agents do not invariably accept and use them; rather, an agent's stance toward a mediational means is characterized by resistance or even outright rejection. Indeed, in certain settings this may be the rule rather than the exception. Resistance and rejection still constitute a relationship between agent and mediational means (a specific form of alterity), they still give rise to mediated action, and they still may have a major impact on the development of the agent. Yet a focus on resistance and rejection leads one to consider a host of issues that do not arise when one assumes that cultural tools are friendly helpers.

In chapter 3, I began to address some of these issues under the heading of appropriation. I began by outlining Bakhtin's notion of making a cultural tool one's own, and I went on to formulate a distinction between appropriation and mastery. In what follows I pursue this general set of issues in more detail in light of ideas outlined by Michel de Certeau (1984). Although there is no evidence that de Certeau was directly influenced by Bakhtin, or vice versa, there are several striking parallels between the account of consumption de Certeau outlined and Bakhtin's analysis of appropriation. In addition, there are some important differences and complementarities, which make their two sets of ideas particularly interesting to explore in juxtaposition. One of these complementarities has to do with the motivations behind their writings. Unlike Bakhtin, de Certeau developed his ideas about consumption largely in response to what he saw as an overemphasis in sociology on the analysis of production.

In this connection, de Certeau (1984, p. xii) questioned "the euphemistic term 'consumers,'" a term that assumes that people are "passive and guided by established rules" (p. xi). When speaking in opposition to this, de Certeau wrote of consumption in terms of "poaching," "renting," and "*ways of using* the products imposed by a dominant social order" (p. xiii). As he notes at one point that has particular salience for studies that focus exclusively on the production of cultural tools, "the presence and circulation of a representation (taught by preachers, educators, and populizers as a key to socioeconomic advancement) tells us nothing about what it is for its users" (p. xiii). Instead of stopping with an analysis of production, de Certeau argued that

> it seems both possible and necessary to determine the *use* to which [representations] are put by groups or individuals. For example, the analysis of the images broadcast by television (representation) and of the time spent watching television (behavior) should be complemented by a study of what the cultural consumer "makes" or "does" during this time and with these images. The same goes for the use of urban space, the products purchased in the supermarket, the stories and legends distributed by the newspapers, and so on. (p. xii)

In de Certeau's view, consumption is such a powerful process that in the end it must be considered to be another form of production, a "secondary production hidden in the process of . . . utilization" (1984, p. xiii). From his perspective, this statement by no means suggests methodological individualism. Indeed, he explicitly warns against "social atomism" grounded in a notion of the individual as an elementary unit out of which "groups are supposed to be formed and to which they are supposed to be always reducible" (p. xi). Instead, his point is that in using or renting representations, rituals, language, and other cultural tools, individuals and groups always shape and transform these cultural tools in particular ways. Just as Bakhtin wrote about words' taking on the accents of those through whose voices they had passed, de Certeau argued that "like tools, proverbs (and other discourses) are *marked by* uses; they offer to analysis the *imprints of acts* or of processes of enunciation . . . ; more generally, they thus indicate a social *historicity* in which systems of representations or processes of fabrication no longer appear only as normative frameworks but also as *tools manipulated by users*" (p. 21).

In de Certeau's view, the power of the users to leave their imprint on tools need not be a matter of conscious resistance or other form of reflective intent. Indeed, it even occurs in cases where agents express a desire to subordinate themselves to a cultural tool and to use it precisely in accordance with socioculturally prescribed norms:

> For instance, the ambiguity that subverted from within the Spanish colonizers' "success" in imposing their own culture on the indigenous Indians is well known. Submissive, and even consenting to their subjection, the Indians nevertheless often *made of* the rituals, representations, and laws imposed on them something quite different from what their conquerors had in mind; they subverted them not by rejecting or altering them, but by using them with respect to ends and references foreign to the system they had no choice but to accept. They were *other* within the very colonization that outwardly assimilated them; their use of the dominant social order deflected its power, which they lacked the means to challenge; they escaped it without leaving it. The strength of their difference lay in procedures of "consumption." To a lesser degree, a similar ambiguity creeps into our societies through the use made by the "common people" of the culture disseminated and imposed by the "elites" producing the language. (1984, p. xiii)

Like Bakhtin, de Certeau based his line of reasoning on the assumption that we can act only by using the cultural tools provided by others. This, in turn, is related to some other assumptions that guided both Bakhtin's and de Certeau's thinking. For example, de Certeau subscribed to the view that cultural tools such as "rituals, representations, and laws" (1984, p. xiii) always belong to someone. They are not neutral cognitive instruments existing outside relations of power and authority. In addition, de Certeau and Bakhtin both examined the relationship between the user of a cultural tool and the other in terms of alterity. Instead of viewing the appropriation of others' cultural tools in terms of benign, uncontested assimilation, de Certeau focused on how struggle and resistance defined this process. His primary concern was with how users of cultural tools are typically "*other* within the very colonization that outwardly assimilate[s] them" (p. xiii).

The writings of de Certeau also complement Bakhtin's in some of the ways he examined issues of power and authority. His point was not simply that we rent, poach, or otherwise use cultural tools that belong to others. It was that these others are typically separated from the consumers of their mediational means in terms of power: some groups are obligated to use the cultural tools that belong to other, more powerful groups. The very term "poach" is instructive in this sense. As de Certeau used it, this term derives its meaning from a practice of illegally trespassing on another's property to hunt or fish. In this case, the other from whom something is taken is typically a party such as a king or the state who possesses greater power than the poacher. Similarly, his discussion of "*ways of using* the products imposed by a dominant economic order" reflects his concern with the power that certain segments or forces in a sociocultural setting have to determine which cultural tools are to be used by people in that setting.

What de Certeau's perspective adds, then, at least in emphasis, to an account of appropriation is an analysis of how the power and authority of various groups play a role in deciding which cultural tools may be employed in particular settings, or scenes. His concern was with how consumers of cultural tools stand in various relationships of alterity to these groups. A central issue is whether consumers belong to the powerful and cultural elite, in which case they use cultural tools belonging to their group, or whether they belong to marginal groups or a counterculture, in which case they use cultural tools belonging to others.

In discussing these issues, de Certeau often relied on a distinction he outlined between "strategies" and "tactics" of consumption:

> I call a *strategy* the calculation (or manipulation) of power relationships that becomes possible as soon as a subject with will and power (a business, an army, a city, a scientific institution) can be isolated. It postulates a *place* that can be delimited as its *own* and serve as the base from which relations with an *exteriority* composed of targets or threats (customers or competitors, enemies, the country

> surrounding the city, objective and objects of research, etc.) can be managed. (1984, pp. 35–36)

In contrast:

> a *tactic* is a calculated action determined by the absence of a proper locus. No delimitation of an exteriority, then, provides it with the condition necessary for autonomy. The space of a tactic is the space of the other. Thus it must play on and with a terrain imposed on it and organized by the law of a foreign power. It does not have the means to *keep to itself*, at a distance, in a position of withdrawal, foresight, and self-collection: it is a maneuver "within the enemy's field of vision," as von Bülow put it, and within enemy territory. (pp. 36–37)

De Certeau's focus was primarily on tactics of consumption, a focus reflected in the dedication of his 1984 volume—"To the ordinary man," that is, the relatively powerless individual who enters into a relation of alterity and must struggle with the "elites." Essential properties of a tactic are that it is "determined by the *absence of power*" (p. 38) and that the agent must operate in the territory of the (more powerful) other. De Certeau employed a set of military and spatial metaphors, some of which have already been mentioned (e.g., "The space of a tactic is the space of the other"). One of these concerned the parallel he saw between tactics, as defined in his writings, and the practices of guerrilla fighters. Like guerrillas, those employing a tactic must operate in the territory of an other who is an enemy or stands in some other position of opposition or alterity.

When taking a "Cartesian attitude" (1984, p. 36) and speaking of space, "one's own place," and so forth, de Certeau had several kinds of space in mind. In what follows, I apply this set of metaphors primarily in connection with written and spoken texts. This means that when considering the issue of whether one is operating in one's own or another's space, I am concerned with whether one is operating with one's own or with the other's language, narrative, "social language" (Bakhtin, 1986; Wertsch, 1991), or other form of textual space.

The Official Soviet History of Estonia

To illustrate some of the issues I have introduced, I turn to another example involving the production and consumption of historical accounts about a nation-state. As in the case of historical texts about the United States, issues of mastery and appropriation are involved in this instance, and in the latter regard processes of resistance play a role, just as they did for some of the U.S. college students. The following illustration of historical representation contrasts, however, in some ways with what emerged in the U.S. case. Specifically, the consumption of history in a small, newly independent (again) country—Estonia—has had a much more contested, and in some ways more complex, past than the United States.

As a small Baltic nation, Estonia and its history have for centuries been shaped by changing relationships with larger neighbors, especially Germany and Russia (or, between 1917 and 1991, the Soviet Union). Since World War I, this history has been one of intermittant periods of independence and domination by these powers, especially the Soviet Union. In the aftermath of the Russian Revolution and World War I, Estonians engaged in what they know of as the War of Independence to free themselves from Russia, and the result was that Estonia existed as a sovereign nation from 1920 until 1940.

This period of independence lasted until the Baltic states of Estonia, Latvia, and Lithuania were forcibly incorporated into the Soviet Union in connection with a secret protocol to the German-Soviet pact of August 1939. A few months after the pact was signed, Moscow demanded that Estonia (as well as the other Baltic states of Latvia and Lithuania) sign mutual assistance agreements with the Soviet Union and allow major Soviet military bases to be established in their territory. After Hitler's successful campaign in France in summer 1940, Stalin demanded that Estonia accept a large number of additional troops and establish a pro-Soviet regime. In June 1940, Estonia was occupied by Soviet forces, and in July Soviet emissaries organized "elections" in which only a single list of Soviet-sponsored candidates was on the ballot. Ignoring the constitution of Estonia, the parliament that resulted from these events immediately voted to be incorporated into the USSR.

After these occurences in 1940 and before summer 1941, when Estonia was occupied by German forces, Soviet authorities arrested large numbers of Estonian political leaders and had them executed or sent to Siberia. Furthermore, Soviet authorities carried out mass deportations of Estonians. Estimates range from 60,000 to 100,000 Estonian men, women, and children who were victims of this forced migration to Siberia or to desert regions of the USSR. This is the equivalent of from 6 to 10 percent of the ethnic Estonian population living in Estonia at that time.

As part of the German attack on the Soviet Union in 1941, Estonia was occupied by Germany. Approximately 200,000 Estonians, including 4,500 Jews, were killed during the next three years, either at the hands of the Germans or while fighting the German or the Soviet army. In autumn 1944, as the Soviet army approached the Baltics once again, between 30,000 and 40,000 Estonians fled to Germany, Finland, or Sweden. By the end of 1944, Estonia was reannexed by the Soviet Union, but guerrilla warfare against Soviet authorities continued until the early 1950s. Estonia was part of the USSR until 1991, when it gained its current status of independence.

Tactics of Consumption and Forms of Resistance

The episode from Estonian history that will be the focus of my analysis concerns events surrounding the incorporation of Estonia into the Soviet Union in 1940. In addition, I focus on the historical accounts that were officially taught and learned in schools and promulgated through other institutions such as the popular media during the Soviet era rather than those that have emerged after independence.

Between 1944 and 1991, the Soviet government devoted massive resources to the effort to promulgate an official history of the Estonian Soviet Socialist Republic, as well as of other parts of the USSR and the world in general. The intent of these efforts was quite clear. For example, even well after the heyday of enthusiasm for creating *Homo Sovieticus*, Soviet authors such as Smirnov (1973, p. 274) continued to make explicit arguments that

> all educational institutions are confronted with the task of giving a clear and convincing account of the mass character of the revolutionary struggle and the need for socialist transformations. It is impossible to bring up true sons of the Motherland [i.e., the USSR], steadfast ideological fighters, without fostering respect for the history of their own people, their own culture. It is essential that every Soviet person should understand that the socialism built in his country according to Lenin's plan acts as the most powerful, effective and humane force which along with the other socialist countries today stands in opposition to imperialism. All Soviet people must fully understand that no mistakes committed in the process of building socialism, no problems of the present day can remove the historic significance of the building of socialism or diminish its achievements.

Among other things, this passage is notable for its focus on *Soviet* people. There is no mention of Russians, Estonians, Uzbeks, or any other nationality, a fact that reflects the very strong effort during the Soviet era to create citizens who would have no source of identity that could effectively compete with their identity as a citizen of the USSR. This constitutes an instance of how a state sought to produce a historical account in the service of its present interests.

As analysts such as Billington (1966, pp. 529–530) have noted, the particular form that this effort took to create loyalty to a new kind of state, a loyalty that was to transcend all other loyalties grounded in nationality or other such phenomena, had roots that extend far back into the history of Russia:

> A . . . borrowing from earlier [Russian] tradition was the subtle Bol-
> shevik adoption of the concept of the "circle" as a new type of
> dedicated community in which all distinctions of class and nation-
> ality were eliminated. Such Bolshevik concepts as sacrificial "party
> spirit" and internal "self-criticism" had been in many ways char-
> acteristic of Russian intellectual circles from the first secret meet-
> ings of Novikov and Schwarz in the eighteenth century.

The detailed implications of such ideology for how the official history of Estonia was written and taught are quite complex, but in general the point is that, when viewed from this perspective, Estonia's
past was interpreted in terms consistent with claims about a homogeneous group of Soviet people making up the USSR. This interpretation relied heavily on notions of an international class struggle and
other Soviet Marxist principles that were presumed to apply regardless of nationality.

As Ahonen (1992, 1997) has outlined, official Soviet history provided an account in which Estonia's, as well as other nations', pasts
were portrayed primarily in terms of general historical laws that naturally and inevitably led to their becoming a part of the USSR. Specifically, it was asserted that the poverty of the workers and peasants in Estonia, along with the rise of a new internationalism and
class consciousness that recognized the advantages of socialism, led
to mass movements to create socialism. Given that the Soviet Union
was next door and had already developed socialism, this analysis
asserted that it was natural that Estonian workers and peasants would
call for the assistance of their counterparts there.

To examine some aspects of the functions, as well as the form
and content, of this official history, Fran Hagstrom and I conducted
a series of interviews in 1993 with several ethnic Estonians, all of
whom lived in Estonia. These interviews were conducted in English
(a language in which all interviewees were fluent or nearly fluent)
and lasted between 20 and 60 minutes each. Three interviewees were
in their twenties, two were in their thirties, and one was in his for-

ties. The amount of detailed information provided in the interviews varied greatly, primarily because the interviewees had encountered official Soviet history at different stages in their lives and under quite different circumstances. The individuals in their twenties and early thirties had relatively little exposure to this history, and this exposure occurred at quite late stages of Estonia's being part of the USSR. As a result, they had been less deeply affected and knew less about this account of the past than the older interviewees.

The interview that provided the greatest amount of detailed information about the official history and the one I examine here was with an Estonian male who was 46 years of age. The wealth of detail is probably a reflection of the fact that he was the interviewee with the most extensive experience in Soviet formal educational settings. In addition, he was the only interviewee to have received all his postsecondary education (eight years) in Moscow, a setting that generally required more ideological vigilence during the 1960s and 1970s than Estonia.

There are numerous indications that this interviewee used tactics of consumption when dealing with the official history of events in Estonia in 1940. These tactics were so consciously used and widely agreed upon that it might be more appropriate to refer to them as "tactics of resistance." In response to the question "How well did you know the official account?" the interviewee replied,

> Well enough to pass my exams. In order to study in Moscow, I had to go through a competitive process based on examinations. For that exam I had to learn or recall the official history version that the teacher in the final grade of high school had made clear to us. There were six applicants for a single spot. The topic could also come up in examinations at Moscow State University on the History of the Communist Party. (taped interview, February, 1993)

So far, this does not sound that different from the way a student in a U.S. high school might approach the study of history; the goal was simply to get through by passing whatever examinations were required. However, a further look at the dynamics of how official history texts were used in classrooms begins to reveal some differences. For example, when I asked the interviewee to recount how he gave oral presentations about the events of 1940 in the presence of his teacher and classmates, he responded:

> The only thing to do openly was to tell the story without any emotion at all so you and everyone else could understand, "Here you have your story, but I am telling it differently than any other sto-

ries I tell you." Actually, another thing you could do was to make the same thing clear in an opposite way: make your story too emotional so that everyone could again understand that you wanted to make it clear that you don't take it seriously. You just change your usual way of speaking.

De Certeau's account of tactics of consumption are quite relevant when interpreting such responses. The space in which the interviewee had to operate was the textual space of another—namely, a text about the past provided by Soviet authorities. The fact that this space was "imposed . . . and organized by the law of a foreign power" (de Certeau, 1984, p. 37) meant that the tactic did not have "the means to *keep to itself*, at a distance"; it had to "maneuver 'within the enemy's field of vision' and within enemy territory." This meant that the interviewee was obligated to recite a text that he clearly viewed as belonging to another and not to him. He did not have the means to confront the other with a countertext but had to struggle in a context of alterity and resistance to the official version.

While such tactics of resistance clearly occurred in the authoritarian setting provided by the USSR, they were not characteristic of everyone's behavior or of most individuals' behavior all the time. Furthermore, they clearly do not occur *only* in such settings. For example, the means that Gamoran (1990) found to avoid participating in civic religion (see chapter 2) clearly qualify as tactics of resistance. And with regard to the teaching of history in the United States, Holt (1990) has outlined ways in which minority and low-income students may view the texts they are required to learn as "someone else's history" and engage in various forms of resistance.

One way in which such examples in the United States differ from what was often encountered in the former Soviet Union, however, is that in places like Estonia the consequences of criticizing the official account of history could be quite high. As a result, it had to be done in private or quite surreptitiously if carried out in the public sphere. Given all this, the task of resisting official versions of history was not left up to students alone. Even in school, a context where teachers and students had to be vigilant about maintaining a facade of loyalty to the USSR, there were ways for teachers to encourage students to develop tactics of resistance. For example, several of the Estonian interviewees reported that teachers sometimes helped them learn how to operate within the textual space of another without appropriating the message. Specifically, they reported that instruction about official history was often accompanied by clear indications from teachers that what they were teaching was not to be believed.[2] As one interviewee noted about his experience in an Estonian school:

> I don't remember, at least from my school, that any of the history teachers would have especially emotionally or somehow tried to bring this official version, so to say, close to the pupils because I guess the reasons were that first of all the teachers knew exactly that it was wrong and the other reason was that they didn't want to provoke the pupils to make comments and things like this. (male, age 46)[3]

Another interviewee reported, "I read the [text]book, and I asked . . . I said [to] the teacher that there is . . . there is not everything right, and this teacher, he said that yes, you read it [the textbook], but you have yourself to find out what is right and what is wrong" (female, age 20).

These reports about the teaching and learning of history in Soviet Estonia reveal a set of tactics employed by students, often with the help of teachers. In all cases, "the space of [the] tactic [was] the space of the other" (de Certeau, 1984, p. 36), the other in this case being the official history texts provided by the Soviet state. Furthermore, the interviewees in this study engaged in these tactics because "a tactic is determined by the *absence of power*" (p. 38). At least in formal instructional and evaluation contexts—contexts controlled by people who "professionally believed" (Estonian interviewee, age 46)—students had little choice but to employ tactics, as opposed to strategies, if they were to resist at all in this public space.

Strategies of Consumption and Forms of Resistance: Official and Unofficial History

One striking feature of discourse in the former Soviet Union was the gulf that distinguished public from private forms of talk (Smith, 1976). An example of this can be found in the wealth of jokes (*anekdoty*) that had a critical political edge. Virtually everyone, including Communist Party members with a reputation for hard line vigilence, told *anekdoty*, but they did so only in contexts that were considered to be private. The public recounting of an *anekdot*, even one that everyone had used or heard in a private setting, could result in very serious consequences, depending on the era and local political climate. In many instances, individuals who were some of the most ideologically vigilent in the public sphere were the best tellers of *anekdoty* in the private sphere. Such patterns are indicative of the widespread "double consciousness" (Ahonen, 1992) that characterized many people in Eastern Europe and the USSR during the Soviet era.

This difference between public and private space did not only manifest itself in connection with *anekdoty*. It also played a major role in other areas of life such as how history was produced and consumed. Indeed, the distinction between the histories that were acceptable in public and private spheres of discourse was so great that some authors (Tulviste & Wertsch, 1994) have found it necessary to distinguish between "official" and "unofficial" history. As I have outlined in previous writings, an official history is approved and produced by the state, and it is assumed to be the only, or at least the only true, history that a state's citizens should learn in settings such as school. As a result, the materials associated with an official history are relatively uniform and accessible to the consumer.

In contrast to all the seeming advantages enjoyed by official histories, unofficial histories are generally not supported by the state. Indeed, in many cases unofficial histories are actively suppressed. One does not have to turn to fictional images from Orwell's *Nineteen Eighty-four* to find instances of attempts to suppress and even obliterate unofficial accounts of the past. Book burnings have been perhaps the most blatant, though by no means the only, method used. Unofficial histories may be political histories that conflict with an official political history, but they may also be social or other types of nonpolitical histories. Even in the latter cases, however, representatives of the state may object to the portrayal on the grounds that it contains an implicit political message. In other cases, an unofficial history of today may have been an official history from a previous period, or vice versa, and the future status of a representation will in turn often be different from what it is today.

Unofficial histories exist in virtually every context where there is an official history. However, their form and content, their status, and their relationship with the official history may vary greatly. For example, the forms of resistance that American college students manifested when producing quest-for-freedom stories about the United States (chapter 3; Wertsch & O'Connor, 1994) can be interpreted as indicating the existence of an unofficial history for these students. In this case, however, the resources for resistance appear to be quite limited and do not take the form of a robust alternative account of American history. The indications of resistance that do exist indicate at least some inklings of an unofficial history, perhaps something like that found in Zinn (1980), but they are not well developed. In contrast, cases such as that of Estonia during the Soviet era reveal that unofficial histories can be quite well developed and can play an effective role in strategies of consumption.

In addition to being asked to discuss their tactics for resisting the official Soviet history of the events of 1940, Estonian interviewees were asked about unofficial histories. In all cases, they distinguished between an official and an unofficial version of these events. Furthermore, they believed that all ethnic Estonians made this distinction. To borrow de Certeau's terminology, this means they engaged in strategies as well as tactics of resistance. They did so by creating a second symbolic space, one "that [could] be delimited as [their] *own* and serve as the base from which relations with an *exteriority* composed of targets or threats (customers or competitors, enemies, the country surrounding the city, objective and objects of research, etc.) can be managed" (1984, p. 36).

The interviewees were first asked to provide the official Soviet version of how Estonia became part of the Soviet Union in 1940. This was followed by a request for the unofficial Estonian version. One interviewee reproduced the official Soviet version as follows:

> (1) For twenty years the Baltic countries were cut off from the Soviet Union, and the workers had to suffer hard under capitalism. All the time they dreamed of being together with Russians and other people of the former Russian empire and now of the Soviet Union again. And then in 1939 the Soviet Union, being afraid of an attack from the side of Germany, made agreements with the governments of all the three Baltic countries—they were usually . . . always called in Soviet literature "bourgeois nationalist governments." And they all signed an agreement with Soviet Union. But then the governments decided . . . decided not to keep the agreement and instead they turned themselves toward Nazi Germany. And the working people in all three countries were very angry with their bourgeois nationalist governments, and they organized . . . socialist revolutions in all the three countries in the summer of 1940. After that they asked the Soviet government . . . and the Soviet Communist Party if they might join the family of the happy Soviet people, if they might join the Soviet Union. And the Soviet Union was ready to accept these three . . . peoples, and that's how the three Baltic countries came into the Soviet Union. That was the official version. (male, age 46)

When the same interviewee was asked to provide the unofficial Estonian version of these episodes, he stated:

> (2) The unofficial versions come generally this way. . . . In 1939 the Soviet Union imposed an agreement on Estonia and the other two

Baltic states which permitted Soviet Union to have military bases in all these three countries. And most people tell stories about the Russians coming in and what was said was that they were very much alike, all of them, partly I guess because at that time just the soldiers and the officers and they were all in uniform. And then in 1940 one day they asked . . . they told Estonia that they had to bring in much more soldiers, and they did it. Estonia didn't resist because it wasn't strong enough for that. Then there were also ironical stories, first about the Russian officers who came in. One of the best known was . . . and I've heard people who have . . . who say that they have seen it with their own eyes . . . that wives of Russian officers bought nightgowns in . . . Tallinn stores and came to restaurants in these nightgowns thinking that these were just the right thing to put on for this occasion. And all kinds . . . of stories. The other stories were about these collaborationists among Estonians who took part in these events in the summer of 1940 and later on. These people were regarded as traitors, and also it was stressed that Russians who had been brought in from the southeast of Estonia played a special role in . . . in these events. What people said was that never had anyone ever in Tallinn seen people in so . . . and any other place in Estonia in so bad clothes. The weapons were taken away from people on the first day when the Russians came in 1940 and very soon arrests began. People began to disappear. One . . . I return now to these collaborationists. What was usually told ironically were stories about people who had been just nothing, who had been criminals or semicriminals and who got to high positions during the Russians. And of course there were stories from the very beginning of people asking questions in these new political lectures, questions which in the later Soviet terminology were called provocative. Or . . . I remember another story about somebody who . . . had a political lesson in a Tallinn school which had to begin with a song "Internationale." And . . . they wanted all the children to sing and as a result the person who organized it had to sing it alone because nobody joined her. By the way, it was the mother of X. Also there were also lots of jokes . . . very early already in 1940 about all these new orders, so. . . . I guess the jokes appeared very early because in the summer of 1941 when the Soviets were out again in newspapers from the very beginning they began to publish jokes and anecdotes about the first Soviet year. (male, age 46)

These two texts obviously differ in many ways, but for my present purposes a couple of basic observations are particularly relevant. First, the interviewee readily recognized the difference between the official and unofficial accounts of these events. Second, rather than representing the internationalist, class-based analysis that serves as the framework of the official Soviet history, the actors in both the official and unofficial accounts provided by Estonians were identified primarily in terms of nationality. This contrasts with the focus on universal material and economic forces that caused "collective persons" (Ahonen, 1992) to act in accordance with class interests. This second point suggests that, in addition to the strategies of resistance provided by operating in his own textual space (i.e., the unofficial history), this interviewee engaged in tactics of resistance when reproducing the official account. The texts produced by all five other interviewees are similarly characterized by these two points.

In terms of the general properties, or assumptions, of official history I outlined earlier, these two texts, as well as responses from the other five interviewees, provide several additional insights. First, all six interviewees clearly recognized that the Soviet account sought to be *the* single, accurate account of how Estonia became part of the USSR. It was equally clear, however, that all six rejected this claim of veracity and authority. All the interviewees knew some version of the official Soviet version of the events of 1940, but in every case they also knew an unofficial version, a version to which they ascribed greater veracity and authority than the official one. This unofficial history provided these interviewees with a textual space that could serve as the basis for a strategy of resisting the official account of the events of 1940.

The picture one gets so far, then, is one in which Estonians who lived during the Soviet era were required to master not one, but *two*, distinct accounts of the events of 1940 and of their nation—an official and an unofficial version. The official history sought to be the single, true account of events in Estonia, but this was not accepted by Estonians. Indeed, they made a clear distinction between knowing an official history and not believing it, on the one hand, and knowing and believing an unofficial history, on the other. The official history was provided by the state, specifically through formal instruction in schools, the media, and so forth. In addition to promulgating the official history, the state went to great efforts to suppress the unofficial one. Through a variety of channels that functioned outside of state control in private spheres of discourse, however, Estonians managed to learn an unofficial history.

Some of the most striking differences between the official and unofficial histories provided by the interviewees have to do with their structure and content. The official history manifested an overarching coherence grounded in a central theme, whereas the unofficial histories seem fragmented, partial, and unorganized. This difference is reflected in texts (1) and (2) provided earlier, and it was in evidence in the productions of all the other interviewees as well. It is a general difference that emerged despite major differences in the amount of detail the various interviewees provided in their texts.

All six interviewees organized their rendition of the official history around three or four basic points. The first, having to do with the positive disposition of Estonians toward the events, was mentioned by everyone. They all stated that according to the official history the people of Estonia voluntarily became part of the USSR and wanted the Soviet Union to come to their assistance (I call this claim A). The second and third points had to do with *why* Estonians wanted this assistance. Five of the six interviewees mentioned that in the official account Estonians were extremely poor (if not hungry) and saw the Soviet Union as a source of social transformation that would alleviate this problem (I call this claim B). Four of the six interviewees mentioned that the official account claimed that the Estonians sought this help as a way of avoiding domination by Germany (claim C). All six interviewees mentioned at least one of these two reasons for why Estonians supposedly wanted to join the Soviet Union. And finally, all six interviewees mentioned in their presentation of the official account that the masses, not just a small group of Estonian people, were in favor of joining the USSR (claim D).

In the official history provided in text (1), the Estonians' voluntary decision to become part of the USSR (claim A) and one of the reasons for holding that opinion (claim B), as well as the claim about the involvement of the masses (claim D), appear at the outset: "For twenty years the Baltic countries were cut off from the Soviet Union, and the workers had to suffer hard under capitalism. All the time they dreamed of being together with Russians and other people of the former Russian empire and now of the Soviet Union again." As part of this same text, the author also touched on claim C in a less direct way when he stated "the working people in all three countries were very angry with their bourgeois nationalist governments [for breaking the agreement with the USSR to oppose Germany], and they organized . . . socialist revolutions in all the three countries in the summer of 1940."

Other interviewees made the points somewhat differently. For example, one commented with regard to claims A and B that "the official [version] was that we were so poor and that we had to go to . . . to join with them. We had to do it and we wanted to do it . . . to join the Soviet Union . . . because we were so poor and they had life and hope" (female, age 36).

In speaking of claim B, one interviewee provided what he termed "the most extreme version," which was "spread by some uneducated occupiers": "I read somewhere that . . . that it was said that Estonians were so poor that they had to find food from garbage boxes and Russians taught us to read and write," (male, age 21).

As noted previously, fear of German domination (claim C) was also included in several interviewees' versions of the official history as a reason for Estonians' wanting to become part of the Soviet Union. An example of this claim is as follows: "the problem was also because, uh, we . . . we . . . Estonia didn't want to join Germany, to be under German influence. Instead of Germans, we chose the Soviet Union" (female, age 36).

Claim D tended to emerge in the course of touching on other issues in the official version. For example, claims about the masses sometimes emerged in comments about the "workers" as in "the workers had to suffer greatly under capitalism" (text 1). In other cases, the use of "we" or "we Estonians" in the offcial version was clearly intended to refer to all Estonians, or at least the vast majority.

In the interviewees' renditions of the official account of the events of 1940, all, or at least the vast majority, of Estonians wanted to join the Soviet Union and their major reasons for wanting to do so were their poverty and hunger as well as their fear of German domination. Some of the interviewees came up with additional details about how and why Estonia became part of the Soviet Union according to the official version of history, but the four claims I have outlined were common to their accounts and provided the framework for generating coherent texts that offered reasons for the actions of the Estonians.

The interviewees' accounts of unofficial history stand in striking contrast to this general picture. Instead of taking the form of an organized narrative with a single general theme, a basic motivation of the main characters, and reasons for that motivation, the unofficial accounts often seemed to have no discernible overarching coherent structure. There was little one can point to as the means for "grasping together" (Mink, 1972) the various actors, events, motivations, and so forth. Instead, the unofficial histories seem to have taken the form of a string of anecdotes or observations. Text (2) is an example of this. This text starts out with a general claim about the Soviets' motivation, but after the first sentence it shifts to anecdotes and observations, with the occasional reappearance of a general claim. In general, this text has nothing like the overarching coherence of text (1) about the official history, which was provided by the same interviewee.

When asked to provide an account of the unofficial version of the events of 1940, several of the younger interviewees were unable to generate an extended text of any sort. Indeed, some of them stated that they had never thought about the overall story concretely. For example, one replied, "I never thought about this. I never reflected on it, but I never thought we joined the Soviet Union because we wanted to" (female, age 20). The initial response of another interviewee to the request to tell the unofficial account was, "we didn't want to join, we were occupied. This is a very emotional issue" (female, age 36).

Thus, unlike the official accounts, the interviewees' unofficial accounts did not seem to be organized around a small set of basic claims. Instead of producing accounts with a single, overarching focus grounded in the motives of the main actors, the interviewees tended to provide a few general statements and then shift to anecdotes or observations or to comments about how someone (usually a family member) told them something that had a very powerful impact on them.

What at first appears to be unorganized in the unofficial histories turns out to be coherent, however, when one considers them from the perspective of their relationship to official versions of the past. Specifically, the source of organization in the unofficial histories is to be found in the fact that they serve as a kind of response—namely, a rebuttal—to the official accounts. This amounts to a form of oppositional alterity between the official and unofficial texts. In particular, the form that alterity takes in this case is what Bakhtin (1984) termed "hidden dialogicality":

> Imagine a dialogue of two persons in which the statements of the second speaker are omitted, but in such a way that the general sense is not at all violated. The second speaker is present invisibly, his words are not there, but deep traces left by these words have a determining influence on all the present and visible words of the first speaker. We sense that this is a conversation, although only one person is speaking, and it is a conversation of the most intense kind, for each present, uttered word responds and reacts with its every fiber to the invisible speaker, points to something outside itself, beyond its own limits, to the unspoken words of another person. (p. 197)

In our case, the "second speaker" is the voice or text of the official history. Of course, the interviewees never mentioned any of the claims of this official history ("his words are not there"), but there is a sense in which the "second speaker [the producer of official history] is present invisibly [in the unofficial history]." The resulting unofficial version of the past is such that "each present, uttered word responds and reacts with its every fiber to the invisible speaker."

From this perspective, it would appear that the alternative textual space provided by the unofficial history did not have an equivalent level of power with that of the official history. Instead, this textual space and the private sphere of discourse in which it appeared occupied a secondary, derivative status vis-à-vis the official text used in the public sphere. Hence at least in one sense the official account can be viewed as continuing to occupy a dominant position, even as it was being resisted and rejected. It set the terms for what had to be addressed in the unofficial historical accounts. What lends coherence to the anecdotes and observations that composed the unofficial accounts is usually the fact that they stood in opposition to the official version. They can be viewed as being organized around *counterclaims*—claim A': Estonians did *not* voluntarily become a part of the USSR, they were coerced; claim B': the Estonians in 1940 were *not* poor and hungry; claim C': the Estonians did *not* seek Soviet help to escape German domination; and claim D': the Estonians who favored joining the Soviet Union were *not* the vast majority, nor did they represent the masses.

Most or all of these counterclaims appeared in every one of the interviewees' unofficial accounts of the events of 1940. Just as all the interviewees included claim A in their account of the official history, all of them included some version of counterclaim A' in their account of the unofficial history. In most cases this was the first point they made. For example, in the first sentence of text (2), the interviewee stated that "the Soviet Union imposed an agreement."

Counterclaim B' also appeared in virtually all of the interviewees' comments. If it did not appear as part of their account of the unofficial version of history (again, many of these were quite short and fragmented), it usually appeared somewhere else in the interview—for example, when we asked about where the interviewee had obtained information for the unofficial history. In response to this question, several interviewees provided extended accounts of how their mother, grandfather, or some other older relative or friend told them that the conditions of life were much better before Estonia became part of the USSR in 1940 than they were after. An example of counterclaim B' can be found in the following statement that began an interviewee's account of the unofficial history: "There was something [existing in 1940 in Estonia] that was good, but we were told it was bad. For example, my grandmother told me about the very old days. It seems that somehow she had a very happy childhood" (female, age 21).

Counterclaim C' did not appear in any explicit form in any of the interviewees' comments. There are several possible reasons for this, at least two of which are worth mentioning. First, of the four basic claims around which the official histories were organized, claim C about the desire to avoid German domination appeared least frequently. Therefore, there may have been less of a need to refute it in the unofficial history. Second, it is clear that the German occupation of Estonia was indeed a tragic event. Many Estonians would have a difficult time deciding whether the German or the Soviet occupation was worse, but it is obvious that the former was not desirable and that from their perspective there was some logic to viewing Soviet assistance as a way to terminate it.

Counterclaim D' appeared in one form or another in every interviewee's comments. Instead of emerging in the form of an explicit and separate assertion, it often appeared in connection with one of the anecdotes or observations. For example, in text (2) the interviewee speaks of "collaborationists" who were viewed by Estonians as traitors, and noted that "what was usually told ironically were stories about people who had been just nothing, who had been criminals or semicriminals and who got to high positions during the Russians' time." As in many other accounts of the events of 1940, the point here is that the only Estonians to collaborate with the Soviets were those who had something major to gain (or in other cases nothing major to lose). They obviously did not represent the masses.

In addition to the striking differences in the contents and forms of the official and unofficial histories, they differed with regard to forces of production. As I have already noted, massive resources went into the production of official history in the Soviet Union. For example, one of the last history textbooks published during the Soviet era for tenth graders was *Istoria SSSR* (History of the USSR), which had a print run of 3,110,000 and cost a very reasonable 70 kopecks. As is typically the case with official texts, it was very accessible and inexpensive. This textbook was intended to be used in schools throughout in the Soviet Union in a lockstep fashion; teachers were to have been teaching the same chapter on the same days across the eleven time zones of this massive state. The clear intent of this effort was to promulgate a single, authoritative text that could be appropriated as part of the process of forming a group identity (Ahonen, 1992) as loyal Soviet citizens.

In contrast, the production of unofficial histories in the Soviet Union was sporadic, fragmented, and often dangerous. After the incorporation of Estonia into the USSR, massive numbers of books having anything to do with unofficial history were burned, and for several decades the mere possession of a written account of an unofficial history of Estonia was punishable by imprisonment. Hence the possibilities for producing unofficial histories in a public space in Estonia were virtually nonexistent. Instead, they had to be produced in private settings, often through discussions with parents and friends. With regard to the events of 1940, this often meant that one learned unofficial history in discussions about what had happened to relatives who had disappeared, fled to Sweden, and so forth. Given that the information for the unofficial versions came from such diverse sources and that these sources tended to focus on personal experiences, it is not surprising that the resulting texts showed neither great internal coherence nor similarity with one another. The unorganized, fragmented production of unofficial history resulted, not surprisingly, in unorganized, fragmented texts.

Summary

Several general observations can be made about the strategies of consumption and the forms of resistance toward official history in Estonia. In one way or another, each of these observations grows out of taking mediated action as a basic unit of analysis. The very definitions of appropriation, tactics of resistance, and strategies of resistance are grounded in the irreducible tension between agent and cultural tool. In addition, the essential role played by mediational means in this approach is what lies behind the concern with how mediational means are produced and consumed. While beliefs held by Estonians about their past were shaped by the official history texts produced by the Soviet state, an examination that focuses solely on production would provide a quite misleading picture of what the consumers of these texts really believed.

As authors such as Ahonen (1992) have emphasized, the production of official history was closely controlled in the Soviet bloc. In addition to being responsible for writing the standard history text (there was basically only one per grade level for the entire USSR, translated into various languages), the Soviet Ministry of Education specified which chapter every student across the entire country was to be studying during each week of the entire school year. This was part of an attempt to control not only the textbook but its uses—

something that was important since, as Wills (1994) has documented, controlling the structure and content of a textbook by no means amounts to controlling how it is employed by teachers. The univocal message students received in formal instruction was also heavily reinforced by the media, the observance of state holidays, commemorative monuments, Communist Party lectures and discussion, and other means.

As many observers of the former Soviet Union have noted, however, even such exhaustive efforts by the state to produce its official history did not result in bringing up "true sons of the Motherland, steadfast ideological fighters" of the sort envisioned by Smirnov (1973, p. 274). Instead, the results of production can be viewed as grist for the mill of consumption. In this connection, de Certeau seemed to be right on target when he argued that "the presence and circulation of a representation (taught by preachers, educators, and populizers as a key to socioeconomic advancement) tells us nothing about what it is for its users" (1984, p.xiii). Instead of appropriating the texts of official history in an uncontested and passive fashion, Soviet citizens often developed quite elaborate forms of "double consciousness" (Ahonen, 1992), "internal immigration" (Zinchenko, 1996), and outright cynicism (Zinoviev, 1984) by engaging in tactics and strategies of resistance. In contrast to a relationship between agent and cultural tool grounded in assimilation, resistance—if not outright rejection—was often the order of the day.

The interviews with the Estonians suggest that their resistance took the form of strategies as well as tactics. In their reports of how history was taught and understood in school, they provided insight into how it was possible to operate on the territory of the other (the Soviet state) while still engaging in tactics of resistance, and they also spoke about using alternative textual spaces, in the form of unofficial histories, that made it possible for them to engage in strategies of resistance. Many Estonians, as well as residents of other areas of the former Soviet Union, report today that virtually no one believed the official history produced by the state.

The relationship between agents and cultural tools envisioned in this case of resistance differs from that outlined in earlier chapters. In particular, some of the U.S. college students' uses of the quest-for-freedom narrative reflected tactics but not strategies of resistance. The most obvious question that arises in the U.S. case is why at least some of the students did not use some other narrative as a mediational means for their performance. In the terminology of the present chapter, this question has to do with why they were restricted to employing tactics of resistance—something that provides a reminder not to underestimate the power of cultural tools. In contrast to the opinion that U.S. schools do not succeed in teaching history, one could argue that the schools have actually done their jobs quite well: they have equipped students with one, and only one, cultural tool to employ in representing the past of their nation-state.

It is beyond the scope of this book to predict whether a particular cultural text will be appropriated in an uncontested manner or will provide a target for tactics and strategies of resistance. Indeed, it is unlikely that any analytic framework in the human sciences can, or should, try to explain or predict such phenomena (Taylor, 1985). However, by beginning with mediated action as a unit of analysis, it is possible to interpret and clarify a great deal about the production and consumption of cultural tools. To paraphrase Burke (1969), the goal in this effort is not to develop an approach that avoids irreducible tensions but an approach that clearly reveals the strategic spots at which such tensions necessarily arise.

When interpreting reports about the knowledge and belief Estonians had about historical texts, I made the point that the irreducible tension between agent and mediational means provided a starting point. An account of cultural tools and how they were produced provided a link to sociocultural context. Cultural tools help set the scene within which human action will occur, and as I have noted at several points these can have a powerful effect on human consciousness and action. On the other hand, even the most complete account of these cultural tools and the forces of production that give rise to them cannot specify how they will be used. Remembering that "the presence and circulation of a representation . . . tells us nothing about what it is for its users" (de Certeau, 1984, p. xiii) leads to a recognition that studies of production need to be complemented with studies of consumption (appropriation, resistance, and so forth), and I would argue that it is possible to gain a great deal of clarity on such issues by approaching them from the perspective of the irreducible tension between agent and cultural tool that defines mediated action.

Appropriation and Resistance: Cultural Stereotypes

As I noted earlier, notions such as tactics and strategies of resistance are relatively easy to envision when dealing with totalitarian settings. Again, Orwell's *Nineteen Eight-four* is perhaps the most famous case in point. Who can read about the exploits of Winston Smith without rooting for him to engage in tactics or strategies of resistance? Indeed, the basic narrative tension of the novel is built around this. Many observers might have similar tendencies when considering the options available to Estonians (or Ukrainians, Russians, or other nationalities for that matter) during the Soviet era. While obvious differences exist between the former USSR and the United States with regard to the uses of history, the findings I reviewed in chapter 3 suggest that the same basic set of constructs can be usefully applied when trying to understand both settings.

A common feature of all these settings is that the official histories that serve as cultural tools are produced by the state and hence have a level of availability and a relative clarity that are not characteristic of many other cultural tools. The general points I wish to make, however, are not meant to apply only to such cases. They are meant to apply more broadly to mediated action and the complex dynamics involved in the relationship between agent and cultural tool. To explore these issues further, I turn to an additional illustration that does not involve mediational means produced and backed up by the power and authority of the state. Indeed, in the cases I examine next the forces of production are quite difficult to specify. As has been true throughout, however, my main concern is with how cultural tools are consumed, appropriated, resisted, and so forth.

The "Microdynamics" of Appropriation and Resistance

My account of appropriation and resistance up to this point has focused on relationships between agents and mediational means that presumably exist *generally*—that is, across various contexts of use. The implicit claim has been that at least certain Estonians generally engaged in tactics and strategies of resistance to official Soviet history, that certain U.S. students generally engage in tactics of resistance to their official history, and so forth. While such issues have some merit and are obviously worthy of detailed investigation, they do not touch on the variability associated with local contexts of usage. As authors such as Billig (1987) have argued, attempts to explain, or even describe, general patterns of human behavior often come up short because they fail to take into account the dynamics of local context, especially social and rhetorical context. For example, the setting in which a statement is made often tells us more about how the statement should be taken than does some general characterization of the speaker. Billig's major concern was with how rhetorical or argumentative encounters provide a setting for any utterance, but his point applies more broadly to other contextual dimensions as well.

In short, when trying to understand human action, it is often as important to know about its local context (its scene with a narrow circumference in Burke's terminology) as it is to have a general description of what the agent is carrying it out.

What this means for an account of mediated action is not that one should give up trying to characterize individuals or groups in some sort of general way and turn to a thoroughgoing contextualism. Carried to its extreme, this would amount simply to replacing one reductionism with another. Instead, my point is simply to provide a reminder of the limits of analyses of human action—limits that I have characterized in terms of Burke's pentad. Most of my comments up to this point have focused on what Burke termed the "agent–instrument" relationship and have largely ignored the pentadic elements of scene, motive, and act. The point to be made here is not that one can escape the limitations of such relationships. Instead, the point is to recognize the limitations as well as insights inherently associated with *any* perspective and to complement it with the insights—and limitations—associated with other perspectives. Like the agents whose mediated action we examine, we too are subject to the affordances and constraints of the cultural tools we use.

In what follows, I outline some of the contextual variability associated with the use of cultural tools. In doing so I employ the term "microdynamics" to index the fact that appropriation and resistance sometimes arise in the flow of action in a matter of seconds. This contrasts with instances, such as those outlined in chapter 4, in which these processes emerge over much longer periods. As is the case with "microgenesis" (Werner, 1948; Wertsch, 1985), the point is to focus on how a process emerges and develops over a very short time span. Furthermore, the microdynamics of appropriation and resistance are "micro" in the sense that they are shaped by factors in the immediate spatial and social context. From the perspective of Burke's (1969a) notion of scene, then, the circumference of what we are examining is quite small in both time and space.

To formulate issues in terms of tightly circumscribed scenes, however, does nothing to lessen the fact that agents, with all their more or less permanent characteristics, are still very much in the picture. Indeed, one of the points I make is that various groups of agents are generally susceptible to different contextual forces. Many dimensions of context could be examined, but I focus on some of the local contexts that shape unique performances of mediated action in what follows.

Stereotype Threat and Appropriation

Stereotypes are "preconceived generalizations about the attributes or traits of people in different social groups" (Laird & Thompson, 1992, p. 499). Most stereotypes are negative, and they are generally recognized as oversimplifications at best, but they are nonetheless widely used in daily life. In a series of recent social psychological studies, Claude Steele and his colleagues (Steele & Aronson, 1995; Spencer & Steele, 1994) have examined how stereotypes may affect their targets. They discuss this under the heading of "stereotype threat," which they define as "being at risk of confirming as self-characteristic, a negative stereotype about one's group" (Steele & Aronson, 1995, p. 797). Steele and Aronson argue that "the existence of such a stereotype means that anything one does or any of one's features that conform to it make the stereotype more plausible as a self-characterization in the eyes of others, and perhaps even in one's own eyes. . . . It is experienced, essentially, as a self-evaluative threat" (p. 797).

As in many discussions in social psychology, Steele and his colleagues formulate their account of stereotype threat in terms of constructs having to do with individuals' mental processes. For example, their argument is grounded in notions such as "self-concept," "frustration," and "protective disidentification." Lying behind their line of reasoning, however, is a set of assumptions about the production and use of cultural tools, and this suggests the possibility of linking their discussion with a sociocultural analysis of the sort being pursued here.

While Steele and his colleagues do not characterize stereotypes in terms of their sociocultural situatedness, they make several comments that suggest precisely this. For example, they refer to "negative *societal* stereotype[s]" (Steele & Aronson, 1995, p. 797, emphasis added), and they write of "stereotypes afoot in the larger society" (p. 810). One simple way to appreciate the sociocultural situatedness of stereotypes is to recognize that the oversimplified generalizations that have great power and authority in one sociocultural setting may have little impact in another. For example, it is about a century too late in the United States to call someone a "carpetbagger" and expect this to be threatening.

Recognizing that stereotypes are tied to particular cultural, institutional, and historical settings raises questions about how they are produced and consumed, and Steele and his colleagues make a few speculative comments about these issues. For example, Spencer and Steele (1994, p. 4) note that "communicative processes play . . . a central role in the acquisition of stereotypes"; in fact, they touch on production as well as consumption when they mention "public and private discourse, the media, school curricula, artistic canons, and the like." A review of how stereotypes are produced provides a reminder that it is certainly possible for the state to be directly involved, something that has occurred more than once in the twentieth century. Indeed, some might argue that this is routinely one function, intended or not, of the official histories found in textbooks.

In many cases, however, negative stereotypes are the products of processes that operate in less overt and official ways. This may make it more difficult to specify the forces that give rise to a stereotype, and it may mean that it is not backed by the power and authority associated with a state, but in many cases this does not make a stereotype any less powerful. Indeed, the specific negative stereotypes examined by Steele and his colleagues are routinely disavowed by representatives of the state and other authoritative institutions, but they nonetheless continue to be "afoot in the larger society" and present a powerful threat to individuals' self-concept. Whatever the particulars associated with specific stereotypes, the general conclusion to be drawn is that it is possible to examine stereotypes, stereotype threats, and related issues only against the background of specific sociocultural settings.

The production of negative stereotypes is an interesting and important topic of study in its own right. However, as has generally been the case in what I have had to say, my primary concern is with issues of how cultural tools are used, and it is in this connection that the findings of Steele and his colleagues have their most important implications from the perspective of mediated action and of sociocultural analysis more generally. In several of their studies, Steele and his colleagues have examined how negative stereotypes about a group might interfere with the cognitive performance of members of that group, especially under conditions of frustration and stress. For example, Steele and Aronson (1995, pp. 788–799) examined the impact of negative stereotypes about African Americans' intellectual abilities on their performance in a test-taking context:

> For African American [college] students, the act of taking a test purported to measure intellectual ability may be enough to induce this threat [of negative stereotypes about their intellectual abilities]. But we assume that this is most likely to happen when the

test is also frustrating. It is frustration that makes the stereotype—as an allegation of inability—relevant to their performance and thus raises the possibility that they have an inability linked to their race. This is not to argue that the stereotype is necessarily believed; only that, in the face of frustration with the test, it becomes more plausible as a self-characterization and thereby more threatening to the self. Thus for Black students who care about the skills being tested—that is, those who are identified with these skills in the sense of their self-regard being somewhat tied to having them—the stereotype loads the testing situation with an extra degree of self-threat, a degree not borne by people not stereotyped in this way. This additional threat, in turn, may interfere with their performance in a variety of ways.

To examine these claims empirically, Steele and Aronson asked black and white undergraduates at Stanford University to take a 30-minute test composed of items from the verbal Graduate Record Examination (GRE). These items were difficult enough to be at or above the limits of most participants' skills and hence were capable of giving rise to frustration. Students in the study were randomly assigned to either the "stereotype-threat condition" or the "non-stereotype-threat condition." In the former, "the test was described as a diagnostic of intellectual ability, thus making the racial stereotype about intellectual ability relevant to Black participants' performance and establishing for them the threat of fulfilling it," whereas in the latter "the same test was described simply as a laboratory problem-solving task that was nondiagnostic of ability" (p. 798).

There were two basic ways in which the general level of the subjects' intellectual abilities in Steele and Arsonson's study was controlled. First, all the subjects were undergraduates at the same institution (Stanford University), with all of its standard requirements for entrance and retention. Second, Steele and Arsonson used self-reported SAT scores as a covariate in their analysis of subjects' performances. This means they employed a technique that statistically adjusted subjects' scores so they could be considered to have equivalent SAT scores.

Having used these techniques to ensure that the black and white students were comparable in relevant ways, Steele and Aronson found a difference between the two groups in the stereotype-threat condition but not in the non-stereotype-threat condition. Specifically, they reported, "with SAT differences statistically controlled, Black participants performed worse than White participants when the test was presented as a measure of their ability, but improved dramatically, matching the performance of Whites, when the test was presented as less reflective of ability" (1995, p. 801).

In a related study (Study 2) Steele and Arsonson (1995) go into further detail about the nature of the depressed performance of the black subjects in the stereotype-threat condition. Specifically, they report that this condition negatively affected both the accuracy and the speed at which black subjects worked. And in Study 4, reported in the same article, the authors provide further information about factors that create stereotype threat. The only difference between the method used in this study and the one used in the studies reviewed so far had to do with what gave rise to the stereotype threat. In the fairly extensive introductory comments to the stereotype threat condition in Study 1, subjects were told that the study concerned "various personal factors involved in performance on problems requiring reading and verbal reasoning abilities" and that they would receive feedback after the test that "may be helpful to you by familiarizing you with some of your strengths and weaknesses" in verbal problem solving (p. 799). In contrast, in Study 4 none of the subjects was told that the test was diagnostic in nature. Instead, all were treated as the non-stereotype-threat subjects had been in Study 1, the crucial treatment in this case being the use of one or another version of a questionnaire:

> The procedure [in Study 4] closely paralleled that of the non-diagnostic conditions in Studies 1 and 2. After explaining the purpose and format of the test, the experimenter (White man) randomly assigned the participant to the race-prime or no-race-prime condition by drawing a brief questionnaire (labeled "personal information") from a shuffled stack. This questionnaire comprised the experimental manipulation. It was identical for all participants—asking them to provide their age, year in school, major, number of siblings, and parents' education—except that in the race-prime condition the final item asked participants to indicate their race. Because this questionnaire was given to the participant immediately prior to the test, the experimenter remained blind to the participant's condition through the pretest interaction. (p. 806)

The findings from this study parallel and extend those from the others reported by Steele and Arsonson (1995). Namely, "Blacks in the race-prime condition performed significantly worse than Blacks in the no-race-prime condition . . . and significantly worse than Whites in the race-prime condition" (p. 807). What these results add to the overall picture is the suggestion that stereotype threat may be induced in a variety of ways. In particular, results from Study 4 indicate that cues that appear to be quite minor or subtle may be capable of giving rise to stereotype threat.

In sum, Steele and Aronson (1995) documented the presence of a stereotype threat to black undergraduate students with regard to intellectual abilities. They explored this phenomenon in a variety of ways and thereby provided a picture made up of several complementary aspects. One of the areas in which they did not provide concrete answers has to do with the precise psychological mechanism or microdynamics that tie the stereotype-threat condition to depressed testing performance. Reviewing the possibilities, they speculate:

> Our best assessment is that stereotype threat caused an inefficiency of processing much like that caused by other evaluative procedures. Stereotype-threatened participants spent more time doing fewer items more inaccurately—probably as a result of alternating their attention between trying to answer the items and trying to assess the self-significance of their frustration. This form of debilitation—reduced speed and accuracy—has been shown as a reaction to evaluation apprehension . . . ; test anxiety . . . ; the presence of an audience . . . ; and competition. Several findings, by suggesting that stereotype-threatened participants were both motivated and inefficient, point in this direction. . . . Together then, these findings suggest that stereotype threat led participants to try hard but with impaired efficiency. (p. 809)

In a related series of studies on "stereotype vulnerability," Spencer and Steele (1994) have documented a similar set of findings on gender differences in mathematics performance. In this study, the authors sought to examine the vulnerability to, or the threat of, "widely known stereotypes in this society [that] impute to women less ability in mathematics and related domains" (p. 4). Their findings are strikingly parallel to those reported by Steele and Aronson with regard to racial differences: "Across four experiments that manipulated stereotype vulnerability—by varying test content, difficulty, and description so as to vary the relevance of the stereotype to test performance—women performed substantially worse than equally-qualified men under stereotype conditions, yet performed equal to them under conditions that relieved stereotype vulnerability" (p. 2).

The findings on stereotype threat and stereotype vulnerability reported by Steele and his colleagues have some interesting implications for the formulation of an account of mediated action. The first point I would make in this respect goes back to the distinction made in chapter 2 between internalization as mastery and internalization as appropriation. The case of stereotypes provides a good illustration of how individuals can routinely master a cultural tool without appropriating it. In this case, the focus is on how it is entirely possible to know a stereotype in the sense of being able to describe it, be able to demonstrate its use in a contextually appropriate way, and be able to explain what it means without believing it or making it one's own in the usual sense.

This leads to a second implication of this body of empirical findings having to do with how the construct of "appropriation" is to be understood. Like terms such as "rent," "employ," or even "use," the term "appropriate" is often understood as carrying some connotations that may not be suitable when considering stereotype threat. The first of these is that some kind of conscious reflection is involved, and the second is that agents use cultural tools voluntarily or willingly. These are connotations that are seldom made explicit or defended. Indeed, they are sometimes overtly denied, as Bakhtin (1986, p. 78) did in his comments about speech genres: "Like Molière's Monsieur Jourdain who, when speaking in prose, had no idea that was what he was doing, we speak in diverse genres without suspecting that they exist." This is not to say that conscious reflection and voluntary use are never involved in the use of cultural tools. They clearly have been in some of the cases I have examined. But they need not be involved. The point is that particular instances of appropriation can be characterized in terms of the degree and type of conscious reflection and voluntary use.

In previous discussions, I have focused on cases in which there was voluntary acceptance or at least an absence of outright rejection of a cultural tool. For example, in the case of the U.S. students' accounts of the origins of their country, many of them appropriated the official quest-for-freedom narrative in an uncontested way, and even those who engaged in tactics of resistance did so in the textual space of this narrative. As I argued in chapter 3, this does not mean that the students' use of this cultural tool was entirely voluntary or based on reflective consideration. Indeed, doing so is probably possible only in the light of having considered alternative mediational means. Of course, the case of the Estonians outlined earlier in this chapter presents a different picture. By creating their own textual space through strategies of resistance, they consciously and voluntarily accepted an unofficial history and rejected the official Soviet version. To be sure, the countertexts they employed were influenced by the official history, but this influence on conscious reflection and volition in their use of cultural tools was indirect.

Yet another set of circumstances surrounding appropriation emerged in the case of instructional discourse modeled on reciprocal teaching that I reviewed in chapter 4. In that case, it seems that appropriation was not a matter of reflection or willful decision. For the students who took on particular patterns of posing questions to others and so forth, appropriation seemed to derive in a relatively unreflective way from practices that students engaged in because they occupied a particular position in a participant structure. It seems that they had been socialized—indeed almost manipulated—into appropriating a cultural tool, and so they bore some similarity to the U.S. college students who employed the quest-for-freedom narrative. In both cases, individuals were using—in a seemingly willing manner—cultural tools that they had not compared with others or held up to critical conscious reflection. And both cases differ from the Estonian one in that the Estonian case involved processes of conscious reflection and voluntary use (or rejection) of a cultural tool.

All this serves as a reminder of the inadequacies of the term "appropriation." The analysis of stereotype threat outlined by Steele and his colleagues adds to these complexities. Many individuals who are the targets of a negative stereotype neither accept it as valid nor believe that it accurately characterizes them. Indeed, the analysis by Steele and Aronson (1995) suggest that it was precisely the subjects in his studies who do *not* accept the negative stereotypes or believe that these stereotypes applied to them whose performance suffers in the stereotype-threat condition. Again, this probably has to do with anxiety and other such factors that interfere with these subjects' performance. Given this set of circumstances, it would seem odd to say that these subjects had appropriated this stereotype. In this case, it seems that a cultural tool shaped agents' action almost in spite of the agents' conscious reflection and volition. Some might be tempted to argue that this is really not a case of appropriation at all, but all that really does is reveal something about our usual interpretation of the term. The fact remains, however, that a cultural tool shaped (to use a neutral term) their performance; the problem (which I leave unresolved) is to arrive at a vocabulary adequate to the complexities involved.

The second general set of implications of Steele's findings for an account of appropriation concerns when and where appropriation takes place. This set of issues falls under the heading of what I am terming the microdynamics of appropriation. Steele's findings show that in many cases the appropriation of a mediational means should not be understood as being tied to the agent independent of context. Instead, it has to do with the local dynamics—or microdynamics—involved in carrying out the immediate action at hand. What the findings of Steele and his colleagues show quite clearly is that stereotype threat does not exist as some kind of constant, pervasive force. Instead, it arises only when induced, or cued, in certain ways.

This needs to be said in the context of remembering that any particular stereotype poses a threat only to members of a particular group. This assumption is reflected, for example, in the findings Steele and Aronson (1995) report about white subjects' performance in stressful test settings. Unlike the black subjects, white subjects showed no difference in their performance in the stereotype-threat and non-stereotype-threat conditions. In this sense, then, an attribute of the agent (group membership) clearly plays a role in the use of this cultural tool. However, the major point of the research by Steele and his colleagues is that stereotype threat is *not* (or at least *not only*) a property of agents. Instead, their emphasis is on how contextual conditions may or may not create this threat.

A further note on terminology is of interest here. In earlier drafts of their papers, Steele and his colleagues referred to the phenomenon of stereotype threat as "stereotype vulnerability." Steele (personal communication, June 1996) reported that they decided to use "threat" instead of "vulnerability" because "threat" points to the context, whereas "vulnerability" implies the agent as the basic source of the effect. The results and the interpretation of these results have persuaded Steele and his colleagues that contextual factors are the primary issue in this case.

So in the end, the discussion of the microdynamics of appropriation in this case draws on at least three pentadic elements: agent, instrument (i.e., cultural tool), and scene (i.e., context). In following the steps that have led to this conclusion, I have elaborated and reformulated the notion of appropriation through several phases. Instead of involving conscious reflection, appropriation oftentimes is almost done *to*—rather than *by*—the agent. Instead of involving willful assent, a cultural tool often affects mediated action in ways the agent neither envisions nor desires. And instead of being an act carried out by an agent and resulting in permanent ownership of a cultural tool, appropriation is often subject to a complex set of microdynamic processes.

Notes

1. Given that conflicting historical representations are the focus of this chapter, I am quite aware that it is important to specify how this version of Estonian history was generated. It was written by myself on the basis of material provided in relatively "objective" sources such as the *Encylopaedia Britannica*. While it is true that no historical account, especially one concerned with a topic such as the relationship between Estonia and the USSR, is uncontested, the historical sketch I have provided seems to be accepted by Estonian and Western observers as the most accurate and has even found increasing support from newly released documents of the former Soviet Union.

2. It is important to note that the teachers and students involved in these cases were in Estonian language schools (and were hence usually ethnic Estonians) rather than the Russian language schools that existed quite independently in Estonia during the Soviet era.

3. The reference in this passage to the desire not to "provoke pupils to make comments and things like this" concerns the teachers' wish to avoid having explicit critical comments about the Soviet Union or the official version of history made in their classrooms. During the Soviet era, when such comments occurred, even in an Estonian school, they usually would have to be reported to Soviet authorities. During this era, all schools were controlled and monitored by these authorities, and overt criticism of the Soviet system by pupils could prove problematic, if not dangerous, to the pupil and the pupil's family.

❋ 6 ❋

Epilogue

Mankind likes to think in terms of extreme opposites. It is given to formulating its beliefs in terms of Either-Ors, *between which it recognizes no intermediate possibilities.*

John Dewey, *Experience and Education*

As I noted in chapter 1, the task of sociocultural analysis is to understand the relationship between human action, including mental functioning, on the one hand, and cultural, institutional, and historical context on the other. Perhaps because of our inclination "to think in terms of extreme opposites," as Dewey calls it, we tend to look at the sides of this relationship as poles of an "either-or" opposition. Specifically, we tend to take either mental functioning or sociocultural setting as fundamental and as giving rise to the other. Methodological individualism assumes that cultural, institutional, and historical settings can be explained by appealing to properties of individuals, and social reductionism assumes that individuals can be understood only by appealing to social fact.

My response to such reductionisms and antinomies has been to seek a way to "live in the middle" (Holquist, 1994). Rather than seeking the key to individual mental processes in sociocultural setting, or vice versa, I have argued that we should employ a unit of analysis that focuses precisely on how these forces come into dynamic contact. Although there are several conceivable ways to formulate this issue, I have done so by examining mediated action, defined in terms of an irreducible tension between cultural tools and active agents. Following Vygotsky, I argue that this unit may be profitably examined by invoking more basic analytic elements—namely, agents and mediational means—but it cannot be reduced to either of these elements in isolation. Following Burke, I argue that these elements must be understood as aspects, or dimensions, of mediated action rather than as independently existing essences.

Such an analytic approach does not reduce the need for specialized methodological expertise. It does, however, call on investigators to define problems in such a way that their analyses can come into productive contact with the analyses of others. Indeed, one of the reasons for choosing mediated action as a unit of analysis is that it does not carve up phenomena into isolated disciplinary slices that cannot be combined into a more comprehensive whole. Because mediated action is grounded in an irreducible tension between elements, it is a unit that at least has the possibility of operating at the crossroads of various academic disciplines.

By way of explicating mediated action, I provided a list of properties in chapter 2. This list is fairly long, but it will need elaboration and further extension in the future. For example, because I focus so heavily on the consumption of mediational means, I have had relatively little to say about the complexities involved in their production. Fortunately, extensive research has dealt with the production of several of the cultural tools I have examined. In the case of the production of historical narrative, for instance, Novick (1988) has outlined a complex set of forces that shape what we believe about the past. In such cases I hope to profit from further contact with others at the crossroads.

After providing my list of properties of mediated action in chapter 2, I focused in subsequent chapters on a subset of issues having to do with the dynamics between agents and cultural tools. This led me to consider a range of issues, but a concern with mastery and appropriation ran throughout them. While recognizing that these two processes are closely linked in many, and perhaps most actual instances, I have considered ways in which they are analytically distinct and have examined several instances in which they operate independently.

In chapter 3, this resulted in an analysis of historical narrative as a cultural tool for representing the past. As studies by Bruner (1990) and others suggest, narrative is an obvious candidate to be examined as a cultural tool since it is so pervasive in human discourse and thought. Furthermore, it is useful to consider narrative for my purposes because it provides an ideal vehicle for exploring several of the properties of mediated action. As I outlined in chapter 3, it is possible to know too little as well as too much about historical narratives. The sense in which it is possible to know too little has to do with issues of mastery, or knowing how to use them. As the research of Beck and her colleagues demonstrates, agents can encounter great difficulty in mastering historical narratives, especially when these narratives are not coherent or when they presuppose too much background knowledge on the part of the agents trying to use them.

Conversely, issues of appropriation come to the fore when examining the national origin narratives produced by American college students. These students appeared to be quite similar with one another in their mastery of the basic quest-for-freedom narrative, but this very mastery seemed to pose difficulties for many of them as they struggled to provide an account of the origins of the United States. Although many of the students seemed content to use the official narrative in a relatively straightforward, uncritical way, others resisted it by employing tactics to deal with the conflict between the official narrative and other accounts they had encountered about the past. The analysis of appropriation in this case actually touched on several aspects of mediated action. For example, the fact that the official narrative shaped the students' accounts even in cases where they obviously resisted it provided an illustration of the power of mediational means to constrain as well as enable human action. Furthermore, it provided a reminder of why it is so important to take into consideration the forces of production that give rise to the cultural tools we employ in mediated action.

In chapter 4, I delved into some further complexities—if not mysteries—of appropriation. There I examined the kind of dyadic and small group interaction Vygotsky had in mind when talking about the intermental functioning that gives rise to intramental processes as outlined in his general genetic law of cultural development. My discussion of these issues reflected the fact that Vygotsky and Bakhtin actually presuppose two levels of social phenomena. First, mediated action is always social in the sense that it involves cultural tools from a sociocultural setting, and second, mediated action is often intermental, or social, in that it involves two or more people acting together in the immediate context. These two kinds of social phenomena interact in complex ways, but in chapter 4 I focused on the issue of how different forms of intermental functioning give rise to different ways of using cultural tools.

I did this by outlining two patterns of intermental functioning and their implications for appropriating speech genres. On the one hand, intermental processes may be characterized by intersubjectivity, as outlined by Rommetveit, and on the other hand, they may be characterized by alterity, as outlined by Bakhtin and others. Like many of the other oppositions I utilized, this one must be understood as a tension between two tendencies that are always both present, at least to some degree, in social interaction. Intermental functioning can come into existence only when at least some minimal degree of intersubjectivity exists, but it also requires various forms of alterity. As I argued in chapter 4, much of the research on intermental functioning to date has focused on intersubjectivity, and this seems to be what Vygotsky primarily had in mind when formulating his general genetic law of cultural development. However, there is growing recognition that resistance, rhetorical opposition, and other forms of alterity need to be taken into consideration when analyzing intermental functioning and its intramental effects. Indeed, it has become increasingly clear that interactional contexts involving resistance and rhetorical opposition may provide some of the most productive settings for developing mastery and appropriation of cultural tools.

In chapter 5, I delved further into the complex relationships that exist between cultural tools and agents. In particular, I outlined instances in which the consumption of cultural tools is characterized primarily by resistance. In the case of Estonians' representation of important events in their past, such resistance took the form of outright rejection of official history. Unlike the American college students dealing with the quest-for-freedom story, the Estonians could produce an unofficial as well as official account of the past, reflecting the fact that they engaged in "strategies" as well as "tactics" of resistance. However, the impact of official production efforts was still in evidence in that the unofficial histories took the form of counterarguments to the official narrative. Again, the power of cultural tools to constrain as well as enable human action is in evidence here, and we are reminded that it is possible to understand mind (in this case that aspect of mind having to do with national identity) only if we understand the cultural tools employed.

My review of the microdynamics of stereotype threat in chapter 5 raised another set of complex issues for appropriation and mediated action. This is so from the perspectives of both the production and the consumption of stereotypes. The production of stereotypes is often more difficult to document and understand than the production of cultural tools, such as the texts that comprise official or even unofficial histories. And as studies by Steele and his colleagues demonstrate, the consumption of stereotypes raises equally intriguing issues. Such consumption is not a process that can be understood independently of the immediate context, or scene, of mediated action. Instead, the very point in analyzing the microdynamics of stereotype threat is that the impact of stereotypes may be "switched" on or off by quite subtle aspects of the context in which agents are acting.

What is perhaps most interesting in this case, serving to distinguish it from many other cases of mediated action, is that it is possible to control the local context in such a way that a cultural tool can have its effect even though the agent actively rejects it. Steele's findings introduce a set of issues not encountered in cases such as pole vaulting, multiplication, or even the use of official histories. The processes involved in stereotype threat still fall under the heading of mediated action in that they are inconceivable without the cultural tool involved. Indeed, the microdynamics of stereotype threat can be studied only because relevant stereotypes exist in a sociocultural setting and only because the agent is a possible target. On the other hand, however, the microdynamics of stereotype threat highlight the fact that the mere existence of a cultural tool does not somehow mechanistically determine an agent's action. Much depends on properties of the agent and of the immediate context.

From the perspective of mediated action, the human condition is to act with cultural tools that are provided by a specific sociocultural setting. Pole vaulting, recounting the past, and individuals' struggles with stereotype threat inherently involve the use of cultural tools. At the same time, however, I have sought to emphasize throughout my analysis of mediated action that cultural tools do not mechanistically determine an agent's action. In the examples I have examined, the mix of contributions from the agent and cultural tools varies, but both are always present in the irreducible tension that defines mediated action.

In the end, the process of analyzing mediated action is perhaps best understood as a form of mediated action in its own right. Such a perspective contrasts with taking it to be part of what aspires to be an elaborated, fixed theory. In the view I have outlined here, constructs such as mediated action and mediational means are cultural tools to be employed in an ongoing process of controlled inquiry into human action in sociocultural settings. Like any other cultural tool, these constructs constrain as well as enable the process, and for this very reason they must be viewed as being provisional and in need of

continual revision and refinement. But as long as they can provide
new insights into the complexities of human action and as long as
they can continue to do this in a way that brings the power of multiple perspectives in the human sciences into productive contact, they
are constructs that I believe can play an increasingly important role
in sociocultural analysis.

References

Ahonen, S. (1992). *Clio sans uniform: A study of the post-Marxist transformation of the history curricula in East Germany and Estonia, 1986–1991*. Helsinki: Suomalainen Tiedeakatemia.

———. (1997). The transformation of history: The official representation of history in East Germany and Estonia, 1986–1991. *Culture and psychology*, 3(1), pp. 41–62.

Appleby, J., L. Hunt, & M. Jacob (1994). *Telling the truth about history*. New York: Norton.

Austin, J. L. (1975). *How to do things with words* (2nd ed.). Cambridge, Mass.: Harvard University Press.

Bakhtin, M. M. (1979). *Estetika slovesnogo tvorchestva* [The aesthetics of verbal creation]. Moscow: Iskusstvo.

———. (1981). *The dialogic imagination: Four essays by M. M. Bakhtin*. Ed. M. Holquist; trans. C. Emerson and M. Holquist. Austin: University of Texas Press.

———. (1984). *Problems of Dostoevsky's poetics*. Ed. and trans. C. Emerson. Minneapolis: University of Minnesota Press.

———. (1986). *Speech genres and other late essays*. Ed. C. Emerson and M. Holmquist; trans. V. W. McGee. Austin: University of Texas Press.

Bartlett, F. C. (1932). *Remembering: A study in experimental and social psychology*. Cambridge: Cambridge University Press.

Beard, C. A. (1921). *An economic interpretation of the Constitution of the United States*. New York: Macmillan.

Bechtel, W. (1993). The case for connectionism. *Philosophical studies*, 71. pp. 119–154.

Bechtel, W., & A. Abrahamsen (1991). *Connectionism and the mind: An introduction to parallel processing in networks*. Oxford: Blackwell.

Beck, I. L., & M. G. McKeown (1994). Outcomes of history instruction: Paste-up accounts. In M. Carretero and J. F. Voss, eds., *Cognitive and instructional processes in history and the social sciences*. Hillsdale, N.J.: Erlbaum, pp. 237–256.

Beck, I. L., M. G. McKeown, & E. W. Gromoll (1989). Learning from social studies texts. *Cognition and instruction*, 6(2), pp. 99–158.

Beck, I. L., M. G. McKeown, G. M. Sinatra, & J. A. Loxterman (1991). Revising social studies text from a text-processing perspective: Evidence of improved comprehensibility. *Reading research quarterly*, 26(3), pp. 251–276.

Billig, M. (1987). *Arguing and thinking: A rhetorical approach to social psychology*. Cambridge: Cambridge University Press.

Billington, J. H. (1966). *The icon and the axe: An interpretive history of Russian culture*. New York: Knopf.

Brown, A. L. (1980). Metacognitive development and reading. In R. J. Spiro, B. Bruce, and W. Brewer, eds., *Theoretical issues in reading comprehension: Perspectives from cognitive psychology, linguistics, artificial intelligence, and education*. Hillsdale, N.J.: Erlbaum, pp. 453–481.

Brown, A. L., & A. S. Palincsar (1982). Inducing strategic learning from texts by means of informed self-control training. *Topics in learning and learning disabilities*, 2(1), pp. 1–17.

Bruer, J. (1993). *Schools for thought: A science of learning in the classroom*. Cambridge, Mass.: MIT Press.

Bruner, J. (1986). *Actual minds, possible worlds*. Cambridge, Mass.: Harvard University Press.

———. (1990). *Acts of meaning*. Cambridge, Mass.: Harvard University Press.

Burke, K. (1966). *Language as symbolic action: Essays on life, literature, and method*. Berkeley: University of California Press.

———. (1968). Dramatism. In D. L. Sills, ed., *International encyclopedia of the social sciences*. New York: Crowell Collier and Macmillan, vol. 7, pp. 445–447.

———. (1969a). *A grammar of motives*. Berkeley: University of California Press.

———. (1969b). *A rhetoric of motives*. Berkeley: University of California Press.

———. (1972) *Dramatism and development*. Worcester, Mass.: Clark University Press.

———. (1984). *Attitudes toward history*. Berkeley: University of California Press.

Carroll, L. (1872). *Through the looking glass: And what Alice saw there*. London: Macmillan.

Cassirer, E. (1944). *An essay on man: An introduction to a philosophy of human culture*. New Haven: Yale University Press.

Cazden, C. (1981). Performance before competence: Assistance to child discourse in the zone of proximal development. *Quarterly newsletter of the Laboratory of Comparative Human Cognition*, 3, 5–8.

———. (1988). *Classroom discourse: The language of teaching and learning*. Portsmouth, N.H.: Heinemann.

Chafe, W. (1974). Language and consciousness. *Language*, 50, pp. 111–133.

———. (1976). Givenness, contrastiveness, definiteness, subjects, topics, and point of view. In C. N. Li, ed., *Subject and topic*. New York: Academic Press, pp. 25–56.

Churchland, P. (1988). Reductionism, connectionism, and the plasticity of human consciousness. *Cultural dynamics*, 1, pp. 29–45.

Clark, A. (1993). *Associative engines: Connectionism, concepts, and representational change*. Cambridge, Mass.: MIT Press.

———. (1997). *Being there: Putting brain, body, and world together again*. Cambridge, Mass.: MIT Press.

Clark, H. H., & S. E. Haviland (1977). Comprehension and the given-new contract. In R. O. Freedle, ed., *Discourse production and comprehension*. Norwook, N.J.: Ablex, pp. 1–40.

Clark, K., & M. Holquist (1984). *M. M. Bakhtin: Life and works*. Cambridge, Mass.: Harvard University Press.

Cole, M. (1996). *Cultural psychology: A once and future discipline*. Cambridge, Mass.: Harvard University Press.

Cole, M., & S. R. Cole. (1996). *The development of children* (3rd ed.). New York: Scientific American Books.

Cole, M., Gay, J., Glick, J., & Sharp, D. W. (1971) *The cultural context of learning and thinking*. New York: Basic Books.

Cornbleth, C. (1995). *The great speckled bird: Multicultural politics and education policymaking*. New York: St. Martin's Press.

D'Andrade, R. (1995). *The development of cognitive anthropology*. Cambridge: Cambridge University Press.

David, P. A. (1986). Understanding the economics of QWERTY: The necessity of history. In W. N. Parker, ed., *Economic history and the modern economist*. Oxford: Blackwell, pp. 30–49.

de Certeau, M. (1984). *The practice of everyday life*. Trans. S. F. Rendall. Berkeley: University of California Press.

del Río, P., & A. Alvarez (1995). Tossing, praying, and reasoning: The changing architectures of mind and agency. In J. V. Wertsch, P. del Río, & A. Alvarez, eds., *Sociocultural studies of mind*. New York: Cambridge University Press, pp. 215–247.

Dewey, J. (1938). *Logic: The theory of inquiry*. New York: Holt, Rinehart and Winston.

———. (1963). *Experience and education*. New York: Collier.

———. (1980). *The middle works, 1899–1924*. Vol. 9. Carbondale: Southern Illinois University Press.

Doise, W., & G. Mugny (1984). *The social development of the intellect.* Oxford: Pergamon Press.

Eisenstein, E. (1979). *The printing press as an agent of change.* Cambridge: Cambridge University Press.

Elias, N. (1991). *The society of individuals.* Ed. M. Schroder; trans. E. Jephcott. Oxford: Blackwell.

FitzGerald, F. (1979). *America revised: History schoolbooks in the twentieth century.* New York: Vintage.

Flanders, N. A. (1970). *Analyzing teaching behavior.* Reading, Mass.: Addison-Wesley.

Frye, N. (1957). *Anatomy of criticism: Four essays.* Princeton: Princeton University Press.

Gamoran, A. (1990). Civil religion in American schools. *Sociological analysis*, 51(3), pp. 235–256.

Gee, J. P. (1991). Social gravity. Paper presented at the American Educational Research Association, New York.

Geertz, C. (1973). *The interpretation of cultures: Selected essays by Clifford Geertz.* New York: Basic Books.

Gerbner, G., L. Gross, N. Signorielli, M. Morgan, & J. Jackson-Beeck (1979). The demonstration of power: Violence profile no. 10. *Journal of communication*, 42, pp. 177–196.

Gibson, J. J. (1979). *The ecological approach to visual perception.* Boston: Houghton Mifflin.

Goodnow, J. (1990). The socialization of cognition: What's involved? In J. W. Stigler, R. A. Shweder, and G. Herdt, eds., *Cultural psychology: Essays on comparative human development.* Cambridge: Cambridge University Press, pp. 259–286.

Gould, S. J. (1981). *The mismeasure of man.* New York: Norton.

———. (1987) *Time's arrow, time's cycle: Myth and metaphor in the discovery of geological time.* Cambridge, Mass.: Harvard University Press.

Gusfield, J. R., ed. (1989). *Kenneth Burke on symbols and society.* Chicago: University of Chicago Press.

Habermas, J. (1970). Toward a theory of communicative competence. In P. E. Dreitzel, ed., *Recent sociology.* London: Macmillan.

———. (1984). *The theory of communicative action: Vol.1. Reason and the rationalization of society.* Trans. T. McCarthy. Boston: Beacon Press.

Halliday, M. A. K. (1967). Notes on transitivity and theme in English, II. *Journal of linguistics*, 3, pp. 199–244.

Heath, S. B. (1983). *Ways with words: Language, life, and work in communities and classrooms.* Cambridge: Cambridge University Press.

Herrenkohl, L. R. (1995). *Enhancing student engagement in the context of school science.* Unpublished doctoral dissertation, Clark University, Worcester, Mass.

Herrenkohl, L. R., & M. R. Guerra (1996). Participant structures, scientific discourse, and student engagement in fourth grade. Unpublished manuscript.

Herrenkohl, L. R., & J. V. Wertsch (in press). The use of cultural tools: Mastery and appropriation. In I. Sigel, ed., *Theoretical perspectives in the concept of representation.* Norwood, N.J.: Ablex.

Hoffer, W. (1985). The Dvorak keyboard: Is it your type? *Nation's business,* 73 (August 1985), pp. 38–40.

Holquist, M. (1981). The politics of representation. In S. Greenblatt, ed., *Allegory in representation: Selected papers from the English Institute.* Baltimore: Johns Hopkins University Press, pp. 163–183.

———. (1994). The reterritorialization of the enthymeme. Paper presented at the International Conference on "Vygotsky and the Human Sciences," Moscow, September 1994.

Holquist, M., & C. Emerson (1981). Glossary. In M. M. Bakhtin, *The dialogic imagination: Four essays by M. M. Bakhtin.* Ed. M. Holmquist; trans. C. Emerson and M. Holquist. Austin: University of Texas Press.

Holt, T. (1990). *Thinking historically: Narrative, imagination, and understanding.* New York: College Entrance Examination Board.

Hutchins, E. (1991). The social organization of distributed cognition. In L. B. Resnick, J. M. Levine, and S. D. Teasley, eds., *Perspectives on socially shared cognition.* Washington, D.C.: American Psychological Association, pp. 283–307.

———. (1995a). *Cognition in the wild.* Cambridge, Mass.: MIT Press.

———. (1995b). How a cockpit remembers its speed. *Cognitive science,* 19, pp. 265–288.

Joas, H. (1985). *G. H. Mead: A contemporary re-examination of his thought.* Trans. R. Meyer. Cambridge: Polity Press.

Kaplan, B. (1983). Genetic-dramatism: Old wine in new bottles. In S. Wapner and B. Kaplan, eds., *Toward a holistic developmental psychology.* Hillsdale, N.J.: Erlbaum, pp. 53–74.

Kuhn, T. (1970). *The structure of scientific revolutions* (2nd ed.). Chicago: University of Chicago Press.

Laird, J. D., & N. S. Thompson (1992). *Psychology.* Boston: Houghton Mifflin.

Lawrence, J. A., & J. Valsiner (1993). Conceptual roots of internalization: From transmission to transformation. *Human development,* 36, pp. 150–167.

Laboratory of Comparative Human Cognition, University of California, San Diego (1983). Culture and cognitive development. In William Kessen, ed., *Mussen's handbook of child psychology* (4th ed.). Vol. 1. New York: Wiley.

Lemke, J. L. (1990). *Talking science: Language, learning, and values.* Norwood, N.J.: Ablex.

Lentricchia, F. (1985). *Criticism and social change.* Chicago: University of Chicago Press.

Leont'ev, A. N. (1981). The problem of activity in psychology. In J. V. Wertsch, ed., *The concept of activity in Soviet psychology*. Armonk, N.Y.: M. E. Sharpe, pp. 37– 71.

Liebowitz, S. J., & S. E. Margolis (1990). The fable of the keys. *Journal of law and economics*, 33, pp. 1–25.

Linell, P. (1982). *The written language bias in linguistics*. Studies in Communication, no. 2. Linköping: Department of Communication Studies.

———. (1988). The impact of literacy on the conception of language: The case of linguistics. In R. Säljö, ed., *The written word: Studies in literate thought and action*. Berlin: Springer, pp. 41–58.

Lloyd, G. (1984). *The man of reason: "Male" and "female" in western philosophy*. Minneapolis: University of Minnesota Press.

Loewen, J. W. (1995). *Lies my teacher told me: Everything your American history textbook got wrong*. New York: New Press.

Lotman, Y. M. (1988). Text within a text. *Soviet psychology*, 26(3), pp. 32–51.

———. (1990). *Universe of the mind: A semiotic theory of culture*. Bloomington: Indiana University Press.

Lucy, J. A. (1992). *Language diversity and thought: A reformulation of the linguistic relativity hypothesis*. Cambridge: Cambridge University Press.

Luczynski, J. (1997). The multivoicedness of historical representations in changing sociocultural context: Young Polish adults' representations of World War II. *Culture and psychology*, 3(1), pp. 21–40.

Lukes, S. (1977). Methodological individualism reconsidered. In S. Lukes, ed., *Essays in social theory*. New York: Columbia University Press, pp. 177–186.

Luria, A. R. (1981). *Language and cognition*. Ed. J. V. Wertsch. New York: Wiley Intersciences.

MacIntyre, A. (1984). *After virtue: A study in moral theory*. Notre Dame, Indiana: University of Notre Dame Press.

Marty, M. (1994). The true believers: Is the end at hand? A serious look at some people who think so [Review of C. B. Strozier, *Apocalypse: On the psychology of fundamentalism in America*]. *New York Times book review* (May 8), p. 16.

Matusov, E. (1996). Intersubjectivity without agreement. *Mind, culture, and activity: An international journal*, 3(1), pp. 25–45.

McKeown, M. G., & I. L. Beck (1990). The assessment and characterization of young learners' knowledge of a topic in history. *American educational research journal*, 27 (4), pp. 688–726.

McKeown, M. G., I. L. Beck, G. M. Sinatra, & J. A. Loxterman (1992). The contribution of prior knowledge and coherent text to comprehension. *Reading research quarterly*, 27, 79–93.

Mead, G. H. (1934). *Mind, self, and society from the standpoint of a social behaviorist*. Chicago: University of Chicago Press.

Medvedev, P. N. (1978). *The formal method in literary scholarship: A criti-*

cal introduction to sociological poetics. Baltimore: Johns Hopkins University Press.

Mehan, H. (1979). *Learning lessons*. Cambridge, Mass.: Harvard University Press.

Middleton, D. (1987). Dance to the music: Conversational remembering and joint activity in learning an English Morris dance. *Quarterly newsletter of the Laboratory of Comparative Human Cognition*, 9(1), pp. 23–38.

Mink, L. O. (1972). Interpretation and narrative understanding. *Journal of philosophy*, 69(9), pp. 735–737.

———. (1978). Narrative form as a cognitive instrument. In R. H. Canary and H. Kozicki, eds., *The writing of history: Literary form and historical understanding*. Madison: University of Wisconsin Press, pp. 129–149.

Mitchell, W. J. T. (1990). Representation. In F. Lentricchia and T. McLaughlin, eds., *Critical terms for literary study*. Chicago: University of Chicago Press, pp. 11–22.

Morrison, T. (1992). *Playing in the dark: Whiteness and the literary imagination*. New York: Vintage.

Norman, D. A. (1988). *The psychology of everyday things*. New York: Basic Books.

Novick, P. (1988). *That noble dream: The "objectivity question" and the American historical profession*. Cambridge: Cambridge University Press.

Nystrand, M. (1993). Dialogic instruction and the social mediation of learning and understanding: A two-year study of classroom discourse in eighth- and ninth-grade English. Paper presented at the convention of the American Educational Research Association, Atlanta.

Nystrand, M. (1997). *Opening dialogue: Understanding the dynamics of language and learning in the English classroom*. New York: Teachers College Press. (with A. Gamoran, R. Kachur, & C. Prendergast)

O'Connor, K. (1991). Narrative form and historical representation: A study of American college students' historical narratives. Paper presented at the Conference for Pedagogic Text Analysis and Content Analysis, Harnosand, Sweden.

———. (1992). *Narrative form and historical representation*. Unpublished master's thesis, Clark University, Worcester, Mass.

Olson, D. R. (1994). *The world on paper: The conceptual and cognitive implications of writing and reading*. Cambridge: Cambridge University Press.

———. (1995). Writing and the mind. In J. V. Wertsch, P. del Río, and A. Alvarez, eds., *Sociocultural studies of mind*. New York: Cambridge University Press, pp. 95–123.

Ong, W. J. (1982). *Orality and literacy: The technologizing of the word*. London: Routledge.

Palincsar, A. S., & A. L. Brown (1984). Reciprocal teaching of comprehension-fostering and comprehension-monitoring activities. *Cognition and instruction*, 1, pp. 117–175.

———. (1988). Teaching and practicing thinking skills to promote comprehension in the context of group problem solving. *RASE* 9(10), pp. 53–59.

Palincsar, A. S., & Brown, A. L. (1989). Classroom dialogues to promote self-regulated comprehension. In J. Brophy, ed., *Advances in research on teaching*. (Vol. 1, pp. 35–72). Greenwich, Conn.: JAI Press.

Palincsar, A. S., A. L. Brown, & J. C. Campione (1993). First-grade dialogues for knowledge acquisition and use. In E. A. Forman, N. Minick, and C. A. Stone, eds., *Contexts for learning: Sociocultural dynamics in children's development*. New York: Oxford University Press, pp. 43–57.

Perret-Clermont, A.-N. (1980). *Social interaction and cognitive development in children*. New York: Academic Press.

Phillips, S. (1972). Participant structures and communicative competence: Warm Springs children in community and classroom. In C. B. Cazden, V. P. John, and D. Hymes, eds., *Functions of language in the classroom*. New York: Teachers College Press, pp. 370–394.

Piaget, J. (1955). *The language and thought of the child*. Trans. M. Gabain. New York: World.

Plunkett, K., & V. Marchman (1989). Pattern association in a back propagation network: Implications for child language acquisition. Technical Report No. 8902, Center for Research in Language, University of California, San Diego.

Quarterly newsletter of the Laboratory of Comparative Human Cognition (1987). 9, 1. [Special issue.]

Reddy, M. J. (1979). The conduit metaphor: A case of frame conflict in our language about language. In A. Ortony, ed., *Metaphor and thought*. Cambridge: Cambridge University Press, pp. 284–324.

Resnick, L. B., J. M. Levine, & S. D. Teasley, eds. (1991). *Perspectives on socially shared cognition*. Washington, D.C.: American Psychological Association.

Resnick, M. (1994). Learning about life. *Artificial life*, 1, pp. 229–241.

Ricouer, P. (1984). *Time and narrative*. Vol. 1. Trans. K. McLaughlin and D. Pellauer. Chicago: University of Chicago Press.

Rogoff, B. (1990). *Apprenticeship in thinking: Cognitive development in social context*. New York: Oxford University Press.

Rogoff, B., C. Malkin, & K. Gilbride (1984). Interaction with babies as guidance in development. In B. Rogoff and J. V. Wertsch, eds., *Children's learning in the "zone of proximal development."* New directions for child development, no. 23. San Francisco: Jossey-Bass, pp. 31–44.

Rogoff, B., & J. V. Wertsch, ed. (1984). *Children's learning in the "zone of proximal development."* New directions for child development, no. 23. San Francisco: Jossey-Bass.

Rommetveit, R. (1974). *On message structure: A framework for the study of language and communication*. London: Wiley.

————. (1979a). On "meanings" of situations and social control of such meaning in human communication. Paper presented at the Symposium on the Situation in Psychological Theory and Research, Stockholm.

————. (1979b). On negative rationalism in scholarly studies of verbal communication and dynamic residuals in the construction of human intersubjectivity. In R. Rommetveit and R. M. Blakar, eds., *Studies of language, thought, and verbal communication*. London: Academic Press, pp. 147–162.

————. (1979c). On the architecture of intersubjectivity. In R. Rommetveit & R. M. Blakar, eds., *Studies of language, thought, and verbal communication*. London: Academic Press, pp. 93–108.

————. (1979d). The role of language in the creation and transmission of social representations. Unpublished manuscript.

————. (1988). On literacy and the myth of literal meaning. In R. Säljö, ed., *The written word: Studies in literate thought and action*. Berlin: Springer, pp. 13–40.

Rosenau, P. M. (1992). *Post-modernism and the social sciences: Insights, inroads, and intrusions*. Princeton: Princeton University Press.

Rumelhart, D. E., & J. L. McClelland (1986a). On learning the past tense of English verbs. In J. L. McClelland, D. E. Rumelhart, and the PDP Research Group, eds., *Parallel distributed processing: Explorations in the microstructure of cognition: Vol. 2. Psychological and biological models*. Cambridge, Mass.: MIT Press, pp. 216–271.

————. (1986b). PDP models and general issues in cognitive science. In J. L. McClelland, D. E. Rumelhart, and the PDP Research Group, eds., *Parallel distributed processing: Explorations in the microstructure of cognition: Vol. 1. Foundations*. Cambridge, Mass.: MIT Press, pp. 110–146.

Rumelhart, D. E., P. Smolensky, J. L. McClelland, & G. E. Hinton (1986). Schemata and sequential thought processes in PDP models. In J. L. McClelland, D. E. Rumelhart, and the PDP Research Group, eds., *Parallel distributed processing: Explorations in the microstructure of cognition: Vol. 2. Psychological and biological models*. Cambridge, Mass.: MIT Press, pp. 7–57.

Rupert, L. J. (1991). Natural contexts of socialization: The zone of proximal development in one child's day. Unpublished master's thesis, Clark University, Worcester, Mass.

Ryle, G. (1949). *The concept of mind*. New York: Barnes & Noble.

Salomon, G., ed. (1993). *Distributed cognitions: Psychological and educational implications*. Cambridge: Cambridge University Press.

Scholes, R., & R. Kellogg (1966). *The nature of narrative*. London: Oxford University Press.

Schrag, F. (1988). *Thinking in school and society*. New York: Routledge.

Scribner, S. (1977). Modes of thinking and ways of speaking. In P. N. Johnson-Laird and P. C. Wason, eds., *Thinking: Readings in cognitive science*. New York: Cambridge University Press, pp. 483–500.

Scribner, S., and M. Cole (1981). *The psychological consequences of literacy.* Cambridge, Mass.: Harvard University Press.

Shklar, J. N. (1991). *American citizenship: The quest for inclusion.* Cambridge, Mass.: Harvard University Press.

Shweder, R. A. (1984). Anthropology's romantic rebellion against the Enlightenment, or there's more to thinking than reason and evidence. In R. A. Shweder and R. A. LeVine, eds., *Culture theory: Essays on mind, self, and emotion.* Cambridge: Cambridge University Press, pp. 27–66.

Silverstein, M. (1976). Shifters, linguistic categories, and cultural description. In K. Basso and H. Selby, eds., *Meaning in anthropology.* Albuquerque: University of New Mexico Press, pp. 11–55.

———. (1980). The three faces of "function": Preliminaries to a psychology of language. In M. Hickmann, ed., *Proceedings of a working conference on the social foundations of language and thought.* Chicago: Center for Psychosocial Studies, pp. 1–34.

———. (1985). The functional stratification of language and ontogenesis. In J. V. Wertsch, ed., *Culture, communication, and cognition: Vygotskyian perspectives.* New York: Cambridge University Press. pp. 205–235.

Simon, H. (1969). *The sciences of the artificial.* Cambridge, Mass.: MIT Press.

Smirnov, G. (1973). *Soviet man: The making of a socialist type of personality.* Moscow: Progress.

Smith, H. (1976). *The Russians.* New York: Quadrangle/New York Times.

Smolka, A. L. B., M. C. R. de Goes, & A. Pino (1995). The constitution of the subject: A persistent question. In J. V. Wertsch, P. del Río, and A. Alvarez, eds., *Sociocultural studies of mind.* Cambridge: Cambridge University Press, pp. 165–184.

Spencer, S. J., & C. M. Steele (1994). Under suspicion of inability: Stereotype vulnerability and women's math performance. Unpublished manuscript, State University of New York at Buffalo and Stanford University.

Steele, C. M., & J. Aronson (1995). Stereotype threat and the intellectual test performance of African Americans. *Journal of personality and social psychology,* 69, pp. 797–985).

Stern, D. (1985). *The interpersonal world of the infant.* New York: Basic Books.

Still, A., & A. Costall (1989). Mutual elimination of dualism in Vygotsky and Gibson. *Quarterly newsletter of the Laboratory of Comparative Human Cognition,* 2(4), pp. 131–136.

Stitch, S. P. (1983). *From folk psychology to cognitive science: The case against belief.* Cambridge, Mass.: MIT Press.

Tanaka, S. (1994). History: Consuming pasts. *Journal of narrative and life history,* 4(4), pp. 257–275.

Taylor, C. (1985). *Human agency and language.* Cambridge: Cambridge University Press.

————. (1989). *Sources of the self: The making of modern identity*. Cambridge, Mass.: Harvard University Press.

Todorov, T. (1984). *Mikhail Bakhtin: The dialogical principle*. Trans. W. Godzich. Minneapolis: University of Minnesota Press.

Tomashevskii, B. V. (1965). Thematics. In L. T. Lemon and M. J. Reis, eds. and trans., *Russian formalist criticism: Four essays*. Lincoln: University of Nebraska Press, pp. 61–95.

Toulmin, S. (1992). *Cosmopolis: The hidden agenda of modernity*. Chicago: University of Chicago Press.

Trevarthen, C. (1979). Communication and cooperation in early infancy: A description of primary intersubjectivity. In M. M. Bullowa, ed., *Before speech: The beginning of interpersonal communication*. New York: Cambridge University Press, pp. 22–45.

Tulviste, P., & J. V. Wertsch (1994). Official and unofficial histories: The case of Estonia. *Journal of narrative and life history*, 4(4), pp. 311–329.

Twain, M. (1989). *Mississippi writings*. New York: Library Classics of the United States.

Valsiner, J. (1997). Magical phrases, human development, and psychological ontology. In C. Lightfoot and B. D. Cox, eds., *Sociogenetic perspectives on internalization*. Mahwah, N.J.: Erlbaum, pp. 78–99.

van der Veer, R., & J. Valsiner (1991). *Understanding Vygotsky: A quest for synthesis*. Oxford: Blackwell.

Voloshinov, V. N. (1973). *Marxism and the philosophy of language*. Trans. L. Matejka and I. R. Titunik. New York: Seminar Press.

Vygotsky, L. S. (1978). *Mind in society: The development of higher psychological processes*. Ed. M. Cole, V. John-Steiner, S. Scribner, and E. Souberman. Cambridge, Mass.: Harvard University Press.

————. (1981a). The development of higher forms of attention in childhood. In J. V. Wertsch, ed., *The concept of activity in Soviet psychology*. Armonk, N.Y.: M. E. Sharpe, pp. 189–240.

————. (1981b). The genesis of higher mental functions. In J. V. Wertsch, ed., *The concept of activity in Soviet psychology*. Armonk, N.Y.: M. E. Sharpe, pp. 144–188.

————. (1981c). The instrumental method in psychology. In J. V. Wertsch, ed., *The concept of activity in Soviet psychology*. Armonk, N.Y.: M. E. Sharpe, pp. 134–143.

————. (1987). *The collected works of L. S. Vygotsky: Vol. 1. Problems of general psychology*. New York: Plenum.

Wartofsky, M. (1973). *Models*. Dordrecht: D. Reidel.

Werner, H. (1948). *Comparative psychology of mental development*. New York: International Universities Press.

Werner, H., & B. Kaplan (1963). *Symbol formation*. New York: Wiley.

Wertsch, J. V. (1979). From social interaction to higher psychological processes: A clarification and application of Vygotsky's theory. *Human development*, 22, pp. 1–22.

———. (1980). The significance of dialogue in Vygotsky's account of social, egocentric, and inner speech. *Contemporary educational psychology*, 5, pp. 150–162.

———, ed. (1981). *The concept of activity in Soviet psychology*. Armonk, N.Y.: M. E. Sharpe.

———. (1984). The zone of proximal development: Some conceptual issues. In B. Rogoff and J. V. Wertsch, eds., *Children's learning in the "zone of proximal development."* New directions for child development, no. 23. San Francisco: Jossey-Bass, pp. 7–18.

———. (1985). *Vygotsky and the social formation of mind*. Cambridge, Mass.: Harvard University Press.

———. (1991). *Voices of the mind: A sociocultural approach to mediated action*. Cambridge, Mass.: Harvard University Press.

———. (1993). Commentary on J. A. Lawrence and J. Valsiner "Conceptual roots of internalization: From transmission to transformation." *Human development*, 36(3), pp. 168–171.

———. (1994a). The primacy of mediated action in a sociocultural approach in psychology. *Mind, culture, and activity: An international journal*, 1(4), pp. 202–208.

———. (1994b). Struggling with the past: Some dynamics of historical representation. In M. Carretero and J. F. Voss, eds., *Cognitive and instructional processes in history and the social sciences*. Hillsdale, N.J.: Erlbaum, pp. 323–338.

———. (1995a). Commentary on I. Arievitch and R. van der Veer, "Furthering the internalization debate: Gal'perin's contribution." *Human development*, 38(2), pp. 127–130.

———. (1995b). The need for action in sociocultural research. In J. V. Wertsch, P. del Río, & A. Alvarez, eds., *Sociocultural studies of mind*. New York: Cambridge University Press, pp. 56–74.

———. (1995c). Sociocultural research in the copyright age. *Culture and psychology*, 1(1), pp. 81–102.

———. (1995d). Vygotsky: The ambivalent Enlightenment rationalist. Volume XXI, *Heinz Werner Lecture Series*. Worcester, Mass.: Clark University Press, 1995, pp. 39–62.

———. (1996). The role of abstract rationality in Vygotsky's image of mind. In A. Tryphon and J. Vonèche, eds., *Piaget-Vygotsky: The social genesis of thought*. East Sussex, England: Psychology Press, pp. 25–43.

Wertsch, J. V., P. del Río, & A. Alvarez (1995). Sociocultural studies: History, action, and mediation. In J. V. Wertsch, P. del Río, and A. Alvarez, eds., *Sociocultural studies of mind*. New York: Cambridge University Press, pp. 1–34.

Wertsch, J. V., N. Minick, & F. J. Arns (1984). The creation of context in joint problem solving. In B. Rogoff and J. Lave, eds., *Everyday cognition: Its development in social contexts*. Cambridge, Mass.: Harvard University Press, pp. 151–171.

Wertsch, J. V., & K. O'Connor (1994). Multivoicedness in historical representation: American college students' accounts of the origins of the United States. *Journal of narrative and life history*, 4(4), pp. 295–309.

Wertsch, J. V., & M. Rozin (in press). The Russian Revolution: Official and unofficial accounts. In M. Carretero and J. Voss, eds., *Learning and instruction in history*.

Wertsch, J. V., & L. J. Rupert (1994). The authority of cultural tools in a sociocultural approach to mediated agency. *Cognition and instruction*, 11 (3 and 4), pp. 227–239.

Wertsch, J. V., & C. A. Stone (1985). The concept of internalization in Vygotsky's account of the genesis of higher mental functions. In J. V. Wertsch, ed., *Culture, communication, and cognition: Vygotskian perspectives*. New York: Cambridge University Press, pp. 162–182.

Wertsch, J. V., & C. Toma (1995). Discourse and learning in the classroom: A sociocultural approach. In L. P. Steffe and J. Gale, eds., *Constructivism in education*. Hillsdale, N.J.: Erlbaum, pp. 159–174.

Wertsch, J. V., P. Tulviste, & F. Hagstrom (1993). A sociocultural approach to agency. In E. A. Forman, N. Minick, and C. A. Stone, eds., *Contexts for learning: Sociocultural dynamics in children's development*. New York: Oxford University Press, pp. 336–356.

White, H. (1973). *Metahistory: The historical imagination in nineteenth-century Europe*. Baltimore: John Hopkins University Press.

———. (1987). *The content of the form: Narrative discourse and historical representation*. Baltimore: Johns Hopkins University Press.

Whorf, B. L. (1956). *Language, thought, and reality: Selected writings of Benjamin Lee Whorf*. Ed. J. Carroll. Cambridge, Mass.: MIT Press.

Williams, M. (1985). Wittgenstein's rejection of scientific psychology. *Journal for the theory of social behaviour*, 15(2), pp. 203–223.

Wills, J. (1994). Popular culture, curriculum, and historical representation: The situation of Native Americans in American history and the perpetuation of stereotypes. *Journal of narrative and life history*, 4(4), pp. 277–294.

Wittgenstein, L. (1972). *Philosophical investigations*. Trans. G. E. M. Anscombe. Oxford: Blackwell.

Wood, D., J. S. Bruner, & G. Ross (1976). The role of tutoring in problem-solving. *Journal of child psychology and psychiatry*, 17, pp. 89–100.

Wortham, S. (1994). *Acting out participant examples in the classroom*. Amsterdam: John Benjamins.

Zinchenko, V. P. (1985). Vygotsky's ideas about units of analysis for the analysis of mind. In J. V. Wertsch, ed., *Culture, communication, and cognition: Vygotskian perspectives*. New York: Cambridge University Press, pp. 94–118.

———. (1996). Vneshnyaya i vnutrennyaya formy: Problemy ikh transformatsii i obratimosti [External and internal forms: Problems of their transformation and reversibility]. *Mir obrazovaniya* [*The world of education*], no. 4, pp. 34–79.

Zinn, H. (1980). *A people's history of the United States*. New York: Harper and Row.

Zinoviev, A. (1984). *The reality of communism*. New York: Schocken Books.

Subject Index

Name Index